In **Rebel with a Cause,** Gary Huey explores the life and times of P. D. East, a white Mississippi newspaper editor whose personal war against racism and bigotry in the 1950s and '60s made him one of the most unusual figures in the modern civil rights movement.

East grew up with the poverty and traditional prejudices of the rural South. In 1953, he left a job with the Southern Pacific Railroad to start a local paper in the town of Petal, Mississippi; though poorly educated, he liked to write and thought the **Petal Paper** would make him a living. At first he avoided controversy, but he was increasingly struck by the senselessness of racial discrimination and began to write about it. In 1954 he ran a mild criticism of Mississippi's efforts to close rather than integrate its public schools after the Supreme Court's **Brown** v. **the Board of Education** decision. Cancelled subscriptions from outraged readers only reinforced his new convictions. East had a fine sense of humor, and when a satirical editorial on racist values was misinterpreted and praised by confused conservatives, he settled on satire as his favorite weapon. No target eluded him; in issue after issue he exposed the bigotry of southern institutions and society with sardonic glee.

The **Petal Paper** began to draw attention from civil rights advocates across the country, who hailed East's work as "a beacon of hope in an otherwise dark area." He was honored with national awards and was encouraged by such men as John Howard Griffin, William Faulkner, Medgar Evers, Hodding Carter, Thomas Merton, Will Campbell, and Steve Allen. Life in Petal, however, was increasingly difficult; East endured death threats, physical abuse, social isolation, and legal harassment. Keeping the paper going drained away his health, destroyed three marriages, and created staggering debts. Though by 1959 he had no local subscribers left, he continued to publish sporadically through the 1960s. The paper and its editor died virtually forgotten in 1971.

East's story gives us a rare appreciation of the courage required to be a lower-class southern liberal in his day. When he took a stand for civil rights, he could scarcely have found a cause more at odds with his own background and environment. Throughout his career he remained an outsider from any organized group or movement, working alone on his paper, making few friends. Poverty, fear, and doubt over the course he had chosen were constant companions. East is a remarkable and haunting figure, and Gary Huey's perceptive study illuminates both the individual and his place in the history of the South and the struggle for racial equality in America.

REBEL WITH A CAUSE

P.D. East,
Southern Liberalism,
and the Civil Rights
Movement, 1953-1971

REBEL WITH A CAUSE

P.D. East,
Southern Liberalism,
and the Civil Rights
Movement, 1953-1971

by Gary Huey

93-118

SR Scholarly Resources Inc.
Wilmington, Delaware

Scholarly Resources Inc.
104 Greenhill Avenue
Wilmington, Delaware 19805

Library of Congress Cataloging in Publication Data

Huey, Gary, 1946–
  Rebel with a cause.

  Bibliography: p.
  Includes index.

  1. East, Percy Dale.   2. Journalists—Southern States—Biography.
3. Afro-Americans—Civil rights—Southern States.   4. Liberalism—
Southern States—History—20th century.   I. Title.
PN4874.E3H83   1985   070.4'1'0924 [B]   84-23516
ISBN 0-8420-2228-7

FOR MY FATHER AND MOTHER
BERWYN AND ELSIE HUEY
MODELS OF TOLERANCE AND UNDERSTANDING

GARY L. HUEY is an assistant professor of history at Louisiana State University at Eunice. A specialist on the social and cultural history of the South, Dr. Huey took his Ph.D. degree from Washington State University in 1981.

Contents

Preface

Despite the American South's long-standing reputation as a conservative, racist monolith, there had always been a segment of white southern society, albeit a very small one, which recognized racial injustices and actually participated in programs designed to improve race relations. Percy Dale East, editor and publisher of the *Petal Paper*, Petal, Mississippi, belonged to this group. Although it is difficult to categorize southern racial liberals, most belonged to the middle or upper classes and found some support by joining organizations that fostered their views. East was one of the exceptions. He came from a rural, lower-class background and refused to join any group that might have given him aid. In November 1953, when East started his newspaper, he paid little attention to the racial situation. Shortly after the 1954 *Brown v. Board of Education* decision, however, he advocated compliance with the law. Local opposition to East grew when he argued that blacks must receive fair treatment and legal equality. He reasoned that to deny rights to any group ultimately posed a threat to the liberties of all. As a result of this stance, East began working with people such as William Faulkner, Lillian Smith, Hodding Carter, Will Campbell, John Howard Griffin, Medgar Evers, and Steve Allen. The White Citizens' Council responded to East by spearheading an effective economic boycott against the *Petal Paper*. By 1959, East had lost all 2,300 local subscribers and most of his advertisers. The paper survived through subscription drives and donations from liberal supporters like Smith, Campbell, Griffin, Allen, Maxwell Geismar, Roy Wilkins, Ralph McGill, Harry Golden, and others throughout the country.

East did not fare as well as his paper. He suffered fits of

deep depression because of the hatred directed at him by his former friends. Under the circumstances, he considered retracting his support of civil rights, but quickly rejected such thoughts. On several occasions, he contemplated suicide as an alternative to his misery, but he always managed to overcome this impulse.

In 1960, East's national reputation grew somewhat when he published his autobiography, and in 1962, it increased further when he received the Florina Lasker Civil Rights Award of the New York Civil Liberties Union. His fame, however, only deepened his difficulties. Obscene telephone calls, social ostracism, and death threats plagued him. To make matters worse, his already troubled and sometimes tragic personal life hit a low point between 1961 and 1963 when he went through two divorces. Throughout these difficult times he maintained his advocacy of civil rights, which added to his woes. The spiraling racial violence in 1963 led a racist group in Mississippi to offer $25,000 for someone to "get East." Fearing for his life, he left Mississippi and moved to Fairhope, Alabama. From his new home, he continued to demand justice for all, but his voice had been weakened. Owing to his shift of location and poor health, he became more of an observer and less of a participant in the movement for racial justice. Nonetheless, he served as a powerful symbol. He had acted in the tradition of a dedicated reformer and racial liberal, and he carried out his mission in the heart of racist territory. He participated in the movement long before it was a popular cause and when the level of danger was especially high. His undisputed courage certainly placed him among those people of conscience and commitment who helped shape one of the most dramatic and significant chapters in American civil rights history.

Acknowledgments

There are many people I would like to thank for their assistance in this project. Howard Gotlieb and the Special Collections staff of Mugar Memorial Library, Boston University, were particularly helpful and patient. Numerous friends of P. D. furnished valuable aid. Maxwell and Anne Geismar, Rev. Will Campbell, and James W. Silver offered many excellent insights into P. D.'s character. East's closest friend, John Howard Griffin, was most helpful. Despite failing health, he answered a multitude of questions and helped me gain access to East's papers. Without him, this study could not have been completed.

Michael Blayney of Wayne State College, Robert Swartout of Carroll College of Montana, James W. Ware of Louisiana State University at Eunice, and Dr. Claude Oubre read the entire manuscript and kept me from numerous errors of fact, interpretation, and style. William Hampes of Louisiana State University at Eunice gave me sound advice on East's psychological state. Anne P. Malone graciously shared her vast knowledge of southern history with me. Although she may not agree with my interpretations, her advice was invaluable. The help and encouragement each of these people gave me went far beyond the courtesies of scholarship and friendship. I am deeply indebted to them.

The suggestions and criticisms of O. Gene Clanton and David Stratton of Washington State University improved the manuscript immeasurably. Edward M. Bennett, also of Washington State University, played two important roles: he offered unfailingly accurate comments, and he recommended P. D. East as a topic. My greatest debt is to Professor LeRoy Ashby under whose guidance this manuscript took shape and matured.

Those who have been fortunate enough to have had Professor Ashby as a graduate advisor can testify to his expert scholarly counsel and the genuine concern he displays for each of his students. Every page of this book reflects his influence on my view of history. Of course errors of fact and interpretation are mine alone.

A note of appreciation is due to my typists: Bonnie Bradley, Debbie Fontenot, Pat Miller, Caletta Soileau, and Donna Tune.

I would like to thank my wife, Bonnie, who has endured this project for eight years while providing a happy home and raising three children. Steven, Amy, and Katie deserve a special thanks too. LaVerne Weber and the late Robert Weber made their special contributions. Finally, I am indebted to my parents, Berwyn and Elsie Huey, for their constant encouragement and support. My entire family's sacrifices made this study possible, and their love made it worthwhile.

1

Introduction:
P. D. East and
Southern Liberalism

On 15 March 1956, the *Petal Paper* of Petal, Mississippi, ran a full-page advertisement, purportedly in behalf of the White Citizens' Councils of Mississippi. It depicted a jackass braying, "Suh, Here's Sweet MUSIC! Yes, YOU too, can be *SUPERIOR*. Join the Glorious Citizens Clan. For only five dollars, GUARANTEED SUPERIORITY!" The "advertisement" listed additional benefits available only to Council members. "Freedom to hunt 'Blackbirds' with no bag limit, and without fear of prosecution! Freedom to take a profitable part in the South's fastest growing business: Bigotry! FREEDOM TO BE SUPERIOR WITHOUT BRAIN, CHARACTER, OR PRINCIPLE! Freedom to wonder who is pocketing the five dollars you pay to join!"[1] Some observers called the publishing of this satirical "advertisement" in the heart of Citizens' Council country an act of rare courage. Others attributed it to sheer lunacy.[2] The man responsible for the advertisement, Percy Dale East, editor and publisher of the *Petal Paper*, accepted neither explanation. He insisted that bravery or insanity had nothing to do with his action. It was the most effective way for him to express his rage against the bigotry of the White Citizens' Council.[3]

As a poor, white, native-born southerner, East did not develop easily or quickly his opposition to white supremacy.

1

He struggled with his conscience on many occasions before he began his campaign for racial justice. Even then he spent several more years battling his own racist feelings. This internal conflict over the race issue culminated in his publication of the "jackass ad." He had finally taken a position from which he would not retreat. As the result of his stand, he became not just the object of his neighbors' scorn and suspicion but also the target of open hostility and an increasingly effective economic boycott. Some good did result, however, as his action won him many devoted allies from every walk of life in both the North and the South.[4]

In his outspoken advocacy of legal and, eventually, social equality for blacks, East did not place himself in opposition to the entire white South. There had always been a small group within southern society that recognized racial injustices and attempted to overcome them. Assuredly, these people were oddities to both southerners and northerners alike. Most white southerners saw them as traitors to a way of life that defended and demanded white supremacy. On the other hand, northern liberals refused to believe that a white southerner would actually speak out in support of the black minority. As a result, southern liberals received no support from the vast majority of southern whites, and their potential northern allies frequently questioned their sincerity. Despite these obstacles East, like his liberal predecessors, provided evidence that the white South was not a conservative, racist monolith that spoke with a single voice.[5]

In determining the criteria for a southern or racial liberal such as East, this study uses a very narrow meaning for the term "liberal." A person's stance on race—not his position in regard to economics or politics—provided the sole test of his liberalism. More specifically, from this perspective, a southern liberal was someone who recognized

> a serious maladjustment of race relations in the South, who recognized the existing system resulted in grave injustices for blacks, and who either actively endorsed or engaged in programs to aid Southern blacks in their fight against lynching, disenfranchisement, segregation, and blatant discrimination in such areas as education, employment, and law enforcement.[6]

Naturally, some southern liberals went further than others in support of blacks. By later standards many would be racists or, at best, paternalists. Yet, in the context of earlier times, they all worked in their own often limited ways to improve the lot of black southerners.

The goals of liberalism have not always reflected concern for black Americans. During the progressive era, numerous liberals advocated such reforms as child labor laws, women's suffrage, and minimum hours and wages, without considering the extension of such benefits to the black community. In the early twentieth century even racist demagogues like James K. Vardaman and Theodore Bilbo of Mississippi enacted liberal legislation in the form of tax equalization, utility and railroad regulations, and greater support for public education, but they obviously meant these to benefit whites only.[7] Therefore, the ultimate test of a southern liberal rested on that person's "willingness or unwillingness to criticize racial mores."[8]

To assure uniformity of meaning, equal precision is essential when defining reform. This term can be as amorphous as that of liberalism. By way of illustration, many Americans viewed the Ku Klux Klan, the American Protective Association, prohibition, and the disenfranchisement of blacks as positive, progressive reforms. Others argued that these actions were anti-reform and that true reform would extend rather than deny political, social, and economic democracy. Still another group held that even some so-called democratic reforms, like cleaning up local governments, fighting prostitution, and providing charity for the needy, were thinly veiled attempts at social control and therefore antidemocratic. Ralph Waldo Emerson pointed up such semantic confusion when he observed that every reformer was both liberal and conservative. He remarked that "We are reformers in the spring and summer, in autumn and winter we stand by the old; reformers in the morning, conservers at night. In a true society, in a true man, both must combine."[9] To avoid such confusion, discussion of positive southern reform will refer only to those programs that tried to help blacks overcome injustices suffered at the hands of whites.

The southern liberal reform tradition to which P. D. East belonged had a long and distinguished, though frustrating, history. At one time the South furnished some of the most eloquent critics of the institution of slavery. Deeply affected by the ideals of freedom and liberty espoused during the American Revolution and by the Enlightenment belief in the perfectibility of man, people like James Birney, George Wythe, and Angelina and Sarah Grimké persuaded many other southerners to support the emancipation of slaves. Such a goal, they argued, was consistent with the themes of democracy and individualism.[10] During the 1820s the South had more antislavery societies than any other part of the country. Membership in the 104 southern societies totaled 5,000, which easily overshadowed that of the 24 northern organizations whose combined membership reached only 1,500. Admittedly, most of these southern antislavery societies supported the colonization of slaves. To this type of abolitionist the blacks were unwelcome residents in the South. The prime motivation of these whites, therefore, was not based on a genuine commitment to equality. This was not surprising since the dominant democratic heritage in the South, drawing upon Jefferson and Jackson, was *Herrenvolk* democracy—for whites only. Within the ranks of such organizations, however, were true liberals who wanted to help blacks as much as whites.[11] These critics of slavery left no aspect of the institution unscrutinized. They exposed its ill effects upon both master and slave as well as on the morals and economy of their society. Part of the South, at least, seemed willing to face courageously its gravest problem.

During the 1830s such fearlessness came to an abrupt end. It was then that the South's liberal, democratic traditions gave way to rigid conservatism. At this time events pointed up sharp differences between the South and the rest of the country. As evidence of the growing regional dissimilarities, southerners only needed to observe the nullification crisis, the beginnings of northern industrialization, and most importantly, the northern abolitionist attack on slavery. The southern way of life no longer seemed compatible with the nation as a whole and for that matter with the Western world. As historian T. Harry Williams later wrote, "Suddenly the Southern states were thrown on the defensive—morally, politically, economically."[12]

At this point most southerners closed ranks and rallied to fend off outside criticism, and in doing so they allowed no dissent at home. The freedom of thought and expression regarding slavery that had existed disappeared. Under attack, the South no longer permitted open debate, since slavery proved too profitable to abolish and too closely tied to the needs of the white culture. Prior to the 1830s many southerners, like Jefferson, had upheld slavery as a necessary evil. Now most supported it as a positive good. It was not enough for one-time opponents of slavery to maintain silence. To stay above suspicion they had to defend slavery zealously.[13] These vigorous demands for conformity proved so effective that by 1837 no antislavery society remained in the entire South. Southerners had left behind much of their open-mindedness and remembered only a distorted individualism, one that allowed them to do as they pleased, thus justifying slavery. In such a stultifying atmosphere, a number of southern liberals moved north.[14]

Although the voice of southern liberals had been reduced to a whisper, rumblings of protest continued in the upper South even in the 1830s. The most celebrated incident occurred in Virginia following the Nat Turner Rebellion. Nearly one-half of the state legislature went on record as opposing slavery, but the spirited debate led to no positive action. In fact, the debate and the rebellion together crystallized opposition to emancipation. Those supporting abolition hoped to use the debate to gain additional allies, but fear of further black violence and loss of valuable laborers made this the last public airing of the slave question in Virginia. People felt compelled to defend slavery more adamantly than in past years. In 1834 a small group of liberals in Tennessee made an abortive attempt to abolish slavery and in 1849 a similar and unsuccessful bid unfolded in Kentucky. The most humanitarian attack on slavery came from an obscure North Carolina preacher, Eli Caruthers. He questioned the moral and historical justifications of slavery, but his ideas found no adherents. Southern liberals had fallen on hard times and the circumstances would not improve even with the end of the Civil War.[15]

Reconstruction gave hope only momentarily to southern liberals. According to the accepted stereotype for the period, white southerners united in their opposition to full citizenship for blacks. Although this was largely true, some white southerners nonetheless attempted to foster cooperation between the races. Most obvious were the white Radical Republicans. Many of these "scalawags" offered political equality to blacks in order to keep themselves in power, but some whites were sincere in their efforts to help the freedmen. Whatever the motivations of whites, blacks under Radical rule participated in government at all levels and the city of New Orleans attempted to integrate its school system.

Even the supposedly united Democrats harbored some racial liberals. The Louisiana Unification Movement of 1873 provided an example. In an effort to entice blacks from the Republican to the Democratic Party, a coalition of southern Louisiana business and political leaders sought to establish a biracial government in their state. In so doing it hoped to regain control of the state from northern and Republican domination. As a part of this scheme the coalition advocated political and legal equality for blacks. Although the Democrats balked at social equality, they had made a major concession. The plan eventually failed for lack of widespread support, but it made clear that a diversity of thought existed during Reconstruction.[16]

The end of Reconstruction brought woe to the liberals. Most of their troubles stemmed from the conservative Bourbon Democrats or Redeemers who controlled the South until the turn of the century. Their grip on the South was so great that C. Vann Woodward has remarked, "It was not the Radicals nor the Confederates but the Redeemers who laid the lasting foundations in matters of race, politics, economics, and law for the modern South."[17] Coming from the old planter, ex-Whig background, these men believed that the future prosperity of the South depended upon industrial progress. To facilitate this the Bourbons emphasized economy in state government, which meant reduced taxes for business and ineffective public service agencies. Also, they advocated a laissez-faire government which would not interfere in social or economic matters unless to help business. They even allied themselves with northern business interests to gain financial support for southern industrialization.

To ensure popular support for their New South, the Bourbons always worshipped at the twin altars of the Old South and the Lost Cause. In giving unqualified praise to the antebellum South and its tragic collapse, they demonstrated their devotion to the southern way of life. The future was important, but to make it successful they could not forget the past.[18] The Redeemers exploited not only southern tradition but the race issue as well. Holding the same basic views on black inferiority as most other white southerners, the Bourbons forced blacks into a caste-like, subordinate position. They did not, however, move to deny all blacks the right to vote. Compassion or true liberal feelings had little to do with this decision. The Bourbons felt that they could control and manipulate this suppressed race to the benefit of the privileged whites, and the plan worked. Through economic coercion, or on occasion by paying blacks off with minor political offices as in Mississippi or South Carolina, the Bourbons for over twenty years crushed all revolts against their authority.[19]

Southern liberals through their attempts at racial cooperation took an active part in various challenges to Redeemer rule. Least effective were the campaigns of lone individuals. Invariably such endeavors failed and frequently at great cost to the insurgents. The convict lease system drew a number of such critics, most prominent among them George Washington Cable, a Louisiana novelist. Under this system, states hired out convicted criminals to work for private companies or individuals. The conditions under which these men labored were deplorable, since state officials seldom enforced laws regulating the number of hours on the job and the type of work performed. All of those trapped in this pernicious system suffered, but blacks received the worst treatment. At times their death rate was twice that of whites. Cable's attack on this virtual reenslavement of many blacks led him to condemn the growing discrimination, oppression, and violence directed against the region's blacks. Cable argued that to demean and degrade blacks in such a manner violated all moral and ethical principles. For his efforts he gained little support and much abuse. In fact the situation became so intolerable that he left the South and settled in Massachusetts. Cable was nonetheless more fortunate than a Georgia legislator, R. A. Alston, who was killed when he revealed the appalling conditions in that state's prison system.[20]

Although individuals caused problems for racists in the post-Reconstruction era, the most troublesome opposition to the Redeemers sprang from group efforts. During the late 1870s and early 1880s one of the first and most notable of these crusades took place in Virginia. The issue that touched off this political revolt centered on the state's debt. Incurred primarily to promote postwar recovery, the debt became so burdensome that Bourbon Democrats cut back on education and other social services to ensure repayment. The opponents of this policy, the Readjusters, took control of the state government by combining the forces of poor whites and blacks. Under the leadership of William Mahone, the Readjusters scaled down the debt, abolished the poll tax, chartered labor unions, lowered taxes on farm lands, built schools for both races, and assured blacks government jobs. Although the Readjusters allied themselves with the blacks mainly for political reasons, Mahone and the other whites attempted to build a biracial party by charting a new course in southern politics. This daring venture worked until 1885, when the Bourbon Democrats finally raised the cry of Negro domination and defeated the Readjusters. Even though this drive ultimately failed, it and other such movements provided future dissidents with a splendid political education.[21]

An even greater challenge to Bourbon rule came with the Populist revolt of the 1890s. The roots of this movement lay in the agrarian discontent of the two previous decades. Its strongest support came from the Southern Alliance, probably the most important liberalizing force in the late nineteenth-century South.[22] The Populists attacked the Redeemers' stranglehold on southern politics and pointed out the growing tenancy problems and the injustice of the crop lien system. Under this latter arrangement, small farmers were forced to purchase food, clothing, and other necessities on credit from the plantation store at exorbitant prices. Even when their crops were sold, many owed so much that they remained in debt to the merchant. Eventually laws required these insolvent farmers to work for their creditors until they repaid their debts. For most this task proved impossible, and they fell into debt peonage. Of equal importance, the Populists tried to halt the encroachment of industrial society in rural America. As Richard Hofstadter, one of the Populist Party's most prominent latter-day critics, admitted,

> Populism was the first modern political movement of practical importance in the United States to insist that the federal government has some responsibility for the common weal; indeed, it was the first such movement to attack seriously the problems created by industrialism.[23]

To achieve these ambitious goals the Populists advocated a variety of specific reforms centering on three issues—land, transportation, and money. The Populists felt that the government had failed in its land policy by allowing large amounts of land to fall into the hands of greedy corporations and foreign interests. In order to rectify this situation they urged the government to reclaim this valuable public treasure. To democratize the transportation and communication networks, that is to reduce the costs, the Populists called for government ownership and operation of the nation's railroads as well as the telegraph and telephone systems. As for the monetary problems, the Populists supported a national currency that was safe, sound, and flexible. Easier credit was a closely related goal that they hoped to achieve through a subtreasury system. In addition to this already ambitious list of proposals the Populists favored the direct election of senators, the secret ballot, the eight-hour working day, and a graduated income tax.[24]

To realize these objectives and wrest control from the Bourbons, the Populists, especially those in the South, believed they had to ally themselves with the blacks. The task was not easy since they drew much of their support from a normally antiblack element, the farmers.[25] To overcome this prejudice the Populists stressed the primacy of class interest over race, suggesting that poor whites had more in common with poor blacks than they did with upper-class whites. As the oft-quoted Tom Watson declared,

> You are kept apart that you may be separately fleeced of your earnings. You are made to hate each other because upon that hatred is rested the keystone of the arch of financial despotism which enslaves you both. You are deceived and blinded that you may not see how race antagonism perpetuates a monetary system which beggars you both.[26]

Such statements were not high-sounding phrases, soon forgotten. Many Populists campaigned, often at great physical risk to themselves, for the right of blacks to vote and hold office, to serve on juries, and to receive justice in court. Also, and most importantly, they denounced the convict lease system, the crop lien system, tenancy, and lynching.[27]

The Populists did not possess an unfettered liberal spirit, however. For many, pragmatism provided the main reason for an alliance with blacks. White Populists needed black support to redress their economic grievances with the Redeemers. As one southern editor proclaimed,

> The Bourbon Democracy are trying to down the Alliance with the old cry "nigger." It won't work though. The Bourbon Democracy have used the Negro very successfully in keeping their supremacy over us and by—our lady! we propose to use him in turn to down them for the good of whites and blacks alike.[28]

Many Populists further displayed their limited racial liberalism by advocating political equality for blacks, but not social equality. Blacks demonstrated their pragmatic tendencies by cooperating with whites, first to obtain protection from prejudice and violence, and only then to attack economic injustice.[29] Despite such limitations, the political partnership of black and white farmers threatened the caste system and Bourbon rule.[30]

Ironically, it was this shaky interracial collaboration that led to the loss of suffrage for most blacks and a deepening of the already strong commitment to white supremacy. The new coalition of whites and blacks presented a genuine threat to the continued power of the Bourbon Democrats. The Bourbons responded by launching a vigorous campaign to thwart the efforts of the Populists. Appealing to the specter of "Negro Domination," the Redeemers ended the somewhat tenuous alliance between whites and blacks. When racial solidarity did not prove to be a more potent force than class solidarity, the Bourbons turned to intimidation, violence, and murder. This divide-and-conquer tactic was not new. There had been a similar response in colonial Virginia, when the upper class had used racism to destroy the common sympathies that existed between poor whites and black slaves.[31]

Seduced by the familiar cry of "nigger," many Populists now joined the Bourbon Democrats in assailing the rights and freedoms of their one-time allies. These agrarian insurgents knew that the upper class had used black votes to maintain office since Reconstruction, and they realized that the Redeemers had continued to use blacks in the 1890s. This occurred despite the genuine efforts of the People's Party, the official Populist political organization, to aid and win the support of black Americans. To people like Tom Watson it now seemed much easier to remove blacks from the political process than to vie for their loyalty. Thus, the Bourbons, with the consent of numerous Populists, systematically disenfranchised blacks.[32]

With the power of the Bourbon Democrats reaffirmed and racism growing throughout the country and in the national government, practically all objections to the further subjugation of blacks disappeared. Most critics of white supremacy either fell silent or left the South. The few voices of protest that remained found their pleas for racial justice ignored, and found themselves stigmatized as disloyal to the "southern way of life." Blacks, devoid of white allies and the vote, discovered sadly that politicians could disregard the most basic human needs of southern Negroes. As a result, the racial caste system, which included the crop lien system, became so oppressive and brutal that it resembled slavery.[33] It would be fifty years before any sizeable group of white southerners would once again publicly advocate racial cooperation. Southern history might have been different had people heeded the call of the Populists; instead, racism remained a key element of southern politics.[34]

The progressive movement of the early twentieth century did not alter the South's racial patterns. This failure resulted not from the absence of progressivism in the region but from the fact that progressivism did little to challenge white supremacy. Throughout the nation progressive reform was primarily for whites. Southern progressives may have supported black disenfranchisement and segregation more openly than progressives elsewhere, but the South's attitudes on the race issue differed from those throughout the nation in intensity, not in kind.[35]

On most issues, in fact, agreement more than disagreement characterized the relationship between northern and southern progressives. Joining their northern counterparts, southern progressives advocated the regulation of utilities, railroads, and other monopolies, penal reform, child labor legislation, municipal reorganization, public health care, improved education, legislation for more representative government, and a host of moral reforms attacking liquor consumption, gambling, and prostitution. The South's role in formulating these goals was not merely to follow the lead of northern progressives. Southerners played an instrumental role in forcing Woodrow Wilson to broaden his program of welfare legislation in order to give additional aid to the politically and economically impotent.[36] Such demands grew out of the attempts by southern progressives to overthrow the entrenched political and economic power of Bourbon conservatives.

Just as northern progressives could not reach total agreement on which issues were important and how they should be handled, southern progressives encountered similar difficulties. Two major wings evolved within the southern branch of the movement. One group, the most conservative, came predominantly from the urban middle class. In general terms, these urban progressives advocated honesty, efficiency, and centralization in business and government, maintenance of white supremacy, and continued attacks upon the Bourbon Democrats.

Led by politicians such as Hoke Smith, Napoleon B. Broward, Charles B. Aycock, and Braxton Comer, and social reformers like Walter Hines Page, Edgar Gardner Murphy, and Alexander J. McKelway, this faction gave southern progressivism its basic character.[37]

Agrarian progressives represented the other major division within the southern movement. In terms of goals and programs, the ostensibly more liberal agrarian progressives differed only slightly from the urban wing. The cleavage between the two groups rested more on style and respectability than anything else.[38] Agrarian leaders like James K. Vardaman, Theodore Bilbo, Ben Tillman, Coleman Blease, and Tom Watson supported credit relief for farmers, antimonopoly legislation, and further attacks on the Bourbons to gain the backing of rural poor whites, a group ignored by the urban progressives. To make their message clear and unforgettable, these men resorted to the most violent, irresponsible race-baiting techniques ever used in American politics. To be sure, the urban progressives were racists, but they never approached the vituperative level of the Bilbos and the Vardamans. At one point, the Mississippi Senate passed a resolution twenty-five to one declaring Bilbo "unfit to sit with honest upright men in a respectable legislative body" and demanded his resignation. Rather than hurting his career such attacks only helped. These demagogues had great appeal to the rural downtrodden. Quite simply, by voicing the bitter frustration and hatreds of their constituents, these agrarian radicals made the submerged whites

> feel important, they stroked the ego of democracy. They denounced in savage diatribes those who they assured the people were their enemies—the Yankees, the Negroes, the patricians—and the people seeing in all this representation of themselves in action against their oppressors, mistook the rhetoric of victory for the reality.[39]

They may have been demagogues, but their economic reform programs placed them squarely in the progressive camp.

Although both wings of southern progressivism scored some formidable victories by improving the quality of life and by establishing the public service concept of the state, neither faction provided substantial assistance to the poor, white or black. One southern historian noted perceptively that urban progressives attacked only the symptoms of the South's problems, such as illiteracy, poor health, and bad roads, instead of the real problems of white racism, maldistribution of wealth, and political and economic powerlessness of the poor.[40] Even the agrarian progressives, the very people cherished by the oppressed whites, failed to help the marginal farmers, as the tenancy rate continued to rise. The biographer of Ben Tillman summed up the unfulfilled promises:

> Tillmanism had more features of the superficial than of a truly radical attempt to uplift the masses. There had been no material improvement, no spiritual awakening, real or illusory. He had aroused certain classes without satisfying them. The tenant farmers and the small landowners were hopping the same clods they had hopped before they heard of Tillman.[41]

Too often, agrarians were corrupted by their racism, subject to bribes from business, and resistant to change.[42] With the 1920s came the rise of business progressivism and its emphasis on efficiency and economic development, but lower-class southerners remained unaffected and continued to languish in poverty. This new strain of progressivism assumed that economic growth would solve the problems of the poor, and if it did not, then solutions most likely did not exist. Despite giving some relief to the underprivileged, progressives made no fundamental changes in the economic and political order of the South.[43]

Under such circumstances racial liberals had little opportunity to ease the burden of blacks. If helping poor whites proved difficult, the task of assisting Negroes was next to impossible. Those who tried to help found themselves forced to make crippling compromises with their bigoted opponents, compromises that made it difficult to distinguish between liberals and racists. For example, practically all southern liberals accepted segregation and opposed social equality. They believed that to do otherwise would only inflame the demagogues and prevent progress for blacks. Edgar Gardner Murphy, an Alabama Episcopal minister and reformer, warned of potential troubles awaiting those who might demand too much, too fast for blacks:

> For these men [the demagogues] to openly attack you would not only be unpleasant but would "drive to cover" men on whom we—and the negroes—*must* depend for

fairness and patriotism. I feel "like a dog" to have to say
these things, but I know our people.[44]

Heeding this warning, most southern liberals accepted the basic
tenets of white supremacy and moved slowly in behalf of blacks,
hoping this tactic would defuse the demagogues and reduce
racial violence. Without such concessions, racial progress
seemed impossible.

Those who dared to exceed these limited goals and break
with racial orthodoxy found themselves in the difficult circumstances that Murphy predicted. The Reverend Andrew Sledd
discovered that his professorship in Latin at Emory College and
his old Virginia family provided little protection when he
stated in a national magazine that southern whites had deprived
blacks of their constitutional rights. Immediate adverse public
reaction forced his resignation. John Hammond, president of
black Prine College in Augusta, Georgia, met privately with
Joel Spingarn of the National Association for the Advancement
of Colored People (NAACP), but word of the meeting surfaced
and Hammond, too, resigned his post.[45] In 1900, Murphy,
ignoring his own advice, organized the Southern Society for the
Promotion of the Study of Race Conditions and Problems in
the South. When his group met for the first time, it excluded
blacks because some participants objected to their presence.
The conference accomplished nothing positive toward improvement of race relations, and plans for a second meeting were
scrapped when no southern city offered to act as host. The
Southern Sociological Congress, organized by a group at Vanderbilt University, tried to lend a helping hand by calling for
equal justice for both races, but then retreated by excluding
blacks from membership and calling segregation laws "wise."[46]

Perhaps the most successful and enduring effort of early
twentieth-century whites to improve the status of blacks came
after World War I. The Reverend Will Alexander, shocked by
the racial violence of 1919, decided that something had to be
done to avert such tragedies in the future. For a while he
traveled throughout the South urging racial cooperation, but
by himself he made little progress. His conversations with
numerous whites confirmed the extreme difficulty of the task.
On one occasion he asked a white minister if his community
had experienced any trouble with Negroes. The man answered,
"No, we had to kill a few of them, but we didn't have any

trouble with them."[47] Realizing that no one person could deal effectively with attitudes as widespread as this, Alexander, with a $75,000 grant from the YMCA, established the Commission on Interracial Cooperation.[48] The Commission wanted to bring blacks and whites together in order to reduce fears and hatreds. Officially, the Interracial Commission accepted segregation, but it broke new ground by allowing blacks to become members and thus to register complaints regarding the harsher aspects of white supremacy. Although few liberal organizations below the Mason-Dixon Line had taken this step and survived, the Commission flourished. As an outgrowth of this organization Jessie Daniel Ames established the Association of Southern Women for the Prevention of Lynching. Together with the Interracial Commission, this group worked diligently to eliminate lynching. They failed, but the number of lynchings declined dramatically during the 1930s.[49]

Most members of Alexander's commission believed that its longevity and limited successes were due primarily to its great caution and restraint in advocating racial change. But in 1926, Alexander made a near fatal slip when he said that he could not defend segregation laws; as to their repeal, he commented that individuals must judge for themselves. Opponents and a large number of allies denounced Alexander's statement immediately. These critics felt that it undermined the "southern way of life." This reaction confirmed the fears of many southern liberals that the slightest opposition to segregation could easily undo any progress they might achieve. Still, a few within the ranks questioned how much good they could do by accepting Jim Crow and merely trying to "humanize" the system. They believed it would eventually weaken the Interracial Commission. Such fears proved correct. The Commission saw its membership and effectiveness diminish by the mid-1930s, but it had made positive contributions. Though timid in action, the Commission on Interracial Cooperation declared that racism was the number-one problem facing the South. Given the circumstances of the era from 1900 to 1930, this was no mean achievement.[50]

Opportunities for southern liberals to effect more significant changes in the South's racial policies and to attack further the conservative power structure increased immeasurably with Franklin Roosevelt's New Deal. In the grip of a devastating national depression the South, more than any other section of the country, required immediate and substantial assistance.[51] The New Deal responded admirably to this great need. Measures such as the Tennessee Valley Authority, the National Youth Administration, the Farm Security Administration, and the Civilian Conservation Corps did not eliminate the economic problems but improved the standard of living and enabled many to survive the worst years of their lives. Going beyond relief, the federal government promoted the growth of organized labor and encouraged the spread of other liberal ideas in an attempt to bring the South in line ideologically with the rest of the nation. Although the New Deal discriminated against black southerners in its relief funds and employment opportunities and passed no civil rights legislation, Roosevelt displayed more sympathy and did more for blacks than any president since Lincoln. Because of these efforts, FDR and his programs aroused unswerving support from the southern masses, both black and white.[52] Even conservatives momentarily put aside their devotion to states' rights in order to take advantage of the federal government's generosity. Some were not comfortable with Roosevelt's economic policies, but before 1936 few had the courage to break with the New Deal. This so-called nationalization of the South broadened the perspective of many southerners and emboldened racial liberals.[53]

These racial liberals now often operated from positions within the federal government, and they did everything they could to help blacks while avoiding any confrontation over race that might undermine their tenuous support. They rarely publicized assistance to blacks and constantly noted that extensive aid came to all in need, especially to poor whites. Through this technique, an old one for southern liberals, they hoped to lure the poor whites away from the "nigger-baiting" demagogues who had been their traditional allies but who had never provided much relief. If this could be accomplished, southern liberals believed they could successfully challenge the racist and conservative leaders of the South.[54]

Ironically, southern liberals ran or held influential posts within the agencies that were most sensitive to black needs. Will Alexander and George Mitchell worked in the Farm Security Administration. Clark Foreman worked in the Interior Department. Aubrey Williams worked with the Federal Emergency Relief Administration and then directed the National Youth Administration. Williams proved to be one of the most effective southern liberals in the New Deal. Under his leadership the NYA achieved the reputation as the most racially enlightened agency in the federal government.[55] To avoid discrimination, Williams ordered white state administrators of the NYA to treat blacks and whites as equals, and he hired black supervisors to see that his commands were carried out. He also found himself, along with Will Alexander and Harold Ickes, providing Eleanor Roosevelt with the counsel she required to fight for black rights.[56] The New Deal had been very good to southern liberals, and through it they began to see that the federal government could bring about positive change in the South.

Unfortunately for the liberals, southern conservatives began to grasp this fact as well. Their uneasiness with Roosevelt finally surfaced after the 1936 election. New Deal relief programs and labor codes and standards threatened the existing social and economic power structure in the South.[57] Even more repulsive to many southern Democrats was Roosevelt's success in winning union and black support. At this point the old Bourbons joined forces with Republicans to form a conservative coalition in Congress that attempted to block further New Deal legislation.[58] This trend most certainly hurt the cause of southern liberals, but they and the New Deal, though crippled, remained an important element in both national and local politics.

In 1938, for example, the New Deal inspired racial liberals to form on a regional basis one of the few broad-based coalitions for reform, the Southern Conference for Human Welfare (SCHW). After meeting with Franklin and Eleanor Roosevelt, Joseph Gelders, southern secretary for the National Committee for the Defense of Political Prisoners, and Lucy Randolph Mason, an official of the Congress of Industrial Organizations (CIO), called for a general conference of all southern liberals to be held in Birmingham, Alabama. The purpose of the meeting was to promote the New Deal, solve the South's economic problems, and improve the lot of blacks. Some of the most prominent racial liberals of the day attended the meeting: journalists Mark Ethridge, Ralph McGill, and Virginius Dabney; academicians Howard K. Beale and Frank P. Graham; political and government officials Aubrey Williams, Hugo Black, Claude Pepper, and Eleanor Roosevelt; and black leaders Mary McLeod Bethune and Benjamin Mays. Added to this list were religious leaders, union officials, and several socialists and Communists. Overall, the middle class dominated the SCHW.[59]

Despite these middle-class ties, the SCHW ran afoul of

southern racial taboos. On the first day of the conference, whites and blacks mingled freely. On the second day, however, City Commissioner Eugene "Bull" Connor ordered the police to enforce the city's local segregation ordinance requiring blacks and whites to sit on different sides of the auditorium. The delegates reluctantly agreed to comply and resolved never to hold another segregated meeting.[60] Even more disturbing to racists and conservatives was the SCHW's attempt to repeal the poll tax. The tax had been enacted in an effort to reduce the number of black voters. Participating states collected the tax in the late winter or early spring when cash was scarce. For most blacks and poor whites the one or two dollar levy made the vote a luxury they could not afford. In some states the poll tax was cumulative—the authorities added previous unpaid taxes to the present year's bill, which further reduced the pool of eligible voters. Since poor whites found themselves hurt by the poll tax, Virginia Durr, leader of the SCHW movement, stressed that the repeal of this undemocratic tax was not a racial issue because it would benefit poor whites as much as blacks. Durr and the SCHW failed in their efforts but the mere fact that they tried set the SCHW apart from most southern liberal organizations. In fact, the SCHW may have been the first southern interracial group to speak out against all forms of segregation and, as such, it anticipated and prepared the way for later more successful assaults against Jim Crow.[61] This stance, however, led to the early demise of SCHW. By 1948 racial "radicalism" and association with American Communists prevented it from attracting large numbers to its membership ranks, so the group finally disbanded.

Although the New Deal brought hope and some progress on the southern racial front, World War II had a more profound impact. The changes were so great that southern liberals found themselves facing a difficult dilemma. Blacks, impatient from decades of accommodation and second-class citizenship, grew more militant and demanded full and immediate equality.[62] Fighting in a war against Hitler's racist regime, blacks called for a double victory abroad and at home. America, they argued, should live up to the ideals for which it was fighting. Most southern liberals, however, believed that blacks should not use this international crisis as a forum to redress their grievances with the Jim Crow system.[63] Fearing that these demands would only intensify racist hatreds and violence, people such as Will

Alexander and Mark Ethridge preferred to maintain their efforts to improve educational and economic opportunities, to stop lynching, and to repeal the poll tax. They did not feel prepared to grapple with segregation and racism, the source of these problems. Southern liberals wanted to continue helping blacks, but most were still reluctant to challenge Jim Crow.

Their fears of a white backlash in response to the more aggressive stance of blacks proved correct, as racial animosities increased during World War II. Riots occurred in Detroit and New York and the number of lynchings grew throughout the country. Southerners considered formally reviving the Ku Klux Klan (KKK), and in Georgia one group filed for a charter of incorporation under the name of "Vigilantes, Incorporated."[64] Senator James O. Eastland of Mississippi constantly berated the efforts of black soldiers, calling their performance an "utter and dismal failure" that "disgraced" the American flag.[65] Tensions became so great that an all-out race war seemed conceivable.

Southern liberals tried to combat this increasingly dangerous trend in race relations. Even before America's entry into the war, Aubrey Williams helped convince Franklin Roosevelt that A. Philip Randolph and other black leaders were justified in demanding an end to racial discrimination in defense industries. In June 1940, Roosevelt responded with Executive Order 8802, which establishd the Fair Employment Practices Commission.[66] Other racial liberals less "radical" than Williams wanted to solve the South's racial problems without involving the federal government. In early 1944 they created the Southern Regional Council to replace the defunct Commission on Interracial Cooperation. Although blacks received a vote in this new organization, it was primarily a middle-class, white liberal effort. Like previous southern liberals, leaders of the Council wanted to shy away from a frontal attack on segregation. This position put them in direct conflict with the new and more vocal critics of Jim Crow, who maintained that the only proper position for a southern liberal was to criticize openly all forms of segregation.[67] World War II had in large part created this split within the movement, as it accelerated demands for total black equality. Many southern liberals, as well as the more prejudiced sector of the country, could not adapt to this bewildering pace of change in human relations. As Walter White, head of the NAACP, remarked, "The highest casualty rate of the war seems to be that of Southern white liberals."[68]

The years immediately following World War II brought little relief to beleaguered southern liberals, as they continued to struggle between the hard-line bigots and those demanding an immediate end to segregation. A conservative resurgence throughout the country saw southern neo-Bourbons regain their grip on power, and as in the past, racist politicians benefited from this conservative control.[69] Southern liberals tried to block this revival whenever possible. They worked diligently for the election of moderate governors such as Kerr Scott of North Carolina, Ellis Arnall of Georgia, Jim Folsom of Alabama, and Sidney McMath of Arkansas, and gave uninterrupted support to proven congressional liberals like Claude Pepper, Lister Hill, Brooks Hays, and Estes Kefauver.[70] The Southern Conference on Human Welfare established the Southern Conference Educational Fund (SCEF) to promote public welfare through improved schooling for blacks and whites. They hoped to appeal to white self-interest by emphasizing that financial advancement for the South would not come until blacks received better education and increased economic opportunities. By 1948, under the leadership of James A. Dombrowski and Aubrey Williams, the SCEF severed its relationship with the parent organization. This move ultimately allowed the SCEF to survive the demise of the SCHW and to challenge segregation more forcefully.[71] This aggressive stand went against the South's conservative trend to such an extent that SCEF members found themselves a minority as most southern liberals rejected this "radical" position.

Nothing brought out this fact more clearly than the SCEF's support of Harry S. Truman's campaign for civil rights. In 1947 his Civil Rights Committee issued a controversial report, *To Secure These Rights,* which condemned in very strong language southern racial practices and attitudes. The report recommended a federal antilynching law, the abolition of the poll tax, laws to prevent discrimination in voter registration, desegregation in the armed forces, prohibition of Jim Crow in interstate transportation, and a halt to federal funds to those practicing segregation.[72] The two southern liberals on the committee, Frank P. Graham and Dorothy Tilly, objected strenuously to what they considered the antisouthern bias in the report. They called for a revision of the harsh language, pleading that such rhetoric only inflamed the racial demagogues and would set back any possible positive racial changes.

Although Graham and Tilly signed the report, they did so with great reluctance, and like many other southern liberals, they felt a growing estrangement from northern liberals and the outspoken SCEF.[73] The 1948 Democratic convention added to the woes of most southern racial liberals. Truman and Hubert Humphrey, mayor of Minneapolis, persuaded the delegates to adopt a stronger civil rights plank in the party platform. After a fierce debate on the issue, many southerners walked out of the convention and shortly thereafter established the Dixiecrat movement, which stressed states' rights and white supremacy. With Governors J. Strom Thurmond of South Carolina and Fielding Wright of Mississippi on the ticket, the party won only four southern states, and its efforts to block Truman's victory failed. In the elections of 1950 and 1952, southern voters retaliated by defeating many racial liberals who had supported the president.[74] Those beyond the reach of the ballot box, James A. Dombrowski, Aubrey Williams, and Virginia Durr, found themselves accused of links with the Communist movement by Senator James O. Eastland and his Senate Internal Security Committee. Even Will Alexander, despondent over this turn of events, became an isolated figure and died alone and disspirited in 1956.[75] At a time when segregation faced its greatest challenge, southern liberals ironically faced similar circumstances due to white backlash and McCarthyism. As one historian noted,

> Operating in a hostile climate, white Southern liberals, if they spoke at all, undertook the unenviable task of opposing Southern school boards, sheriffs, politicians, White Citizens' Councils, and resurrected Ku Klux Klans in their own bailiwicks and at unfavorable odds. Theirs would be a lonelier, more dangerous struggle than the one Southern liberals had faced when Jim Crow had appeared impregnable.[76]

The Cold War had only one positive effect for racial liberals. To help the United States live up to the role of leader of the free world, some politicians worked hard to promote equality.

Aware of the difficulties and hazards of their position, most southern reformers turned to programs less controversial than those concerning race. Like the business progressives of the 1920s, they advocated generous pensions for the aged, better roads, public hospitals, improved educational systems, and antimonopoly legislation. In short, they once again attacked the symptoms of problems instead of root causes: racism, urbanization, and industrialization.[77] To do otherwise would invite personal disaster. As Virginia Durr wrote to her brother-in-law, Hugo Black,

> I am seeing down here this deathlike conformity building up, when to speak out, to take action of any kind, to protest, to write a letter, to hold a meeting brings down on your head both social and economic ruin and there is no recourse in the law.[78]

It was at this time, though, one of the worst for southern liberals, that P. D. East chose to speak out against segregation. Like some of the southern liberals who preceded him, East's liberalism grew more aggressive with time. He began in the 1950s by supporting legal equality only, but within a few years he advocated social equality as well. As a result, he paid a heavy price for his beliefs.

Notes

[1] P. D. East, *Petal* (Miss.) *Paper*, 15 March 1956, 4.

[2] Neil R. McMillen to the author, 5 August 1977; Alfred Hassler, "South by East," *Fellowship*, November 1956, 14–15; "White Mississippi Editor Pokes Fun at Jim Crow," *Jet*, 14 March 1957, 12–15.

[3] P. D. East, *The Magnolia Jungle: The Life, Times and Education of a Southern Editor* (New York: Simon and Schuster, 1960), 178.

[4] Some of the people supporting East were historians Frank Freidel and Arthur M. Schlesinger, Jr., Eleanor Roosevelt, Senator Paul Douglas, comedian Steve Allen, and newspapermen Ralph McGill and Hodding Carter.

[5] This is the theme of a number of important studies. The best of these works include: Morton Sosna, *In Search of the Silent South: Southern Liberals and the Race Issue* (New York: Columbia University Press, 1977); Carl Degler, *The Other South: Southern Dissenters in the Nineteenth Century* (New York: Harper and Row, 1974); Dewey W. Grantham, *The Democratic South* (Athens: University of Georgia Press, 1963); T. Harry Williams, *Romance and Realism in Southern Politics* (Athens: University of Georgia Press, 1961); C. Vann Woodward, *Origins of the New South, 1877–1913* (Baton Rouge: Louisiana State University Press, 1951); William H. Chafe, *Civilities and Civil Rights: Greensboro, North Carolina, and the Black Struggle for Freedom*

(New York: Oxford University Press, 1980); Charles E. Wynes, ed., *Forgotten Voices: Dissenting Southerners in an Age of Conformity* (Baton Rouge: Louisiana State University Press, 1967); Hugh C. Bailey, *Liberalism in the New South: Southern Social Reformers and the Progressive Movement* (Coral Gables, Florida: University of Miami Press, 1969); Herbert J. Doherty, Jr., "Voices of Protest from the New South, 1875–1910," *Mississippi Valley Historical Review* 42 (June 1955): 45–66.

6 Sosna, *Silent South*, viii. See also Chafe, *Civilities*, 6; Numan V. Bartley and Hugh D. Graham, *Southern Politics and the Second Reconstruction* (Baltimore: Johns Hopkins Press, 1975), 23.

7 Grantham, *Democratic South*, 49–50. The subject of race and the progressives will be discussed in more detail later in this chapter.

8 Sosna, *Silent South*, viii.

9 Ralph Waldo Emerson, *The Collected Works of Ralph Waldo Emerson*, ed. Robert E. Spiller and Alfred R. Ferguson, Vol. 1: *The Conservative* (Cambridge: Harvard University Press, 1971), 186. For additional discussion see the following works: Ronald G. Walters, *American Reformers, 1815–1860* (New York: Hill and Wang, 1978); Clyde S. Griffin, *The Ferment of Reform, 1830–1860* (New York: Thomas Y. Crowell, 1967); Norman H. Clark, *Deliver Us From Evil: An Interpretation of American Prohibition* (New York: W. W. Norton and Company, 1976); Jack Temple Kirby, *Darkness at the Dawning* (New York: J. B. Lippincott Company, 1972); Louis Filler, *A Dictionary of American Social Reform* (New York: Philosophical Library, 1963); Robert H. Walker, *The Reform Spirit in America: A Documentation of the Pattern of Reform in the American Republic* (New York: G. P. Putnam's Sons, 1976); John Higham, *Strangers in the Land: Patterns of American Nativism, 1860–1925* (New York: Atheneum, 1963); Christopher Lasch, *The New Radicalism in America, 1889–1963: The Intellectual as a Social Type* (New York: Vintage Books, 1965); Kenneth Kusmer, "The Functions of Organized Charity in the Progressive Era," *Journal of American History* 60 (December 1973): 657–78.

10 George Brown Tindall, "Southern Mythology," in *The South and the Sectional Image: The Sectional Theme Since Reconstruction*, ed. Dewey W. Grantham (New York: Harper and Row, 1967), 16; Grantham, *Democratic South*, 7, 18; Williams, *Romance and Realism*, 10–11; Garry Wills, *Inventing America: Jefferson's Declaration of Independence* (Garden City, New York: Doubleday and Company, 1978); Leonard W. Levy, *Jefferson and Civil Liberties: The Darker Side* (Cambridge: Harvard University Press, 1963).

11 Carl Degler, "The Peculiar Dissent of the Nineteenth-Century South," in *Dissent: Explorations in the History of American*

Radicalism, ed. Alfred F. Young (DeKalb: Northern Illinois University Press, 1968), 113; Degler, *Other South,* 21; C. Vann Woodward, *The Burden of Southern History* (New York: Vintage Books, 1960), 178. See also George M. Frederickson, *The Black Image in the White Mind: The Debate on Afro-American Character and Destiny, 1817-1914* (New York: Harper and Row, 1971).

12 Williams, *Romance and Realism,* 8.

13 Ibid., 11; Grantham, *Democratic South,* 18.

14 Degler, "Peculiar Dissent," 119.

15 Ibid., 116-19.

16 Williams, *Romance and Realism,* 17-44.

17 Woodward, *Origins of the New South,* 22. For views opposing Woodward see Jonathan M. Wiener, *Social Origins of The New South: Alabama, 1860-1885* (Baton Rouge: Louisiana State University Press, 1978); Roger L. Ransom and Richard Sutch, *One Kind of Freedom: The Economic Consequences of Emancipation* (Cambridge, England: Cambridge University Press, 1977).

18 Williams, *Romance and Realism,* 46-47; Grantham, *Democratic South,* 23.

19 Williams, *Romance and Realism,* 48-50. For further details see Grantham, *Democratic South,* 23-24; Joel Williamson, *After Slavery: The Negro in South Carolina During Reconstruction* (Chapel Hill: University of North Carolina Press, 1965): Guion Griffis Johnson, "The Ideology of White Supremacy," in *The South and the Sectional Image,* ed. Grantham, 73-74. Johnson notes that the paternalism of whites led them to believe it was their duty to protect and guide the blacks to a higher plane of civilization, and that the blacks in return would accept the status assigned them by whites. See also Paul M. Gaston, *The New South Creed: A Study in Southern Mythmaking* (New York: Alfred A. Knopf, 1970).

20 Sosna, *Silent South,* 2; Wynes, *Forgotten Voices,* 11-12; Doherty, *Voices of Protest,* 50-52. For a discussion of the convict lease system see Woodward, *Origins of the New South,* 212-15.

21 Woodward, *Origins of the New South,* 94-106; Degler, "Peculiar Dissent"; Degler, *Other South,* 269-304.

22 Theodore Saloutos, *Farmer Movements in the South, 1865-1933* (Berkeley: University of California Press, 1960).

23 Richard Hofstadter, *The Age of Reform: From Bryan to F.D.R.* (New York: Vintage Books, 1955), 61; Grantham, *Democratic South,* 33-34.

24 Woodward, *Origins of the New South,* 250; Kirby, *Darkness,* 9; Sheldon Hackney, ed., *Populism: The Critical Issues* (Boston: Little, Brown and Company, 1971), 4-6; Lawrence Goodwyn, *Democratic Promise: The Populist Moment in America* (New

York: Oxford University Press, 1976).

[25] Woodward, *Burden of Southern History*, 114; Williams, *Romance and Realism*, 53.

[26] C. Vann Woodward, *Tom Watson: Agrarian Rebel* (New York: Oxford University Press, 1938), 220.

[27] Williams, *Romance and Realism*, 53; Woodward, *Burden of Southern History*, 114.

[28] Goodwyn, *Democratic Promise*, 284.

[29] William Chafe, "The Negro and Populism: A Kansas Case Study," *Journal of Southern History* 34 (August 1968): 404.

[30] Goodwyn, *Democratic Promise*, 294; Sheldon Hackney, *Populism to Progressivism in Alabama* (Princeton: Princeton University Press, 1969). For an opposing point of view see Robert Saunders, "Southern Populists and the Negro, 1893–1895," *Journal of Negro History* 54 (July 1969): 240–61.

[31] Edmund S. Morgan, *American Slavery American Freedom: The Ordeal of Colonial Virginia* (New York: W. W. Norton and Company, 1975), 316–37; Grantham, *Democratic South*, 38–41; Williams, *Romance and Realism*, 54–58; Goodwyn, *Democratic Promise*, 299–300.

[32] Goodwyn, *Democratic Promise*, 304–6; Woodward, *Origins of the New South*, 323; Williams, *Romance and Realism*, 55–57; Grantham, *Democratic South*, 41–42; Johnson, "White Supremacy," 78.

[33] Goodwyn, *Democratic Promise*, 305–6; Pete Daniel, *The Shadow of Slavery: Peonage in the South, 1901–1969* (Urbana: University of Illinois Press, 1972).

[34] Goodwyn, *Democratic Promise*, 305; T. Harry Williams, "Huey, Lyndon, and Southern Radicalism," *Journal of American History* 60 (September 1973): 269.

[35] I. A. Newby, *The South: A History* (New York: Holt, Rinehart and Winston, 1978), 360; Dewey Grantham, "The Progressive Movement and the Negro," *South Atlantic Quarterly* 54 (October 1955): 461–77; Kirby, *Darkness*, 1; Bailey, *Liberalism in the New South*, 51–53, 129; Woodward, *Origins of the New South*, 373. It should be noted that some social reformers among the progressives believed that progressivism should deal with the race issue, but they were less influential on this than on other reforms they promoted. Notable in this group were, for example, Jane Addams and John Dewey.

[36] George Brown Tindall, *The Emergence of the New South, 1913–1945* (Baton Rouge: Louisiana State University Press, 1967), 10; Arthur S. Link, "The South and the New Freedom," *American Scholar* 20 (Summer 1951): 314–24; Grantham, *Democratic South*, 56–58. For an opposing point of view see Richard Abrams, "Woodrow Wilson and the Southern Congressmen, 1913–1916," *Journal of*

Southern History 22 (November 1956): 417–37.

37 Newby, *The South*, 360; Tindall, *Emergence of the New South*, 18; Woodward, *Origins of the New South*, 371–72; Kirby, *Darkness*, 3; Grantham, *Democratic South*, 53.

38 Newby, *The South*, 363; Tindall, *Emergence of the New South*, 20; Williams, *Romance and Realism*, 58–59; Monroe Lee Billington, *The American South* (New York: Charles Scribner's Sons, 1971), 324.

39 Williams, *Romance and Realism*, 63; Newby, *The South*, 363.

40 Newby, *The South*, 361.

41 Francis Butler Simkins, *Pitchfork Ben Tillman: South Carolinian* (Baton Rouge: Louisiana State University Press, 1944), 485.

42 Newby, *The South*, 363; Williams, *Romance and Realism*, 263–64.

43 Williams, *Romance and Realism*, 63–64; Tindall, *Emergence of the New South*, 32.

44 Sosna, *Silent South*, 12–13.

45 Sosna, *Silent South*, 14; Charles Flint Kellogg, *NAACP: A History of the National Association for the Advancement of Colored People, 1909–1916* (Baltimore: Johns Hopkins Press, 1967), 216.

46 Sosna, *Silent South*, 17–18. Blacks did sit in on the meetings of the Southern Sociological Conference but that was as far as this white group would go.

47 Ibid., 21.

48 For a thorough discussion of the Commission on Interracial Cooperation see Sosna, *Silent South*, 20–41. Also, one should consult Wilma Dykeman and James Stokely, *Seeds of Southern Change: The Life of Will Alexander* (Chicago: University of Chicago Press, 1962).

49 Sosna, *Silent South*, 33–34. The group organized by Jessie Daniel Ames broke away from the Interracial Commission because it supported a federal antilynching law and Ames did not. She preferred local solutions rather than ones imposed from outside. This stance was taken frequently by racial liberals and was not the sole preserve of the white supremacists. For a penetrating analysis of this organization see Jacquelyn Dowd Hall, *Revolt Against Chivalry: Jessie Daniel Ames and the Women's Campaign Against Lynching* (New York: Columbia University Press, 1979). See also Charles W. Eagles, *Jonathan Daniels and Race Relations: The Evolution of a Southern Liberal* (Knoxville: University of Tennessee Press, 1982), 57–59.

50 Sosna, *Silent South*, 38–41.

51 Frank Freidel, "The Conservative South," in *The South and the Sectional Image*, ed. Grantham, 99; Grantham, *Democratic South*, 71.

52 Grantham, *Democratic South*, 70; Newby, *The South*, 428; Sosna, *Silent South*, 66–67.

[53] For a discussion of those uneasy with FDR's program, and those opposed from the beginning, see Tindall, *Emergence of the New South*, 608–25.

[54] Sosna, *Silent South*, 63, 86.

[55] Ibid., 63, 71. For an excellent study of Williams see John A. Salmond, *A Southern Rebel: The Life and Times of Aubrey Willis Williams, 1890–1965* (Chapel Hill: University of North Carolina Press, 1983).

[56] Joseph P. Lash, *Eleanor and Franklin* (New York: W. W. Norton and Company, 1971), 688–97.

[57] Tindall, *Emergence of the New South*, 618.

[58] James T. Patterson, *Congressional Conservatism and the New Deal* (Lexington: University of Kentucky Press, 1967).

[59] Thomas Krueger, *And Promises to Keep: The Southern Conference for Human Welfare* (Nashville: Vanderbilt University Press, 1967), 21–23.

[60] Ibid., 26–27.

[61] Ibid., 194.

[62] Newby, *The South*, 435.

[63] Tindall, *Emergence of the New South*, 717–18.

[64] Ibid., 716–17; Sosna, *Silent South*, 107.

[65] Sosna, *Silent South*, 110.

[66] Tindall, *Emergence of the New South*, 713–15.

[67] Ibid., 719–21.

[68] Sosna, *Silent South*, 109.

[69] Grantham, *Democratic South*, 74–75; George E. Mowry, *Another Look at the Twentieth-Century South* (Baton Rouge: Louisiana State University Press, 1973), 61.

[70] Grantham, *Democratic South*, 75.

[71] Krueger, *And Promises to Keep*, 187–90.

[72] Sosna, *Silent South*, 150–51.

[73] Ibid., 149–52.

[74] Francis Butler Simkins, *A History of the South* (New York: Alfred A. Knopf, 1965), 605.

[75] Sosna, *Silent South*, 170–71.

[76] Ibid., 171.

[77] Numan V. Bartley, *The Rise of Massive Resistance: Race and Politics in the South During the 1950's* (Baton Rouge: Louisiana State University Press, 1969), 21.

[78] Sosna, *Silent South*, 171.

2

The Formative Years

Before he started the *Petal Paper* in November 1953, P. D. East rarely objected to the second-class citizenship of most blacks in the United States. Even with his newspaper as a sounding board, it took him another year and a half to present, haltingly at age thirty-three, his public opposition to racial prejudice. This long silence, given his economic background and the virulent racism pervading his home state of Mississippi, was not surprising.[1] That he finally spoke out forcefully in support of minority rights set East apart from most lower-class Mississippians who were unsympathetic to civil rights; for that matter it set him apart from most southerners. In a region that placed a premium on conformity to its mores,[2] East stood out as a rebel against one of the most deeply cherished southern traditions, white supremacy.[3] Because he spoke out in this fashion, he found himself embroiled in controversy, something to which he had become accustomed. Throughout most of his previous thirty-three years he had been at odds with the people and circumstances around him. His stance on race represented just one more expression of his rebellious nature. In fact, East felt so alienated from his immediate surroundings that he came to see himself as a perpetual outsider—a judgment his early years seemed to confirm.

When he was only five days old, his natural mother, Laura Battle Hopkins, gave him up for adoption. She had just left her second husband, Dr. M. D. Hopkins,[4] and started home to her father's farm on the Mississippi Delta. On 26 November 1921, en route from New Orleans, she gave birth to a son in Columbia, Mississippi. Because she had one daughter from a previous marriage already living with her parents, Laura Battle Hopkins decided not to burden her family with an additional child.[5] She told the attending physician of her decision; he located the adoptive parents, James and Bertie East. Upon reaching her family's home, Laura Hopkins kept the birth a secret for nearly a year. Once her father, Richard T. Battle, learned of his grandson's existence, he visited the Easts asking them to return the infant to his mother who now regretted her decision. The Easts refused, even when offered a large sum of money as compensation. Later, Larson Z. Battle, M.D., Laura Hopkins's brother, visited his nephew's home but met with no more success than his father. The Battles, though socially prominent and financially secure, made no trouble for the Easts and never contacted them again.[6] Understandably, the adoption and the circumstances surrounding it profoundly affected P. D. East's life. One of the most dramatic and visible consequences concerned simple economics.

East's adoptive father, James, although a hard worker, barely eked out a living as a blacksmith in the sawmill camps of southern Mississippi. His wife, Bertie, helped by running a raw-planked boardinghouse in each new camp, but even with her assistance the family's financial condition remained tenuous. The Easts, like thousands of other Mississippians, found themselves disadvantaged economically in the nation's poorest state.[7] Escaping this fate proved difficult because Mississippi differed little from its neighbors; the entire South lagged behind the rest of the country in per capita income. Even by 1930 the South's average annual income was only 60 to 70 percent of that enjoyed by the remaining states. In dollars and cents, this meant the average independent southern farmer received an annual return of $519. In industry the average annual income from cotton goods totaled $619; in lumber and timber, $748; and in southern industry as a whole, $823.[8]

Although the Easts avoided the worst ravages of poverty, Mississippi style, life in the sawmill camps was nonetheless destitute. This misery resulted from the robber-baronish attitudes of most southern timber men who operated on the proposition of "cutting and getting out," laying waste to much of Mississippi's vast lumber resources in less than sixty-five years. Few knew the meaning of conservation. To accelerate this exploitation, the owners moved their sawmill camps from one stand of virgin timber to the next. With profit the overriding concern, companies gave little consideration to the workers' welfare. Owners exacted the most strenuous labor from their men for sixty hours a week at an average wage of twenty-three cents an hour.[9]

The sawmill camps, according to one study in 1930, lacked "many of the comforts and conveniences which even the dweller in the cotton mill village [found] absolutely essential."[10] Few offered the luxuries of a licensed physician and proximity to hospitals and schools. Decisions to locate the camps placed railroad service to the timber holdings over the needs of the labor force. For those requiring medical attention, home remedies most often prevailed.[11] The rudimentary education that white camp children received was provided by nearby communities or the workers themselves, never by the mill owners—and black camp children probably received no formal education at all. Houses in these temporary settings barely fit the definition. East remembered vividly their basic construction:

> There wasn't a single painted house, nor was there a single building with wall paper or paint inside. The houses, every last one of them, were built of rough lumber, each board six to eight inches wide. The wide planks were nailed onto a frame of rough two-by-fours. A strip of rough lumber about two inches wide was nailed over cracks where the larger planks joined together. The roofs were of "tar paper," a black material of some sort, easily torn and punctured. There was not one roof in the camp without several leaks. Every house had extra pails for use during rain.[12]

To these stark quarters families added a stove purchased from the company store, which deducted its money from the workers' paychecks. Companies, unconcerned about life's necessities, made no provision for the people's free time, either, Most community residents found their recreational options reduced to drinking, gambling, viewing an occasional movie, and, for saint and sinner alike, attending the annual revival meetings.

Life in these sawmill camps was "at best a rude sort of existence."[13] William Faulkner in *Light in August* described graphically what the lumber companies had done to the land and the people. They left it "a stump-pocked scene of profound and peaceful desolation . . . gutting slowly into red and choked ravines beneath the long quiet rains of autumn." As for the shacks in these deserted sawmill villages, they were "not even remembered by the hookworm-ridden-heirs-at-large who pulled the buildings down and burned them in their cookstoves and winter grates."[14] Poverty and ignorance tied most of those who lived and worked in such places to this industry all of their lives.[15]

James East proved the exception as he managed to break away from the sawmill camps, but his departure did not signal new-found prosperity. Instead, it reflected the effects of depleted forests and the Great Depression.[16] With the best timber stands gone and profit margins reduced, large lumber companies left southern Mississippi, abandoning all of their workers. By 1935 this two-fold dilemma left East unemployed and, after the bank in Lumberton collapsed, with no savings. Penniless, the family moved to Bartan, Mississippi, where East went to work for Chester Hare, a small-time lumberman who cut trees for use as utility poles. Despite East's suitability for the job, he remained with Hare only a short time. One day while at work in the woods, East was bitten by a copperhead snake. The deadly venom did not claim his life, but left him incapacitated for nearly a year.

Once back on his feet he joined an old friend, Sol Barber, in the stump-hauling business.[17] P. D. East noted that his father's poor financial sense led, in part, to this endeavor's failure. Too often, it seemed, the senior East gave his small share of the profits to his hard-pressed employees. Hard work alone kept the concern operating for three years. Then, from 1938 until the summer of 1939, James East served as night-watchman in Pleasant, Mississippi. The summer of 1939 marked the end of his job-hunting odyssey when he found steady employment in his wife's hometown of Columbia, Mississippi.

The hardships of this nomadic poverty took a heavy toll on young P. D. East. In the first seventeen years of his life he moved eight times and was never in one place more than five years. Not surprisingly, he thought of himself as an outsider.[18] In 1927 he first experienced the full impact of this status when he entered the public school system in Carnes, Mississippi. That year a large number of children from the sawmill camps registered to attend classes. To the Carnes residents, these young people were undesirable intruders. As East remembered, "The resentment was not great, but it was present, and we didn't need extrasensory perception to know it. I was treated by the teachers at the school, as well as by the students, like a bastard child at a family reunion."[19]

East refused to accede to even the mild discrimination encountered at Carnes. When local students insisted on forcing the "sawmill kids" to the end of all school lines, he resorted to fisticuffs to maintain his position.[20] East later remarked, "As far back as I can recall—I've been plagued with a human weakness of sort. If someone didn't like me, I didn't like him."[21] He turned frequently to physical violence and, although he won few fights, he always felt better for having made the effort. Despite this small satisfaction, his battles failed to give him that crucial sense of belonging. If anything, they increased his loneliness.

As he grew older, the sense of being an outsider intensified. His freshman year in high school at Pleasant, Mississippi, provided a case in point. Throughout the entire year, East had only one pair of pants, one pair of shoes, and two identical shirts. Classmates teased him constantly, asking if he ever changed his clothes. They called him a "Beau Brummell" and a "fashion plate." Only thirteen and the youngest student in school, East could not cope with such remarks. Now, instead of lashing out constantly at his adversaries as he had done previously, he withdrew more and more into himself.[22]

At best, this new tactic was a limited success. East could not keep the hurt and anger inside himself indefinitely. Although less frequent, his responses were more bellicose than before, even on the most trivial matters. Once, for example, he had a nearly disastrous confrontation with his chemistry instructor who accused him of setting off stink bombs. Denying the charge, East began a heated debate which ended in an exchange of punches and his expulsion for a month.

Out of school and with little to occupy his time, East began to wallow in self-pity. This brought on fits of deep depression, and at one point he decided to commit suicide. He hoped that by doing so others would finally feel sorry for him. To accomplish the task, he stole poison from a local physician. When Dr. S. L. Olden, who had befriended East, realized what had happened, he went directly to the young boy's home and finally convinced East that no one had the right to take a human life, even his own. The doctor's genuine concern bolstered East for a while, but within a few weeks loneliness and depression returned. During his five years in Pleasant, P. D. East never felt a part of his high school or the community. Later, he recalled, "I was not a part of anything. I was alone no matter how many persons were around."[23] This sentiment deepened throughout his life and haunted him until his death.[24]

East's religious convictions no doubt added to this sense of isolation. Even from an early age, he seldom felt comfortable with his mother's fundamentalist Methodist faith, but for him to question religion was to cast doubt on one of the cornerstones of southern society. The South during East's youth had, and would continue to have, no equal in terms of church attendance and religious zeal.[25] Historian Kenneth Bailey has written, "Protestantism reigns supreme in the South to an extent unmatched in this hemisphere. Nowhere else, almost surely, is there a Protestant population of equal size so renowned for its piety or for its committment [sic] to old-fashioned Scriptural literalism."[26] In the Southeast of the 1920s, 61.5 percent of all white adults belonged to a church, in contrast with 54.3 percent for the nation as a whole.[27] By 1952 this percentage had risen to 72 percent for the entire South.[28]

Although fundamentalism as practiced by East's mother was not synonymous with Protestantism, such beliefs did play major roles within the three major denominations of the South—Methodist, Baptist, and Presbyterian.[29] For years southern poverty produced small and underfinanced churches that turned, out of economic necessity, to an undereducated, anti-intellectual, and often emotional clergy. These ministers only reinforced their congregations' adherence to biblical literalism. Lacking any substantial intellectual content, this particular southern theology championed a personal salvation based solely on an emotion-laden conversion experience. Feeling, not thought, provided the key to eternal life. This southern orthodoxy also placed major emphasis upon the doctrines of original sin and human depravity, in sharp contrast to less literal Protestants elsewhere who often stressed the ideas of Christian love and forgiveness. Saddled with guilt for innumerable sins, each fundamentalist Christian felt an overriding obligation to find forgiveness with God, nothing less and nothing more.[30] In support of this quest, the devout took a hard line on private morality of a particular kind. This moral restrictiveness shaped fundamentalist southern churches into austere institutions opposed to such "sins" as drinking alcoholic beverages, smoking cigarettes, dancing, and divorce.[31]

Questions concerning what should be done to alleviate poverty and racism carried little weight with southern fundamentalists. They expended their moral energy fighting the devil's temptations and worrying about the evil that an all-seeing God might uncover in their lives.[32] When confronted with certain aspects of the New Testament that appeared to demand solutions for worldly problems, most southern Christians sidestepped the contradictions and condemned the social gospel.[33] This did not mean that they totally neglected earthly problems; they simply cared more about saving souls, especially their own.

Parodoxically, white southern Christianity did not confine itself to spiritual matters. Its immense popularity also sprang from the fact that it helped to justify the temporal white "southern way of life."[34] The church's conservative theology buttressed a conservative social philosophy that advocated the preservation of traditional southern values. Usually this meant upholding ideals like the supremacy of a conservative anti-industrial, antiurban agrarian society, the inferior status of blacks, and the unparalleled holiness of southern churches. As one minister remarked, "We have the most righteous people, the friendliest society, and the purest churches anywhere."[35] Southerners had little doubt that God favored their society, so few cared to tamper with near perfection. The church proved no exception. Thus, it reflected rather than shaped southern attitudes.

Southern religion best displayed its mirror-like quality by defending white supremacy. Many liberal Christians failed to understand how any true believer could practice racial discrimination, but no contradictions existed for most devout southerners. Having emphasized the sinfulness of each individual, fundamentalists believed that God's supreme command directed His children to seek forgiveness. This decree took precedence over every other aspect of life. It mattered more how a person stood before God, saved or damned, than whether social and legal equality existed between races. Some paternalistic concern for the physical welfare of blacks existed, but the status of their souls meant more. As one Baptist asserted, "Shall a preacher be interested in the community welfare? Certainly, but the greatest service he can possibly render is to bring wrong-hearted men to Jesus."[36] Tragically, "the main impact of the churches' message [did] not penetrate the racial situation of the South." Religion, therefore, helped legitimize the white "southern way of life."[37]

With religion playing such a crucial role in the South, heavy, often compulsive pressure forced people to affiliate with some church. As Samuel Hill noted in his book *Religion and the Solid South*, "Cultural forces give the unchurched person the impression that he is somehow a threat to the entire society, a traitor to the cause, an inauthentic member of the regional community."[38] No observation could more accurately describe P. D. East. Although the South's religious fervor never appealed to him, his final repudiation of southern Methodism, and its obsession with sin and guilt, evolved painfully and slowly. Some of his worst childhood memories centered around the yearly revival meetings[39] at which the minister, Brother Hull,[40] called upon all listeners to repent and accept Jesus Christ as their savior. To hasten conversions, Hull stressed relentlessly the wretched sinfulness of every human being and the fact that no transgression escaped God's vigilant eye. During each service young East agonized over his misdeeds. In his autobiography he recalled his reaction to a typical sermon:

> My mind would wander as I listened to the words of the Lord being spoken to me, and I knew they were directed right at me—an awful sinner. Well, let's see, what sins had I committed since the revival of the past summer. Yes, I did plan to kill Mort McPhail for breaking my nose. True, I'd called him a son-of-a-bitch, but he'd deserved it. I wondered if the Lord took into account the fact that Mort was indeed a son-of-a-bitch.

> After a good hour of sweating it out, and I thinking several times the Lord was likely to take me any time with a bolt of lightning or something. Brother Hull would call a halt to the sermon.[41]

East never understood why God would want someone as evil as himself. Even at home he could not escape the irrational guilt stirred up by such emotional meetings. His mother, who dragged him to each service, never allowed him to forget his wickedness. He always resented this treatment and, as late as the 1960s, he described her as "a real, honest-to-God witch who pumped me so full of fear of hell-fire and brimstone that I would often cry myself to sleep at night."[42]

To make matters worse, Brother Hull usually stayed with

the East family since Bertie East ran the sawmill camp's boarding-house. As a result, East found himself under the constant and critical scrutiny of both his mother and the traveling evangelist. When he failed to play the role of the "little angel," his mother would beat him.[43] Once Bertie East caught her son with his head unbowed during the mealtime blessing. His transgression and punishment were compounded by his asking how she could see him without unbowing her head.[44] Both zealots tried to convince the young boy that if he did not support God he automatically favored the devil. In a desperate attempt to encourage East to commit himself to Jesus, they told him that, until he reached the age of twelve his sins were held against his mother. The plan went awry. As East recalled,

> I must confess that while I wasn't too happy about my mother's getting my sins chalked up against her, I used it to my own advantage many times. When my mother and I would have a difference of opinion, which was too often, I'd "get even" by going out and sinning all over the place. I'd smoke—sinful. I'd steal Coke bottles from the commissary and break them on the railroad. I'd sit and curse as long as I could think of words; then I'd repeat myself. What's more, running out of known sins, I'd commence to sit and think evil thoughts. Why not? I'd ask myself. When she finds out the sins against her, she'll let me have my way about a few things. It was simple logic.[45]

On occasion East's father tried to defend his son. He would tell his wife to leave the boy alone, but the respite would last only a few days.

Finally, the pressure to march forward and accept Jesus grew too great to resist. Each time he failed to make the commitment, East could hardly bear the burden of guilt and ostracism. "It was a frightening thing to me. Knowing how very wicked I was, I often left the tent to walk a few yards home, knowing full well I'd never make it. How lonely I was! How long I'd lay awake at night! How I wept."[46] Thus at the age of twelve, long before he felt ready, P. D. East acknowledged Jesus Christ as his personal savior. The decision evoked only more despair and bitterness:[47]

> With the promise of a new suit, and with the threat of going to hell, and with several nudges in the side, I walked the sawdust trail. I gave my heart to Jesus with hesitation

and reluctance—and with disgust for myself. There must have been much joy in Heaven that night, but there wasn't any joy in my heart. I had sold out.[48]

In less than two years, East renounced his forced conversion and declared himself an atheist. He revolted not just against his mother's intensive indoctrination, but also because reality failed to square with his religious expectations. For example, he had been taught that God provided for the impoverished, but his own life argued against this claim. He longed for someone to explain how his father, "a man who had never in his entire life done an injustice to any living soul, a man who had worked with his hands and back to provide for his family, a man who had never lied or cheated anyone—how was it that such a man had nothing?"[49] No one could provide the answer to this and similar questions. So, feeling betrayed by God and man, East broke with religion during his freshman year in high school. He dramatically announced the decision in his science class. He explained that God was a figment of mankind's imagination, conjured up out of weakness, and declared his refusal to worship such an imaginary and capricious deity. This stand, in a conservative, deeply religious environment, opened East to ridicule from his teachers as well as his classmates. He could not comprehend why his opinion created such hostility, but he declined to recant. "Having taken what I considered a reasonable point of view, it was only natural that I defend it, which I did. I stood alone, and it was a lonely stand, but to back down was out of the question."[50]

Once he made this resolution, P. D. East never truly returned to the Christian faith. There were times when he tried to rekindle, at least outwardly, his devotion to religion, but each attempt failed.[51] He also turned to Unitarianism and Judaism but with little satisfaction.[52] Although he continued to share some ethical stances more typical of some of the more socially concerned churches, such as the emphasis on humanitarianism and love in worldly relationships, he based his beliefs on philosophy rather than theology.[53] Religion and people devoted to their faith always intrigued East,[54] but he could never again accept the simple doctrines of his childhood, if indeed he ever had. His stand on religion only bolstered his general self-image as an outcast of southern society.

Despite intense loneliness and growing feelings of alienation toward certain aspects of southern society, East maintained, beneath a cynical exterior, a compassionate and sensitive nature. Over a period of years these humane qualities led him to identify with other southern outcasts.[55] For P. D. East the so-called "Golden Rule"—do unto others as you would have them do unto you—represented more than a meaningless cliché. As early as 1927 he endeavored to apply these words to his daily life, even when dealing with blacks,[56] but his environment made this task most difficult. Prior to entering high school East had never heard the word Negro because the sawmill camp residents called all blacks "niggers." East also used the term since he knew no other, but he claimed to have rejected the idea that blacks were inferior, a rather enlightened attitude for a white Mississippian. Recalling his childhood East remarked, "I was superior, yes—but I didn't know it. I have always treated a Negro as I treat a white man."[57]

Not many white southerners could make a similar claim because white supremacy constituted one of their most distinctive and fundamental values.[58] No economic class and few aspects of life escaped the influence of racism and segregation. Even in the face of black accomplishments in scholarship, the fine arts, and the professions, and even after the racist excesses of Nazi Germany were public knowledge, "virtually all whites remained convinced that segregation and white supremacy were essential to the well-being of the South."[59]

Politics best reflected the all-consuming nature of white supremacy. As V. O. Key wrote, "In its grand outlines the politics of the South revolves around the position of the Negro. ... Whatever phase of the Southern political process one seeks to understand, sooner or later the trail of inquiry leads to the Negro."[60] Key further noted that the greater the concentration of blacks the deeper the concern about upholding white supremacy. This had special meaning for P. D. East. During his youth, Mississippi had a higher proportion of blacks than any other state in the union. Due to this concentration of blacks, Key wrote, "Mississippi undoubtedly ... harbored the most unrestrained and continuous advocates of white supremacy."[61]

White Mississippians mastered quickly the art of maintaining their exalted position. Through their 1890 constitution they had legally and effectively disenfranchised blacks. Each prospective voter had to interpret a passage of the constitution to the satisfaction of the white registrar. Of course, few or no blacks succeeded. Senator Theodore Bilbo boasted that the state constitution was a "document that damn few white men and no niggers at all can explain." This procedure proved so successful that other southern states adopted a similar scheme, dubbing it the "Mississippi Plan."[62]

In the social sphere Mississippi, like many other states, implemented innumerable Jim Crow laws to keep the races separated as much as possible. These statutes applied to public accommodations, schools, transportation systems, and even cemeteries. Where legislation proved inappropriate, social customs regulated interracial relationships. Southern whites expected blacks to "be content, law abiding, hard working, peaceful, and happy in their subordinate status."[63] From the other side of the color line, social prohibitions existed that kept whites from addressing blacks as Mr., Miss, or Mrs., and even forbade a simple handshake.

Many southerners believed that violation of these or any other taboos represented an attack on the whole "southern way of life." They held that questioning any part of the system eventually led to questioning the entire system, so they demanded total conformity to southern values.[64] Sociologist Howard Odum has commented that the South fell victim to a "state of mind similar to that commonly manifested in war times. . . . There was little freedom of feeling and little freedom of speech in matters relating to religion, race, industry or several social and moral sanctions."[65] To ensure compliance with their wishes, white southerners sometimes resorted to wholesale violence and intimidation; Mississippi led the way. Between 1853 and 1959, white Mississippians lynched an acknowledged 538 blacks— one-sixth of all such deaths in the United States.[66] The southern homicide rate for the 1920s and 1930s ran "two-and-a-half times higher than in the rest of the country."[67] Feeling besieged, southerners reasoned they had to fight to preserve their way of life, whatever the costs.

Unlike his rejection of organized religion, P. D. East's initial rejection of militant racism did not result in a grand declaration of principles.[68] His opposition was quiet but unflinching. Bertie East gave her son, at age six, his first bitter taste of racial prejudice. During the family's one-year stay near Maxie, Mississippi, East began to ride with the Italian fruit and vegetable peddler when he paid his weekly visit to the camp. The man allowed the boy to honk the truck's horn and ring a bell to attract customers. East delighted in this privilege, and the peddler enjoyed his young assistant. To show his appreciation, the man treated East to fresh bananas and other fruit, but the budding friendship ended quickly. Bertie East took her son aside and told him that he could no longer ride with the man. When asked why, she responded, "He's a 'Dago' and he's different from us—and now that's all."[69] Unable to comprehend this reasoning, East asked for further explanation. His mother answered this question with a spanking. East commented later, "Even with a blistered tail, I couldn't understand what it was all about. I saw only a man, a nice man who was kind to me and whom I liked."[70] Despite his objections, East had taken his last ride with the vegetable man.

Bertie East worked relentlessly to instill in her son the racial mores of the South. The struggle between the two was unceasing and the vegetable peddler incident marked only the beginning. East's next maternal lesson on race occurred several years later at the Carnes camp. There he became close friends with a young black boy, Tee Williams. As this friendship grew, P. D. wanted Tee to spend the night at his home. When he asked his mother for permission, she emphatically refused. Surprised, East again questioned her decision, and Bertie East once again applied the rod. For emphasis she told her son, "Tee is a nigger. That's why he can't spend the night and that's all there is to it."[71] Thereafter, East kept his objections to himself, but they existed nonetheless. As he stated,

> Tee may have been a "nigger," but I could see no difference
> in the two of us. It mattered not one iota to me; first Tee
> was a friend, and I enjoyed his companionship, and that
> was all there was to that. It was the same with the "Dago"
> at the Maxie camp. I didn't give a damn.[72]

East might not have given a damn, but southern society certainly did. Tee Williams could not even walk into the camp commissary and charge a nickel's worth of candy to his father, so East always purchased enough for himself and his friend, not a significant act by some standards, but an important one for a seven-year-old boy. Still, East's conscience troubled him because, as he pointed out, I "failed to speak up for Tee....I committed sin by my silence."[73]

The violence employed by some whites to maintain white supremacy may have prompted East's silence. He certainly had the opportunity to witness such actions. One especially frightening incident occurred when he entered the sixth grade. The new principal, Elmo Rand, arranged for the boys to play basketball with several neighboring towns. On the way to a game in Lumberton, Rand's car had a flat tire. He pulled into a service station that the young East recommended. The black attendant, Sam, asked Rand very politely to move the car slightly to avoid blocking the gas pump. Rand flew into a rage, screaming, "No goddamned nigger's going to tell me what to do!" And with that, he split open Sam's head with a tire iron. After recovering from the shock of what he had witnessed, East ran to summon a doctor while the other boys remained seated in approving silence. Appalled, but fully helpless, East did not protest. He had little choice. As he noted, "Nothing was done about the incident. As a matter of fact, Mr. Rand was something of a hero at school after that. To be a 'regular fellow' and to split the skull of a Negro who'd done nothing whatsoever was what heroes were made of in those days."[74]

East also did not condone the sexual abuse of black women by whites. As a senior in high school, he sat in on many conversations detailing someone's latest bedroom or backseat conquest. On one occasion a boy named Ed Sanders bragged about the satisfaction he found down in the "nigger quarters." He told his awe-struck audience, "Just give a can of snuff. Them niggers are always glad to give a white man a piece." A roar of laughter from all gathered around followed this bit of advice. From all except East, who, in a boiling rage, shouted "Ed, you're a damned liar," and accused his friend of rape. Sanders, now upset himself, demanded, "What the hell is it to you?" Although he never understood his own action, East replied, "Ed, by God, any time anybody is done a wrong it's my business." The crowd immediately called East a "nigger lover." Ignoring these fighting words, he stormed out of the room. The matter was finished, even though East wondered for days why he had spoken out. He never found an acceptable answer, but he believed vaguely that it had something to do with the value and the dignity of human life.[75]

This deep compassion also nurtured within East a fierce sense of justice and a genuine devotion to its implementation. Between 1935 and 1939, while working in Jesse Wild's Pleasant, Mississippi, general store, East applied his ideals whenever possible, often at considerable physical and financial risk. Wild was a greedy, unscrupulous man who constantly cheated his customers and expected his employees to follow the example. In filling sacks with sugar, coffee, rice, cornmeal, and seeds, Wild always put in less than advertised. When he sold block ice, he disregarded the fact that the ice melted down. Soon after East began working for Wild, the task of filling sacks fell to him. As long as Jesse watched, East did as instructed, but the minute the boss turned his back the boy filled the bags beyond the prescribed weight. As East put it, "I undertook to play God. When I knew Jesse cheated a person in some way, I'd give him an extra measure of whatever I was selling him. . . . Naturally, I did not make my dishonesty known to anyone."[76] He sold the ice, meat, and other products by their actual weight.

Finally, his employer caught East selling ice by the actual weight to a black minister. Confronted with the evidence, East could not deny the charge. Without warning, Wild hit the boy squarely on the jaw, knocking him into a refrigerator. It would not be the last time that Wild administered such a beating, but East kept coming to the aid of cheated customers. Again, Wild detected East's efforts, on this occasion discovering some excessively heavy sacks. Instead of striking his clerk this time, he weighed every bag in the store and charged the overweight items to East. It took the boy the entire summer to pay the debt, and receiving no salary meant no new clothes for school that fall and few, if any, textbooks. Never one to back down, East continued to "play God," despite the odds. He insisted, "Justice was not abstract with me; it was real and personal. . . . How could I with full knowledge of what I was doing cheat a man who needed every cent he had to take care of his family?"[77] Apparently, neither threats nor punishments could weaken his commitment to justice.

Age and maturity only strengthened East's personal code of ethics and alienation from southern society. In 1939, at Pearl River Junior College in Poplarville, Mississippi, East wasted no time in demonstrating his stubborn, rebellious temperament.[78] The school had a compulsory ROTC program that included drill sessions three mornings each week. East had to work to stay in school, and the only job he found required staying until midnight. As a result, he slept through most of the early morning drill sessions. When asked to explain his absences, East replied that he came to school for an education, not for military training. The regular army colonel in charge of the ROTC unit reported him to the administration, and East received an automatic one-week suspension.

At the beginning of the second semester, East, citing his economic plight, pleaded for exemption from the program. When his request was firmly rejected, he called the colonel a stupid "son-of-a-bitch" and stalked out of the office. Seething with anger, he composed, mimeographed, and distributed a four-page vitriolic attack on the military and the local ROTC program. To no one's surprise, the school expelled him the following day.[79] East had once again exercised his gift for opposing what most southerners held dear, in this instance the military.[80] During the 1920s and 1930s, when military drilling lost favor throughout much of the country, it remained popular in the South,[81] much to East's chagrin.

East's pattern of casting himself as an outsider continued. After his expulsion, he worked for several months for the local newspaper, *The Weekly Democrat,* writing a column for the social page entitled "Puttering with Percy."[82] He then moved to Hattiesburg and went to work for the Greyhound Bus Lines in the baggage department. This position lasted for nearly a year until he took a higher paying job with the Southern Railway System. As a ticket clerk he made $40 per week, an excellent wage by Mississippi standards,[83] but East never felt a part of the company. He noted, "from the day I reported to work at Southern Railway, I didn't fit. It was April 18, 1942, when I began and August 1, 1951, when I left, and that's a long time not to fit. Somehow, through it all, I never cared whether a train was on time or not."[84] He stayed with the company, however, because he had married Katherine McNeese in March 1942, and felt he had to support his family.

Dissatisfaction with his job and with life itself heightened on East's twenty-first birthday—for it was then that Bertie East revealed to her son that he was adopted. East had suspected the truth for a number of years. Once Jesse Wild had called him "a little adopted bastard," and on another occasion, a distant relative introduced him as "Jim and Bertie's adopted boy." Each incident troubled East, but he had been too ashamed and too numb emotionally to question his parents. Yet these suspicions failed to prepare him for the actual story. As he admitted, it "literally knocked the props from under me."[85]

For all of his twenty-one years, East had felt like an outsider and now that isolation and insecurity seemed total.

Recalling the many family reunions he had attended as a youth, he now realized why most relatives ignored him or pushed him aside.[86] He suddenly felt a certain distance between himself and his adoptive family. Even the love provided by Jim and Bertie East could not bridge the gap, and, understandably, he did not feel a part of his natural mother's family either.[87] Regarding his blood mother, Laura Battle Hopkins, his feelings were mixed. He confessed,

> I almost hated her. How could a mother give away her child? What kind of woman would do such a [*sic*] thing? I was confused and resentful and disgusted. As hard as I tried, I could not get the woman off my mind. . . . I never wanted to see her. Frustration was my fate; there were too many questions to which I could find no answers.[88]

Engulfed by depression, East, who had always possessed a temper that hovered near the boiling point, found it increasingly difficult to control his emotions. In this state of mind, he entered the army in December 1942.

From the beginning of his military duty, East experienced untold adjustment difficulties. In less than twelve months, the army transferred him five times, and on no occasion did he see combat in either the European or Pacific theaters. Like most Americans, East wanted to contribute to the war effort, and his feelings, like the South's, ran deep. No section of the country gave stronger support to the United States' role in the Second World War than the South.[89] In fact, the region's dedication to the conflict helped reunite the Democratic Party, which had split over Roosevelt's New Deal.[90] From the southern viewpoint, no effort was too great to defeat Nazism, Fascism, and the Japanese. Ironically, the one time East followed his southern instincts, his wishes were denied:

> I was confused and angry and disgusted. Why? Over and over I asked the question. Why, since I had to be in the Army, could I not at least be sent overseas where I might feel that I was doing some small amount of good, instead of being aimlessly shipped hither and yon about the United States, from one meaningless job to another.[91]

To make matters worse, the last job to which he had been assigned at Camp Butner, North Carolina, no longer existed by the time he arrived. With nothing to do but wash dishes and drink beer, East's despondency increased. Remembering this time, he lamented, "What a lonely, miserable feeling it is to be some place and not know a single person with whom you can talk."[92] Adding to this already heavy psychological load was word that his natural mother had died recently. At first he tried, unsuccessfully, to be happy about her death; he then attempted, likewise without success, to summon up pity. Finally, his emotional burden overwhelmed him.

P. D. East started to experience complete and total lapses of memory. This had occurred several times before he arrived in North Carolina, but never with the frequency and duration of his latest episodes. The most frightening incident, and the one that prompted him to seek medical attention, took place as he walked to the PX for a beer. He remembered leaving the barracks, but the rest was a total blank until he found himself standing in the middle of a busy street. Upon returning to the base, he received permission to report to the hospital.

Once there, he saw a psychiatrist, Felix Goldberg. Goldberg prescribed a sedative, and for the first time in months East spent a restful night. The following day the doctor began questioning him in an effort to discover the source of his problem. After two weeks of this therapy and only two lapses of memory, East requested his release from the hospital. Goldberg agreed reluctantly. Within two weeks, East returned more frightened than ever. Shortly thereafter, in late 1943, Dr. Goldberg suggested that his patient accept a medical discharge. He explained that East "was temperamentally unsuited for the rigid discipline demanded by the military."[93] East inquired if this indicated a serious mental problem. The psychiatrist informed him that the lapses only reflected East's attempt to escape an unbearable situation; some people turned to drugs or alcohol, while East allowed his mind to act as a safety valve. To prevent a total nervous breakdown, and to help him adjust to civilian life, Goldberg advised East to contact a psychiatrist after leaving the army.[94]

Despite continued therapy, the expected cure failed to materialize. When he tried to return to work with the Southern Railroad, the company doctor refused to certify him as medically fit. East admitted that the responsibility for this state of affairs rested with him alone, "The fault was mine, of course, because I refused to talk with [the doctor] freely. . . . I could not bring myself to talk about my family. The question of why a mother would give away a child haunted me day and night, but I discussed it with no one."[95] Wracked by mental anguish and thoughts of suicide, East finally told the psychiatrist about his adoption. The doctor advised him to communicate with his blood relations. Feeling he had nothing to lose, East contacted his uncle, Larson Z. Battle. A warm relationship developed from the moment the two men met. East recalled, "Here was a man to whom I could talk. I knew that without having to think about it. . . . We were friends without sparring to find out what the other thought."[96]

Dr. Battle revealed to his nephew what he knew about the boy's mother and father. East, in turn, unburdened himself to his uncle, disclosing many problems. The doctor, in an effort to help his troubled nephew, offered to pay his way through college and even invited him to live with him in Jackson, Mississippi. Although tempted, East refused to accept the offer of a college education because he felt inadequate intellectually. Since Battle's wife and daughter resented East's presence in their home, he also declined the invitation to live with his uncle. Like his numerous future visits to Jackson, this one was confined to only a few days.

Eventually, East summoned up enough courage to go to his mother's grave while visiting, for the first and last time, his half-sister in Houston. Not knowing what to expect at the cemetery, he approached the trip with apprehension. His fears proved groundless. Remembering his thoughts at the time, he wrote, "As I stood in the cemetery beside the grave I felt the deepest compassion I've ever known, before or since. . . . It was, as a matter of fact, a relief of some sort. For the first time in my life, I knew full well I didn't hate my mother."[97] This emotional release and his uncle's warm friendship seemed to have a therapeutic effect on East. His memory lapses disappeared and within six months of his discharge the railroad's psychiatrists recommended he be allowed to return to work. The company complied.

With his new-found peace of mind, East struggled to overcome his self-image as an outsider. He now wished to provide his wife Katherine, whom he married in March 1942,[98] with all the material rewards of success. As he put it, "I decided to become an outstanding young man."[99] To accomplish this task, he joined the Hattiesburg civic clubs, contributed to the right charities, spoke to people he despised, and stayed sober. Soon, the local country club asked him to apply for membership. He declined reluctantly for financial reasons. In fact, his quest for success had forced him into debt. It took nearly two years before East grew disenchanted with his new life. Reflecting on this period, East commented, "I thought I was a happy man who enjoyed every second of it. I must have been sicker than anyone thought."[100]

By the mid-1940s, the Southern Railroad promoted East from ticket clerk to traveling passenger representative on the "Southerner" and the "Tennessean." In this position, his old attitudes began to reassert themselves. His job required him to write a thorough report of each trip no matter how routine the journey. Never able to compose these documents, East started to concoct absurd accounts. One such report read, "On this trip the train was wrecked and everyone was killed." Another one stated, "I traveled from New York to New Orleans and back to Washington and I didn't open my mouth to a single person. The train was on time, and I was glad, glad, glad! Do you hear? I was glad!" Naturally, the management did not appreciate such narratives.[101]

Although railroad officials questioned East's unorthodox reports, they never threatened to dismiss him. When he began to violate southern laws and company policy regarding the seating of blacks in Jim Crow cars, however, trouble ensued. Some northern states had overturned such laws, but southern states, owing to strong public support, adhered to these practices. Those unwilling to comply, either train personnel or passengers, faced arrest and the railroad itself could be sued.[102] East first sensed the illogical nature of segregation in the train's dining car. There curtains surrounded each table allowing blacks and whites to sit in close proximity without making contact. Although East did not comprehend why whites were willing to sit within a few feet of blacks separated only by a flimsy piece of material, he at first said nothing. He rebelled eventually, however, over the issue of special cars for each race. As passenger representative, the duty of moving blacks to the Jim Crow cars fell to East. He carried out this chore with no complaint for several years until finally, in 1949, a black refused to move. The man asked very politely why he should move, and proceeded to note that his money was the same color as that belonging to the white passengers. Satisfied with this argument, East allowed the man to remain in the car reserved for whites.[103]

Few people on the train approved of East's actions. The conductor, hostess, and some passengers reported the incident to the railroad's management. When asked to explain his behavior, East told his superiors that he agreed with the black man's reasoning. At that point, East believed he could have regained his employer's confidence by repenting and promising never to let it happen again. East found himself unable to choose this alternative. "I could not bring myself to repent; to do so would have been completely dishonest, and I knew it."[104] By persisting in his viewpoint, East knew he had jeopardized his job. To keep from being fired, he resigned his position as passenger representative and returned to the Hattiesburg ticket office.

Still dissatisfied with working for the Southern Railroad, East decided to try to develop his talent as a writer. Between 1947 and 1949, while remaining with the railroad, he enrolled in writing courses at Southern Mississippi College. During this period, East wrote a number of feature articles for various newspapers in the South.[105] In his most ambitious venture, he wrote a novel, *To the Memory of One of De Lawd's Most Remarkable Chillun, Roark Bradford.* East had been impressed with Bradford's work, especially his *Ol' Man Adam an' His Chillun,* which was used as the basis for the play and movie, *The Green Pastures.* Bradford's writing dealt mainly with blacks and their interpretation of the Bible. In treating this subject, Bradford had captured brilliantly the dialect of southern blacks. Copying this formula, East's novel centered on the sermons of a fictitious black minister. After several years of searching, East found no one willing to publish his work.[106]

The pleasure and money brought by East's free-lance writing did not diminish his aversion to the railroad. By July 1951, he made $80 per week and, with over nine years seniority, had job security; but such advantages meant little to him. As he remarked, "One day it suddenly came to me that if I had to spend another hour in the place I would go raving mad. I was . . . miserable and sick of the whole thing." Thus, on the morning of 15 July 1951, P. D. East submitted his resignation, effective 1 August 1951. When asked about this rash move, East could not articulate his reasons for quitting. "I couldn't explain it to anyone. I didn't know why I'd done it, after all, I was in debt, as usual, and had no prospect of another job."[107] At this point, his wife, Katherine, left him and took their seven-year-old son, Byron, with her. Despite pleas from East to return, she never reconciled with her husband. As a result, he charged her with desertion and was granted a divorce in February 1952.[108]

Within a week he married Billie Porter.

East tried to subsist on the money he earned as a writer, but with little success. Finally, in December 1951, a friend informed him that a local labor union, the Coke and Chemical Workers, needed someone to edit its newspaper, *The Union Review*. Armed with his journalistic experience, East campaigned for the opening and won. The chief steward of the union and East split the profits from the paper on a 40–60 percent basis. In theory, East ran the publication, but in practice, the chief steward approved every detail, economic and editorial. East did not like this situation, but his substantial income provided the inducement to remain. In fact, *The Union Review* was so successful that the local garment workers' union approached East to edit its paper, *The Local Advocate*. Together, the two papers proved so financially rewarding that East climbed out of debt for the first time in his life. Money, however, had limited appeal for him. Freedom of thought and action meant more than security. He concluded,

> It had nearly reached the point that I had to call him [the chief steward] before I went to the bathroom. Slowly and painfully I realized that I had simply swapped one millstone—punching a clock at the railroad—for another—the ever present demands of the chief steward.

Like that first millstone, East also cast this one aside by quitting in early 1953.[109]

To find freedom to act and speak as he pleased, East concluded that he must be self-employed. The perfect solution seemed to lie in starting his own newspaper. "After some thought, I decided I would like to own a small town weekly newspaper. That way I could be my own boss, all profits would be mine, and I'd be completely independent—no clocks to punch, and no boss making demands." Thus, in November 1953, taking his $3,000 in savings, East established the *Petal Paper* in Petal, Mississippi, a town three miles outside of Hattiesburg. The local merchants welcomed East with enthusiasm. They promised mass advertising and as much support as he needed.

At this point, P. D. East believed he had at last achieved economic independence, and he was quite pleased with himself. He noted that he had "finally found a means of getting somewhere from nowhere."[110] For a short time his prediction appeared correct, but after the *Brown v. Board of Education* ruling his relentless conscience would push him once again into the role of rebel and outcast.

Notes

[1] As a poor white, P. D. East was not automatically condemned to a life dominated by racial prejudice. Some southerners from the lower economic strata, "rednecks," like East, eventually rebelled against their heritage of racial hatred, e.g., Rev. Will Campbell and Senator Fred Harris. V. O. Key, Jr., in his classic, *Southern Politics in State and Nation* (New York: Alfred A. Knopf, 1949), 5, stated that the black's worst enemies were upper-class whites. Professor Key's conclusion, however, does not reduce the hardships endured by blacks at the hands of the sometimes manipulated poor whites.

[2] I. A. Newby, *The South: A History* (New York: Holt, Rinehart and Winston, 1978), 417.

[3] Key, *Southern Politics*, 5, 229–30. See also Herbert Blumer, "The Future of the Color Line," in *The South in Continuity and Change,* ed. John C. McKinney and Edgar T. Thompson (Durham, North Carolina: Duke University Press, 1965), 328; M. Elaine Burgess, "Race Relations and Social Change," in McKinney and Thompson, 338–39; George Brown Tindall, *The Emergence of the New South, 1913–1945* (Baton Rouge: Louisiana State University Press, 1967), 731; Newby, *The South*, 403, 420–74, 474–79; Francis M. Wilhoit, *The Politics of Massive Resistance* (New York: George Braziller, 1973), 238–39.

[4] There is some question as to whether East's parents were ever married. He told his friends, the Rev. Will Campbell and others, that his mother was rather promiscuous and that she never married his father. East wrote to a friend that possibly his uncle had lied about his mother being married to spare his feelings. P. D. East to Orvin Alfred; no date, P. D. East Papers, Box 26, Mugar Memorial Library, Boston University. Yet, in his autobiography, he clearly states that legal bonds did exist, so I have chosen to accept this account. If East was illegitimate, that fact could only have strengthened his opinion that he was an outsider. It is also interesting to note that East never tried to contact his father or his father's family. He never gave a reason for this inaction on his part.

[5] There is ample evidence that Laura Hopkins Battle was an emotionally unstable person. This unstability, no doubt, influenced her prompt decision to put her son up for adoption. She was often subject to temper tantrums and violent outbursts.

Mississippi Women's College expelled her twice for such actions. She married three times and had one child from each union. Two of the children were raised by her father and brother; East was the third child. As a pianist touring the South, her temper led her to cancel performances on more than one occasion. P. D. East, *The Magnolia Jungle: The Life, Times and Education of a Southern Editor* (New York: Simon and Schuster, 1960), 105-7.

6 Ibid., 99; Will D. Campbell, *Brother to a Dragonfly* (New York: Seabury Press, 1977), 215.

7 Joseph J. Spengler, "Southern Economic Trends and Prospects," in McKinney and Thompson, 109-12; Tindall, *Emergence of the New South*, 480. See also Neal R. Peirce, *The Deep South States of America: People, Politics, and Power in the Seven Deep South States* (New York: W. W. Norton and Company, 1974), 164; Joseph J. Spengler, "Demographic and Economic Change in the South, 1940-1960," in Allan P. Sindler, ed., *Change in the Contemporary South* (Durham, North Carolina: Duke University Press, 1963), 35-37.

8 Tindall, *Emergence of the New South*, 319-20. See also Thomas D. Clark, *The Emerging South* (New York: Oxford University Press, 1968), 107.

9 Thomas D. Clark and Albert D. Kirwan, *The South Since Appomattox: A Century of Regional Change* (New York: Oxford University Press, 1967), 139-41. The South produced nearly 50 percent of the nation's timber at this time, with Louisiana, Mississippi, Arkansas, and Alabama among the top producers.

10 Abraham Berglund, George T. Starnes, and Frank T. de Uyuer, *Labor in the Industrial South: A Survey of Wages and Living Conditions in Three Major Industries of the New South* (Charlottesville: University of Virginia Press, 1930), 53-68.

11 As an illustration of the primitive nature of medical care, East was treated for stepping on a nail by having a long rod wrapped in cotton and soaked in iodine inserted into the wounds. As a result he contracted blood poisoning instead of lockjaw. East, *Magnolia Jungle*, 24.

12 Ibid., 18.

13 Berglund, Starnes, and de Uyuer, *Labor in the Industrial South*, 53-68.

14 William Faulkner, *Light in August* (New York: Vintage Books, 1972), 3.

15 Tindall, *Emergence of the New South*, 329.

16 Clark and Kirwan, *The South Since Appomattox*, 142.

17 The stumps of the trees left by the large timber concerns would be blasted from the ground with dynamite and then hauled to companies that extracted resin, turpentine, and other by-products. East, *Magnolia Jungle*, 58.

[18] During the first seventeen years of his life, East moved a total of eight times. Ibid., 26. On this idea of East as an outsider, see also P. D. East, "Look Back in Pain," undated text of speech given by East, 4, Box 54, East Papers. Hereafter cited as East, "Look Back in Pain"; John Howard Griffin, taped response to questions submitted by the author, Fort Worth, Texas, 6 December 1976. Hereafter cited as Griffin, taped response.

[19] East, *Magnolia Jungle*, 26.

[20] East, "Look Back in Pain," 1.

[21] East, *Magnolia Jungle*, 26.

[22] Ibid., 56-57.

[23] Ibid., 74-79.

[24] Griffin, taped response.

[25] Samuel S. Hill, Jr., *Southern Churches in Crisis* (New York: Holt, Rinehart and Winston, 1966), xii. See also Samuel S. Hill, Jr., "The South's Two Cultures," in Samuel S. Hill, Jr., ed., *Religion and the Solid South* (New York: Abingdon Press, 1972), 24-25; Newby, *The South*, 414; Francis B. Simkins and Charles P. Roland, *A History of the South*, rev. ed. (New York: Alfred A. Knopf, 1972), 411; John S. Reed, *The Enduring South: Subcultural Persistence in Mass Society* (Lexington, Massachusetts: D. C. Heath and Company, 1972), 63-68.

[26] Kenneth K. Bailey, *Southern White Protestantism in the Twentieth Century* (New York: Harper and Row, 1964), ix.

[27] Tindall, *Emergence of the New South*, 197.

[28] Joseph H. Fichter and George L. Maddox, "Religion in the South, Old and New," in McKinney and Thompson, 363.

[29] In the South between 1950 and 1964, the Baptists, Methodists, and Presbyterians totaled 80 percent of those people claiming church membership. Reed, *The Enduring South*, 59; Hill, *Southern Churches in Crisis*, 23.

[30] Newby, *The South*, 410-12; Tindall, *Emergence of the New South*, 196-98; Hill, *Southern Churches in Crisis*, 99-102.

[31] Reed, *The Enduring South*, 69.

[32] Ibid., 60-61.

[33] Newby, *The South*, 411-13.

[34] Hill, *Religion and the Solid South*, 36, 43.

[35] Ibid., 50.

[36] Tindall, *Emergence of the New South*, 198.

[37] Hill, *Religion and the Solid South*, 33-35, 43. It might be noted that the early colonist felt free to enslave blacks since it was assumed they had no souls. Winthrop D. Jordon, *White Over Black: American Attitudes Towards the Negro, 1550-1812* (Chapel Hill: University of North Carolina Press, 1968), 179-215.

[38] Hill, *Religion and the Solid South*, 54.

[39] The traveling revivalists were usually the most theologically and

socially conservative in the South. Tindall, *Emergence of the New South*, 197; Simkins and Roland, *History of the South*, 421.

[40] East, *Magnolia Jungle*, 45.

[41] Ibid., 41, 43.

[42] East, "Look Back in Pain," 4.

[43] Griffin, taped response.

[44] East, *Magnolia Jungle*, 45.

[45] Ibid., 47.

[46] Ibid., 49.

[47] Griffin, taped response.

[48] East, *Magnolia Jungle*, 49.

[49] Ibid., 64.

[50] Ibid., 57.

[51] At times East tried to develop a religious faith out of genuine spiritual need, but often, especially when he began to publish the *Petal Paper*, he adopted the outward trappings of religion because he believed such actions would help him financially.

[52] Campbell, *Brother to a Dragonfly*, 219.

[53] Griffin, taped response. Campbell, *Brother to a Dragonfly*, 217–28; Millard Fuller to the author, 20 June 1977; Sarah Patton Boyle to the author, 1 August 1977.

[54] John Howard Griffin noted that some of East's closest friends were deeply religious, e.g., Jacques Maritain and Thomas Merton, both Catholic priests, Rev. Will Campbell, Rev. Clarence Jordan, and Griffin himself. Griffin, taped response.

[55] Griffin, taped response. P. D. East, interview held with reporters from *Time Magazine*, New York, New York, February 1957, 1, Box 53, East Papers. Hereafter cited as East, interview with *Time Magazine*; East, "Look Back in Pain," 8–9; Ralph McGill, review of *The Magnolia Jungle: The Life, Times and Education of a Southern Editor*, in *New York Times Book Review*, 14 August 1960, 7; John Howard Griffin review of *The Magnolia Jungle: The Life, Times and Education of a Southern Editor*, in *Sepia*, December 1960, 13.

[56] East, *Magnolia Jungle*, 27.

[57] East, interview with *Time Magazine*.

[58] This topic receives extensive discussion in the previously cited works by Key, Newby, Tindall, and Wilhoit. See also Morton Sosna, *In Search of the Silent South: Southern Liberals and the Race Issue* (New York: Columbia University Press, 1977); C. Vann Woodward, *The Strange Career of Jim Crow*, 3rd rev. ed. (New York: Oxford University Press, 1974).

[59] Newby, *The South*, 432.

[60] Key, *Southern Politics*, 5. Key notes that issues other than race were in fact crucial to southern politics. This was possible since practically all southerners agreed on the policy of white su-

premacy, but to the outside world race appeared the dominant factor in all political discussions.

61 Ibid., 233.

62 Peirce. *Deep South States,* 169.

63 Newby, *The South,* 435.

64 Peirce, *Deep South States,* 169. See also Hortense Powdermaker, *After Freedom: A Cultural Study of the Deep South* (New York: The Viking Press, 1939), 43–55.

65 Howard W. Odum, *An American Epoch: Southern Portraiture in the National Picture* (New York: Henry Holt, 1930), 321.

66 Peirce, *Deep South States,* 169.

67 Newby, *The South,* 418.

68 East, interview with *Time Magazine.*

69 East, *Magnolia Jungle,* 25.

70 Ibid.

71 Ibid., 40.

72 Ibid., 39.

73 P. D. East, "The South, Collectively, is a Patient Most Ill," *Vital Speeches,* 15 May 1957, 477.

74 East, *Magnolia Jungle,* 31–32.

75 Ibid., 89–90.

76 Ibid., 71.

77 Ibid., 84–85.

78 East had a very poor education throughout his life. Mississippi's schools received very little funding from the state. In 1940 the average national expenditure was about $144.00 per pupil. The southern average was far below this figure and Mississippi ranked last with $47.49 per pupil. Throughout his five years in high school, East never had enough money to purchase all the necessary textbooks. For an in-depth discussion of southern education see Tindall, *Emergence of the New South,* 473–504.

79 East, *Magnolia Jungle,* 96–97; East, "Look Back in Pain," 5.

80 Traditionally, historians and the general public have regarded the South as possessing a martial character. This spirit of militarism, they argue, led southerners to support every major military conflict involving the United States. For works supporting this viewpoint see John Hope Franklin, *The Militant South, 1800–1861* (Cambridge: Harvard University Press, 1956); Rollin G. Osterweis, *Romanticism and Nationalism in the Old South* (New Haven: Yale University Press, 1949); C. Vann Woodward, *Origins of the New South, 1877–1913* (Baton Rouge: Louisiana State University Press, 1951); Pat Watters, *The South and the Nation* (New York: Pantheon Books, 1969). Within the last few years, there has been a challenge to this thesis of a martial South. The revisionists point out that the South was not always or unanimously in support of the military. For example, the

deep devotion to the armed forces and its rigid discipline has risen more from the upper class than the lower class. For a detailed discussion see the excellent article by Robert E. May, "Dixie's Martial Image: A Continuing Historiographical Enigma," *Historian* 40 (February 1978): 213–34.

81 Arthur A. Ekirch, *The Civilian and the Military* (Colorado Springs: Ralph Myles Publisher, 1972), 217–19.

82 East's actual name was Percy Dale but he preferred to use his initials since Percy did not sound very masculine.

83 Sindler, ed., *Contemporary South*, 34. The average annual wage in Mississippi for 1940 was $218.

84 East, *Magnolia Jungle*, 98.

85 Ibid., 99.

86 East, "Look Back in Pain," 4.

87 P. D. East to Maxwell Geismar, 23 April 1961, Box 28, East Papers.

88 East, *Magnolia Jungle*, 100.

89 Wayne S. Cole, "America First and the South, 1940–1941," *Journal of Southern History* 22 (February 1956): 36–47; Monroe Lee Billington, *The Political South in the Twentieth Century* (New York: Charles Scribner's Sons, 1975), 33–37; Key, *Southern Politics*, 353–54; Tindall, *Emergence of the New South*, 687–731.

90 Tindall, *Emergence of the New South*, 687.

91 East, *Magnolia Jungle*, 100–101.

92 Ibid., 101.

93 Ibid., 102.

94 Ibid., 101–3.

95 Ibid., 104.

96 Ibid., 105.

97 Ibid., 107.

98 Before 1959 few references were available on Katherine East. The most important was the divorce complaint filed by P. D. East on 19 February 1952. Her name appeared on one other occasion when she co-authored an article with her husband. Even though the marriage lasted nearly ten years and resulted in one child, Byron Percy, East never mentioned Katherine or the boy in his autobiography.

99 East, *Magnolia Jungle*, 108.

100 Ibid.

101 Ibid., 109.

102 Sosna, *Silent South*, 134–36; Charles S. Mangum, Jr., *The Legal Status of the Negro* (Chapel Hill: University of North Carolina Press, 1940), 182–87.

103 East, *Magnolia Jungle*, 108–10.

104 Ibid., 110.

105 At least once East shared the by-line of an article with his wife, Katherine.

[106] P. D. East, rejected pages for the *Magnolia Jungle*, 236, Box 11, East Papers. East said the reason given by the publisher for the rejection was the criticism by the NAACP of Roark Bradford's work. Since he had used the black dialect, the group charged him with emphasizing the stupidity of the southern black. They told East that publication of this similar book would create an explosive situation.

[107] East, "Look Back in Pain," 5; East, *Magnolia Jungle*, 112.

[108] *P. D. East v. Katherine East*, Chancery Court of Lauderdale County, Mississippi, number B2391, 19 February 1952, Box 45, East Papers.

[109] East, "Look Back in Pain," 5-6; East, *Magnolia Jungle*, 112-15; East, interview with *Time Magazine*, 2-3.

[110] East, *Magnolia Jungle*, 114.

3

Conscience Over Profit: The Development of a Racial Liberal by Chance and by Choice

P. D. East began publishing the *Petal Paper* for one basic reason: to make money. He never intended to involve himself in any fight for human rights or the airing of controversial opinions.[1] At first he did not even have an editorial policy, and when one finally emerged it seemed totally inoffensive. He promised simply to maintain fairness and a willingness to compromise. On occasion he offered some of his viewpoints, but most often he avoided taking sides. Even this restrained position created trouble for East, however. As black Americans began to attack segregation successfully through the courts in cases such as *Brown v. Board of Education of Topeka,* his subscribers and advertisers began asking him for his feelings on court-ordered desegregation. He tried to steer a middle course by supporting segregation and at the same time by noting the difficulties and consequences of disobeying the Supreme Court. This position satisfied few. East's fellow Mississippians would not allow him to straddle the editorial fence on this issue. They demanded unequivocal support for the "southern way of life," and considered anything less traitorous. Soon they began to pressure him into adopting their rigid racial attitudes, but the more they did so, the more East resented their actions.

Finally, and almost inevitably, his old rebellious nature and sense of decency led him to speak out against blind devotion to white supremacy, although he still supported segregation. Such moderate views outraged the hard-line segregationists who stepped up their bitter criticism. East tried to avoid a running fight with these professional southerners, as he called them, since it cost him money. When they refused to accept his peace offerings, East grew more outspoken. In March 1956, when he published the "jackass ad," he reached a point from which he could not retreat. He had become an ally of black Americans and had embarked upon a crusade that would continue for the rest of his life.

It was a strange turn of events from those early days in November 1953, when publication of the *Petal Paper* had begun under the most pleasant of circumstances. Citizens of Petal warmly greeted P. D. and Billie East's newspaper. The Easts hoped to make a comfortable income from their paper and keep the Petalites happy as well. According to East, the formula for success was quite simple: love American motherhood and hate sin. The policy had worked for the other weekly papers, and he knew it would work for him.[2] To implement this plan, East hired six women to collect community news. Prominent among these reports were social events, high school athletics, hospital notes, stories on local men in the armed forces, and business developments in Petal. East himself took photographs to accompany these articles. For potential readers with a religious bent he arranged with several ministers to write a "Prayer and Meditation" column, and for those interested in country and western music, the paper carried a piece each week called "Low Down on the Hoe Down" by country radio singer Jimmy Swan.[3] An additional ploy to raise circulation involved mentioning the names of as many people as he could each week. Every issue carried a column entitled "Citizen of the Week." In this feature East praised some local notable's devotion to the well-being of Petal. As he later admitted, these people were usually "village businessmen whose sole contribution, like mine, was to figure out how to make a dollar from the citizens of the area."[4] Wanting to slight no one, he mentioned in his column, "East Side," the names of people not honored as "Citizen of the Week." He assumed that people loved to see their names in print and would buy the publication that took advantage of this weakness.

It also seemed reasonable to East that for people to buy and advertise in his paper the local economy had to remain strong. To help foster a favorable economic climate, if only psychologically, he praised ceaselessly the economic and cultural resources of the community. He rivaled even George Babbitt in his boosterism. In one piece he boasted,

> Sort of thought we might write in our editorial this week something about the needs of Petal, like civic clubs, churches, better school facilities, better streets and the like.

> But in looking around we have decided that such a subject would be a poor choice. And the reason is this *[sic]* Petal has everything that anyone in Mississippi's large cities has. We've more than enough to meet our needs.[5]

East thought that no right-thinking Petalite would argue with such a statement.

With this philosophy East should not have had to worry about offending anyone, but he worried nonetheless. To avoid any possible misunderstanding, he emphasized in his first issue that the *Petal Paper* was to serve the citizens of Petal and nothing more. His policy statement left little doubt on the matter: "The primary purpose of the *Petal Paper,* which you are now holding in your hand, is to be of service to you. We have no bones to pick with anyone; therefore, there will be no crusades, except when in the public interest."[6] East wasted no time putting this innocuous policy into action. On the hotly debated issue of incorporation for Petal he wrote:

> Almost from the first day the office of the *Petal Paper* was opened, we have had the question of "Incorporation" called to our attention. We have heard parts of both sides of the question, and are convinced the question certainly has two sides, both with good points.

> Now, we have been asked by advocates of both sides what we thought about the question of Incorporation. We think it's a good subject, and intelligent subject, and feel that it should be discussed not only in the barber shops, the grocery stores, the service stations, but in your paper, which after all, is the place for such a discussion.

> As a newspaper our job is not to discuss the question; our job is to report your discussions, be they pro or con. As a newspaper our job is not to make news, but to report it accurately and as unbiased as is humanly possible.[7]

After this so-called editorial, he went on to note the remarks of several people on incorporation. Looking back on this fence-straddling type of journalism, East said, "Too many Mississippi editors have cast-iron guts; nothing makes them ill. As for me, I was probably the only one with a stomach made of solid brass."[8]

To ingratiate himself further with the community and make money, East, while seeking additional advertising revenue, spent sixteen to eighteen hours a day talking with anyone who would listen. He also joined the Kiwanis Club to help promote his paper. He remarked that "each Tuesday I attended the meeting and dutifully ate the green peas and mashed potatoes, shook hands, smiled and listened to my peers discuss the weather and the world situation."[9] To enable himself to maintain this hectic pace, he began to take Dexedrine; then at night to counteract the stimulant, he took sleeping pills. By mid-January this regimen put East, suffering from exhaustion, in the hospital.

Upon his recovery and return to work, East made his first editorial mistake, quite unintentionally. In honor of Abraham Lincoln's birthday, East ran a front-page story praising the former president and calling his assassination unfortunate. Almost immediately several readers cornered the editor and told him the only unfortunate aspect of Lincoln's death was that it had not come sooner. Shocked by this response, East refused to apologize. He learned quickly that even mild disagreements such as this caused financial repercussions as he watched his February income drop sharply.[10]

Equally troublesome were psychological problems he encountered as he grew increasingly dissatisfied with his membership in the Kiwanis Club. The forced congeniality began to irritate him. At one meeting, he removed his obligatory name tag. When a fellow Kiwanian asked about his first name, East replied, "You can just call me mister." Failing to see the humor in this comment, his acquaintance requested that he wear the name tag. East complied as he did not want to lose more money. He forced himself to continue smiling, shaking hands, and being, as he put it, a joy-boy. But the income he derived from such activities failed to alleviate his disenchantment with this lifestyle. As he noted, "In the midst of laughter and good fellowship, I suffered the deepest loneliness."[11] This mental anguish led eventually to frequent outbursts of temper.

The first episode occurred when a local merchant and advertiser told East that his business would improve if only he attended church. East snapped back, "I appreciate your suggestion, but I'm damned if I'll use the church for business purposes."[12] He then stormed out of the man's store; the man, in turn, withdrew his advertisement from the paper for the next two weeks. Disturbed by this loss, East apologized, saying he had felt ill that day. The peace was short lived. Later, the same individual asked him why he did not live in Petal. East explained that his wife preferred Hattiesburg since Petal, as an unincorporated area, had no police or fire protection. This answer proved unsatisfactory as the merchant told him that setting up residence in Petal would make the paper more profitable. Once more East exploded, "By God, if I have to be subjected to the whim of every bastard with three bucks to buy my paper, I'll quit publishing the damn thing."[13] This time East returned to apologize before the man had the opportunity to cancel his advertisement.

The fear of losing money enabled East to keep his depression and resulting temperamental outbursts under control, at least during the remainder of 1954. In fact, he was so busy promoting his newspaper that he overlooked the Supreme Court's momentous *Brown* decision. On that day, Monday, 17 May 1954, East spent his time photographing a quarter-pound egg laid by a local hen. As he remembered, "I was more concerned with the size of a hen's rump than I was with the basic rights of one man in every ten."[14] Over a month would pass before he commented upon the case, but his fellow southerners felt impelled to speak out immediately.

On 19 May 1954, John Bell Williams, United States representative from Mississippi, gave a speech to the House in which he condemned the ruling and used the epithet "Black Monday" to describe the day the court handed down its decision. Another Mississippian, Circuit Court Judge Tom P. Brady, delivered his own "Black Monday" address condemning the court and calling for organized opposition. His audience, the Greenwood, Mississippi, chapter of the Sons of the Revolution, received his message with such enthusiasm that he expanded it into a booklet, *Black Monday*. His call for formal resistance proved so powerful that Robert B. Patterson, a plantation manager from Indianola, Mississippi, together with several local businessmen, started the first group dedicated to fighting the court desegregation order, the White Citizens' Council of Mississippi (WCC). Patterson had called for a similar association in November 1953, when he learned of the case pending before the court, but few responded to his pleas. Now, with the ruling as an impetus and Brady's pamphlet as an official handbook, the Council began a vigorous campaign to thwart any attempts at integration.[15]

In undertaking this effort the WCC had ample support. Most southerners, 75 percent according to a reliable poll, opposed efforts to integrate schools. This same poll, taken in the early 1950s, revealed that nearly 70 percent of the white South saw blacks as lacking morals and ambition; 73 percent believed that blacks had an underdeveloped sense of responsibility; and nearly 60 percent believed that blacks were inferior intellectually.[16] In more blunt terms, most Mississippians agreed with a farmer from Calhoun County who said, "The best way to understand how people here feel is to put it the way my daddy put it: The nigger has no soul. He is like a duck, a chicken, or a mule. He hasn't got a soul." Or as a logger stated, "Let's face it; the nigger is a high-class beast."[17] The Yale-educated Judge Brady provided an equally pessimistic picture of blacks.

> You can dress a chimpanzee, house-break him, and teach him to use a knife and fork, but it will take countless generations of evolutionary development, if ever, before you can convince him that a caterpillar or a cockroach is not a delicacy. Likewise the social, political, economic, and religious preferences of the Negro remain close to the caterpillar and the cockroach.[18]

Such attitudes made it clear why whites objected so strongly to the *Brown* decision. They feared that interracial contacts at school would result inevitably in similar contacts outside the classroom, and this in turn would bring about interracial marriage, inferior children, and mongrelization of the white race. At that point the United States—like the once powerful civilizations of Egypt, Greece, Rome, and Spain—would supposedly fall victim to the destructive character of Negro blood.[19]

To prevent this potential tragedy, the White Citizens' Council and its allies urged all white southerners to close ranks in opposition to integration. Reasoning that nothing short of total agreement could bring victory, they worked to stamp out all dissent. No one could voice the slightest doubt about the wisdom of white supremacy or advocate compliance with the law. The WCC attempted to marshal every segment of southern society to this position. "To break ranks in any way branded the offender a communist and a traitor to the South."[20] No politician who hoped to remain in office dared to oppose the Council. Many, like Senator James O. Eastland, needed little prompting since they already believed in segregation. Eastland told a cheering crowd, "You are not required to obey any court which passes out such a ruling. In fact, you are obligated to defy it."[21] The Mississippi state legislature fulfilled its role by creating the Legal Educational Advisory Committee (LEAC) to maintain segregated schools in order "to preserve and promote the best interests of both races."[22]

The Council also enlisted the clergy in its fight to preserve white supremacy. It did not succeed with the hierarchy of most southern churches who appealed to their members to obey the law, but many local congregations and their ministers repudiated the official position. The sympathies of the majority of white southerners lay with the WCC, not with the denominational authorities.[23] This religious support proved so strong that the Council began to take on a religious character. Every chapter had its own chaplain and began and ended each meeting with prayerful pleas for God's blessings. Taking a cue from their congregations, Protestant clergymen had become active participants in the WCC and now comprised a sizeable portion of the organization's leadership. In line with this religious tendency, a persistent WCC theme emphasized God's alleged support of segregation. Relying on Noah's curse on his son Ham and his descendants, a passage from Leviticus in which the faithful were told to keep their animals, crops, and cloth from mingling with diverse kinds, and numerous other Biblical citations, the preachers tried to demonstrate that white supremacy and applied Christianity were the same.[24]

The White Citizens' Council further delighted in using carefully selected quotations from Thomas Jefferson and Abraham Lincoln to support its cause. The Council's newspaper, the *Citizen Council,* devoted an entire issue to Lincoln and his views on race. For those not receiving the paper, the WCC launched a nationwide advertising campaign to publicize Lincoln's ideas.[25]

Perhaps the most emotion-filled segregationist tactic was one that raised the time-honored specter of black men sexually violating southern white women. Southern men rationalized the need for racial separation as the only means available for protecting the virtue of their beloved women. Rekindling the cult of southern womanhood from the antebellum period,[26] these men looked to Judge Tom P. Brady as one of their most vocal spokesmen. In hyperbolic prose he expressed the admiration of southern men for their women. "The loveliest and purest of God's creatures, the nearest thing to angelic being that treads this terrestrial ball is the well-bred, cultured white woman or her blue-eyed, golden-haired little girl."[27] The WCC believed that no red-blooded southerner could resist protecting such a fair flower through the maintenance of rigid segregation.

In waging this war for the hearts and minds of white southerners, the Citizens' Council and its allies offered a large number of reasons to support white supremacy. Foremost among them were the supposedly disastrous consequences of integration. Taken together these motives left little room for neutrality or unenthusiastic support. The Council knew how to compel compliance and the pressure to conform was tremendous.

In this intolerant atmosphere East's subscribers and advertisers began to ask that he comment on the *Brown* decision. Initially he gained time by noting that he had to find out what verdict the court had rendered before offering his sentiments.[28] Upon reading the court's opinion, he remained neutral. He did not oppose the ruling, but he did not champion it either. Although he believed in segregation, he could not do so with the enthusiasm of most white southerners. He knew this stance would fail to appease their strident demands,[29] but he nonetheless tried to cling to the middle ground. As if to emphasize his devotion to segregation without condemning the Supreme Court, he printed a critical account of Adlai Stevenson's appearance with Mississippi Governor Hugh White at a Jimmy Rogers Day celebration. East rebuked White for presenting Stevenson as a friend of the state despite the former Illinois governor's stand against segregation.[30] His readers only increased their demands for stronger statements.

Unable to resist the pressure, a week later East finally published information on the *Brown* decision. It was a fence-straddling masterpiece. He ran two editorials on the subject, one from the *Christian Science Monitor* favoring the decision and a second from Gulfport, Mississippi, in opposition. In an editor's note accompanying the two pieces he wrote:

The important question of segregation is indeed good
editorial material, and possibly we should take a stand for
or against the recent Supreme Court ruling. We feel that
more important than segregation is the right of every
individual to decide for himself, to seek his own destiny,
express his own thoughts, follow his own reasoning. So,
Segregation or Non-Segregation—the thing that makes it
right or wrong is your opinion.[31]

He had decided that the safest position, and the most profitable,
was to straddle the issue. "I tried to ignore the whole thing at
first," he recalled. "I could anticipate what it would lead to. I
was trying not to think anything that would cost me money."[32]

East continued to take jabs at integrationists while supporting their opponents. In a particularly nasty piece, he attacked
Eleanor Roosevelt. At the time, her son, James, had been sued
for divorce by his second wife. Capitalizing on this circumstance,
East recounted the considerable marital difficulties of the
Roosevelt children and closed by stating, "Thus, while Mrs.
Roosevelt was trying to destroy segregation and preaching the
immorality of racial 'discrimination' in the South, her children
ran wild."[33] He followed this article the next week with reprints
of editorials supporting James O. Eastland for the Senate.
Subsequently, he wrote two editorials of his own in which he
portrayed Eastland as a friend of labor and a man who had
worked for the people of Mississippi and the nation. He also
supported William Colmer for the House of Representatives.[34]
Colmer was every bit as racist as Eastland and would later help
to initiate the Southern Manifesto, a 1956 declaration by nineteen senators and eighty-one congressmen in which they pledged
to resist desegregation by all lawful means. East even stooped to
reprinting some of the White Citizens' Council propaganda
regarding Abraham Lincoln's racist pronouncements.[35]

This racist material, although a regular feature, did not
dominate the paper. East concerned himself with many other
issues, some significant, most trivial. Of the more important
variety, he favored an end to an open range which resulted in
numerous collisions between livestock and automobiles.[36] When
a local packing company came under fire for mistreatment of
the animals it slaughtered, East jumped to its defense with his
own editorial and a reprint from another. The fact that the
Dixie Packing Company advertised in the *Petal Paper* and
provided numerous jobs in Petal did not endanger East's

standing locally.[37] He also endorsed the Southern Railroad, his former employer and current advertiser, when the company decided to discontinue passenger service between Meridian, Mississippi, and the Louisiana state line. Here, too, he remained on safe ground, as the only ones objecting strenuously to this action were the politicians.[38] On other topics, he opposed socialized medicine, favored taxing the Tennessee Valley Authority, and supported national defenses to oppose communism.[39]

Staying with such relatively safe stories and advocating the maintenance of segregation, East finished his first year of publishing on solid financial footing. As he recalled, "God was in His heaven, all was well in Petal, and nothing else mattered to me. I was still a Kiwanian in good standing, and the paper showed a profit. I had two automobiles, a nice white house, a hearty handshake, and a toothy smile for all customers."[40] He wanted to hold a party in celebration, but his wife, Billie, demurred on the grounds that such antics were somewhat excessive. Instead, he ran a full-page advertisement with his and Billie's picture along with an obsequious thank you.

> Before we organized the paper we planned for something like a year; we tried to take into consideration every conceivable possibility—and one thing that was then, and has during our first year, been predominant in our efforts was the downright, honest-to-goodness friendliness of those whom we have tried to serve. From us, to everyone of you who have so graciously given your help and encouragement, we thank you from the bottom of our hearts.[41]

East's first-year success failed to quell his vague feelings of insecurity and dissatisfaction that had surfaced in the spring. He felt uneasy, even though he had achieved most of the goals he set for himself in 1954. Financial success and popularity seemed inadequate to him. Publicly, he kept his temper outbursts under control, but sleep came only with the use of sedatives. He tried to avoid dwelling on his mental state whenever possible and to banish unpleasant thoughts.[42] Even with himself, it seemed he preferred evasion to confronting difficult issues.

Events, along with actions by the governor, the legislature, and the WCC, forced East off the fence with his readers and himself. Mississippi Governor Hugh White, anticipating trouble with the federal government after the *Brown* decision, tried to gain the support of his state's conservative black leaders, mostly ministers and educators, to continue the segregated school system. Not only did the scheme fail, it failed miserably. By a vote of eighty-nine to one the blacks rejected the governor's proposal and thereby delivered a shocking blow to the white establishment. As one black argued,

> Gentlemen you all should not be mad at us. Those were nine white men that rendered that decision. Not one colored man had anything to do with it. The real trouble is that you have given us schools too long in which we could study the earth through the floor and the stars through the roof.[43]

Reeling from this nearly unprecedented action, Governor White called a special session of the state legislature to devise a plan for evading forced integration. White requested a constitutional amendment authorizing the legislature to abolish the state's public schools to avoid desegregation. The legislature responded without hesitation. Governor White, when questioned about this drastic measure, replied that the major responsibility lay with the blacks because they refused voluntary segregation. They "must suffer the responsibility for their actions."[44] The amendment was then placed on the December ballot for public approval.

When debate on the issue began, East tried the old tactic of fence-straddling. In November 1954, he published two editorials of differing viewpoints. The first, written by former Mississippi governor and Dixiecrat Fielding Wright, stated that a vote against the amendment meant a vote for integration. Those opposed declared this untrue. They favored segregation but felt that this amendment would not ensure its perpetuation and might make possible the destruction of the entire state educational system.[45] As East admitted later, he had no opinion on the matter at the time.[46] As more news releases crossed his desk, however, he began to give the issue some thought and decided that those against the amendment were correct. He found the argument of Joel Blass, an attorney and state legislator, most persuasive. Blass contended that if the amendment went into effect, blacks could sue for admittance to school and win since it made no reference to maintaining the separation of the races. This would result in the destruction of the public schools, leaving private ones to take their place, an unsatisfactory alternative for many whites. Blass also believed that some legislators feared the higher taxes needed to equalize education between whites and blacks; the amendment provided an easy way out of the dilemma with little regard for segregation. According to Blass and his supporters, the Friends of Segregated Public Schools, a more viable solution involved use of the state police power granted by the Tenth Amendment to the United States Constitution. Under the amendment the state would maintain segregated schools in order to prevent riots and chaos that would surely follow attempts at desegregation.[47] Although East agreed with Blass, he wanted to remain uninvolved. Without explanation, however, and in conflict with his neutrality, he ran only articles by Blass and editorials opposing the amendment. He had started to get down from his fence, however unconsciously.[48]

Increasingly disturbed by the possible abolition of schools and the gross inequality of education for blacks, East, in December 1954, finally spoke out against the amendment. He stated quite clearly that he supported segregation, hoping this would deflect criticism, but aware of the risk he was taking. The self-proclaimed leading merchant in Petal, one of East's biggest customers, had made it clear that such a position would result in cancellation of his advertisement. East did not want to lose the man's business, but he also felt he had a right to his own opinion and a compelling inner need to present it publicly. "I could no more keep myself from writing on the matter than I could control an act of nature," he recalled.[49] Less than one week before the election he printed his beliefs in "Mississippi's Brain Department." Displaying both caution and racism, East declared, "From our point we oppose the measure, and we know darned well that we do not favor integration. We favor segregation because we think integration would be detrimental to both white and colored races."[50] He went on to say that he opposed giving so much power to the state legislature; such power would come at the expense of individual freedom. East felt that no one group should be trusted with such far-reaching authority. Furthermore, he warned that disobeying the Supreme Court was both illegal and unnecessary. Legal ways existed to challenge the court's ruling. By going to court, he argued, the case could be drawn out for years, thus permitting the continuation of segregation.[51]

Despite his strong defense of segregation, East lost his top advertiser. As an additional consequence of his stand, his stringers, the local newsgatherers, quit their jobs. He paid them twice the going rate for their reports, but the generous salary could not erase their employer's deviation from the southern way of life. East harbored no ill will towards the women: "I don't criticize these people for not providing news for me. I couldn't buy their souls.... They have principles."[52] The editorial also cut short his budding association with James O. Eastland. As late as 1 November 1954, the senator had written a very friendly letter to East complimenting him on his tribute to a recently deceased mutual friend. Eastland closed by saying, "If you ever get up to Washington or to Ruleville, please come to see me. Friendship such as yours is not common in this world and I hope some day I can be worthy of it as well."[53] Upon reading "Mississippi's Brain Department," Eastland cancelled his subscription and never had another kind word to say to or about P. D. East. Even though East suffered his first round of economic pressure as a result of his editorial statement, he felt better psychologically and was rewarded with his first good night's sleep in months.[54]

As expected, the voters of Mississippi approved the school amendment. The Friends of Segregated Public Schools, who had worked to defeat the measure because they felt that such a law would ensure desegregation, wrote a generous thank-you note to the *Petal Paper* for its efforts on their behalf.[55] Leaving no doubt as to his continued opposition to the amendment, East printed two short paragraphs on an otherwise blank paper. They read,

> Now that the Mamas and Papas of Mississippi have given Uncle Hugh and the boys the "big stick" they wanted so badly for Christmas—Long will it wave.

> But not over the head of the United States Supreme Court as the Mamas and Papas have been told, but over the heads of the same Mamas and Papas who so generously have given away their public school system for Christmas.[56]

In light of East's stand on the amendment, many of his acquaintances began to ask suspiciously what his editorial policy was. Since he was uncertain about "what an editorial was,"[57] he talked to the man whose newspaper printed the *Petal Paper*, Easton King. As the publisher of the *Chronicle Star* in Pascagoula, Mississippi, King had earned a reputation as a solid and fair journalist. He gave East some very simple advice: be honest. The *Petal Paper* soon reflected this counsel, as an

editorial policy based on fairness emerged. In making judgment
on any issue East pledged to back the position he considered
fairest to everyone. He made it clear, however, that once he took
a stand he was not wedded to it permanently. If additional
information arose to prove him wrong, he promised to change
his opinion. When unable to reach conclusions, East swore to
remain neutral. In line with his fairness doctrine he would
maintain a tolerant attitude and hear all the differing perspec-
tives that might arise over any given issue. Emphasizing the
eternal value of fairness he wrote,

> We have supported measures which we knew would be
> defeated. We supported them because we thought them to
> be right and fair. And here and now we would like to say
> that fairness is never defeated—the infection is ever present,
> and sooner or later that which is fair, and is defeated, will
> have to be done over.[58]

He noted that this editorial policy might create financial problems if advertisers withdrew their notices from his paper after
failing to control his opinions. He added, "We knew, because it
has happened to us."[59] In closing, he denied charges that he
sold his editorials to the highest bidder. Although this policy
statement proclaimed a bolder stance than the one he issued in
November 1953, it did not raise the red flag of rebellion.

Quite simply, East wanted to state his own opinions so
that he could be honest with himself as well as others. He had
no intention of marching forth on one crusade after another,
but he did believe in freedom of speech.

> In my utter simplicity, I thought my decision would be
> acceptable to my subscribers. I thought honestly and sin-
> cerely, that with rare exception a man could say what he
> wished without fear of reprisal, especially a man with a
> newspaper who was seeking to expand his commercial and
> unhappy soul in a direction that was, for a change, decent
> and honest. I had a lot to learn.[60]

If he had a lot to learn, his neighbors had much to teach.
Subscription renewals failed to materialize and advertising levels
dropped. Avoiding unpleasant thoughts, he attributed the problem to an after-Christmas slump. Nonetheless, he tried to
refrain from making any more controversial statements.[61]

His efforts proved fruitless. By late January 1955, he spoke
out again. This time he took a good-natured jab at the liquor

laws of Mississippi. Legally, prohibition still existed in the state. Despite this law, people bought and sold substantial amounts of alcohol and paid a state tax on this bootleg liquor. In 1954, the people of Forrest County, where East lived, purchased approximately fifty thousand gallons of whiskey worth one million dollars. The hypocrisy of voting "dry" and drinking "wet" baffled East. Trying to explain this contradiction, he suggested that somewhere in the county there existed a large hole into which the "drys" poured the illegal liquor. They did this to protect these people who might be tempted by the illegal substance. He finished by saying, "Assuredly that's what has happened—because we could never believe that in the County of Forrest there would be 5856 little holes [the number of registered voters] into which all that whiskey could be poured—Never!"[62] East learned quickly that his comment failed to amuse everyone. One advertiser told him, quite nicely, that this criticism of prohibition hurt the *Petal Paper*. East let the matter drop, but his courteous critic cancelled his advertisements. Several Baptist ministers attacked him as well, using the epithets "boozehead and liquor hound."[63]

East's associates felt that he was assaulting their entire value system. His every action, no matter how innocuous, brought increased criticism. The Kiwanis Club held a booster tag sale in which each member was to participate. Whether by going from door to door or by working the sidewalks, members had to sell a certain number of tags. Not liking this type of sales approach, East at first refused to contribute his efforts. Faced with the uncompromising hostility of club members, he bought his quota of booster tags and promptly threw them in the river.[64] He further angered the Kiwanians when he refused to donate time to repaint the club's headquarters. This action cost him additional revenue. One fellow Kiwanian, who had advertised in the *Petal Paper* from its inception, ignored East the next time the editor paid a business call at his store. Making East wait for over an hour, he finally asked, "P. D., you waiting for something?" Struggling to control his anger, East responded calmly, "Yes, sir. I was just standing here waiting for the second coming of Jesus. I knew damned well his pappy wouldn't let him come to Petal without first checking in with you."[65]

To make matters worse, he criticized politicians who campaigned only on the issue of segregation. To East, the candidates spent so much time saying how they would continue to keep blacks in their place that they said little about their other policies. After making this point, he added,

> Don't misunderstand this statement, I think segregation must be and will be maintained, but it has become the topic of many office seekers who use it for the purpose of arousing all of us to indignation, when actually, the biggest problem with the candidate is lack of qualifications for office.[66]

East found that he could not voice even such minor complaints. His income for February 1955 slid to an all-time low. Once again, he backed down but the damage had been done.

Distrust of East's motives grew so strong that his endorsement of state and local politicians in the spring primaries created even more turmoil. On 3 March 1955, he declared for three candidates. At the outset of the editorial, he remarked that his position would no doubt cost him money since those he did not support would probably refuse to run advertisements in his paper. In spite of this possibility, East believed that he needed to be honest with his readers. Anything he might write about the elections would reflect his bias, so it was important for the public to know his preferences. He backed Paul B. Johnson for governor, Luther Lee for county supervisor, and Bob Waller for sheriff. East made it clear that he would support his candidates by emphasizing their strengths and not by tearing down their opponents.[67]

Almost immediately adverse reactions poured in. Within a few days, East had been charged with trying to run the state and the world, and selling his endorsement to the three men in question. As predicted, several politicians refused to do business with him and one man removed his advertising. In fielding this criticism, East reiterated his faith in a policy of honesty: "I still am just country enough to believe that by being as straight forward and honest in your convictions as possible, it will pay in the long run."[68] His grand hopes never came close to fruition. So great was the negative reaction that when one candidate whom East had failed to endorse ran his political advertisement in the *Petal Paper*, East awarded him a page-one thank you.[69]

Further difficulties confronted East when he defended a prominent local family, the Tatums, who were charged with greed and attempts to keep out industry. The Pontiac Refining Company had offered to purchase land for a new refinery from the considerable Tatum holdings, but the family refused to sell. Many outraged local people accused the Tatums of blocking progress for the Hattiesburg area, and they demanded the sale of the land, even if it required condemning the property in question. Sensing an effort to violate the Tatums' property rights, East came to their defense. He did not want to create any additional trouble for himself. He already had enough of that, but he felt compelled to say something. On 10 March 1955, he argued that if a wealthy family's property rights were vulnerable, his were as well.[70] Having warmed to the subject, he followed this column the following week with an especially critical piece. In it, he presented the theme that individual property rights took precedent over a few dozen jobs for Hattiesburg. Stealing from one private concern to give to another, he contended, failed to provide a sound basis on which to develop Mississippi's industrial potential.

Reaction to the second editorial came rapidly. Petroleum companies doing business with the *Petal Paper* cancelled their advertisements, which resulted in a substantial loss for East. Two local businesses followed suit on grounds that East opposed economic growth. One bank president cornered him and demanded, "Tell me, East, how the hell do you propose we get industry in the area?" Shortly thereafter, the banker cancelled his account with the *Petal Paper*. The Tatums eventually won their fight, but for East the episode resulted in one more economic reversal.[71]

Shaken by the financial results of this incident, East once again pledged to remain silent on all controversial issues and to work, instead, on rebuilding his paper's circulation and advertising. His personal opinions would have to take a back seat to the financial stability of this enterprise. As he later put it, "I'd felt a touch of social and economic pressure, and found it unpleasant."[72] He tried as best he could neither to see nor hear any local problems. Each week he attended the Kiwanis meetings and dutifully reported the proceedings in the paper. Business improved but his mental attitude did not. By mid-April 1955, fits of depression and temper outbursts returned, and they came frequently. The state legislature, however, soon helped him regain peace of mind.

In defiance of the *Brown* decision, Mississippi politicians amended their constitution making it even more difficult for blacks to vote. As Mississippians and other southerners recognized, effective resistance to the Supreme Court's ruling required keeping the number of black voters to a minimum. Having performed this task in the past, the Magnolia State intended to stand even stronger during this time of trial, and it succeeded. In 1955, blacks comprised 41 percent of the state's voting age citizens, but as a result of past practices and the amendment only 4 percent were registered.[73] Whites achieved this goal by changing only one word in the constitution. In the past, voters had been required to read *or* interpret the state constitution. Now they had to read *and* interpret the document. Any enterprising voting registrar could find fault with the most learned explanation.[74]

For blacks who managed to have their names placed on the voting books, the White Citizens' Council had another solution. Local newspapers published the names of all registered black voters or distributed such lists throughout the community. These blacks often found themselves fired from their jobs, unable to get credit, and evicted from their rented houses. If such tactics failed, WCC members then visited the recalcitrants' homes urging them to take their names off the registration list in order to remain on peaceful terms with the rest of the community. In the Yazoo River town of Belzoni, 126 blacks were registered in the spring of 1955. Using pressure tactics the Council reduced the number to 35.[75]

Those still refusing to cooperate could contemplate the fate of Gus Courts who was shot and severely wounded; or that of the Reverend George Lee who was killed by a shotgun blast. Incredibly, the sheriff who investigated Lee's murder first claimed that the lead shotgun pellets taken from the victim's face were dental fillings. Finally, he concluded that another black had killed Lee in an argument over a woman.[76] Few blacks failed to understand the meaning of such incidents.

East also found it difficult to ignore a decision of the Board of Trustees for the state universities to screen outside speakers appearing on the campus of any state school. Reportedly, the trustees gave lists of prospective speakers to the White Citizens' Council and the American Legion for final approval. Academic freedom had little support in Mississippi or the South.[77] The state legislature went so far as to censure Hodding Carter, editor of the *Delta Democrat-Times*, by a vote of eighty-nine to nineteen, for writing an article critical of the WCC.[78] As historian James W. Silver noted later, Mississippi was rapidly becoming a closed society tolerating even less dissent than in previous years.

Unable to suppress his disgust over such events, East noted, "I felt that if I didn't say something about what was stuck in my craw I'd explode."[79] Instead of writing a scathing editorial, however, he composed the first of many satirical columns, "Us—And Them Other Crawfish." In this piece, he suggested changing the state symbol from the magnolia to the crawfish because of its tendency to walk backwards. This he claimed was synonymous with the progress made by the state of Mississippi.

> Here in the state of Mississippi we are making progress, progress such as no state heretofore has known. Our sagacious leaders are showing us how; they are leading the way. Their aim is to protect us from those crawfish who haven't the intelligence to move backwards, (as any sane crawfish knows) backward toward the mud from which we came.[80]

From this point he praised as "progressive" the constitutional amendment restricting voting, the screening of speakers on college campuses, and the censure of Hodding Carter, the "Delta Demon." The writing and publishing of the article provided excellent therapy for East, but he expected an avalanche of criticism to follow in its wake. To his great surprise, the editorial failed to elicit any hostile reaction. Even more astonishing, he received two calls complimenting him on "telling them niggers where their place is."[81] These bigots even bought subscriptions to the paper and, as East recalled, "Without comment, I took their money."[82]

Heartened by the lack of a negative reaction, East decided that now he might be able to comment on other issues of importance without endangering his already tenuous economic situation. Of special importance to him was the recent strike against Southern Bell by the Communication Workers of America (CWA).[83] In general, East supported the union movement, opposed right-to-work laws, and, of course, had edited two union papers; but his first editorial on this strike criticized certain actions of the union.[84] He directed his anger not at the right to strike, something he believed in; instead, he condemned the violence that union members had allegedly committed.

> From our very first issue, this paper has supported organized labor; we will continue to support labor, so long as we think it is right. We believe the labor movement as a whole

to be right, but the business of violence as has been displayed in the current strike is not right, and in no way will we try to convince anyone that it is.[85]

This revulsion against violence on East's part was a sincere and long-term belief, but it won him few friends in the CWA.

The day after the editorial appeared in the *Petal Paper,* the local union president demanded a retraction and an apology. When East refused, the union threatened to go to an attorney regarding a possible lawsuit. The telephone calls began. Some requested subscription cancellations, others were obscene, and a large number threatened physical violence. "I was warned not to go out of my house at night, or 'something will happen to you that ought not happen to a dog.' "[86] Ironically, the first threats of bodily harm came from East's long-time allies. In spite of the pain this caused, East tried to keep a sense of humor about it all. He related one telephone conversation with an irate woman who asked,

> Are you P. D. East?
> Yes, I answered.
> You're a no-good bastard and a stooge for the telephone company. You are supposed to be a pro-labor editor. I don't think you're an editor at all—you're a no-good bastard.
> And a phone-company stooge, I injected.[87]

Finally, even humor could not relieve the tension. To get relief from the constant harassment, he took his phone off the hook. He could not relieve his self-inflicted anxiety, however; he felt like a traitor. He had always supported unions but would not tolerate violence for any reason. Hurt by labor's antagonistic response and torn between two strongly held beliefs, he remained silent for the next several weeks.

His attempt at an uneasy neutrality ended with the death of a young girl in Laurel, Mississippi. The child had fallen from a tree, injuring herself severely. When her parents tried to call for an ambulance the line was dead because the telephone cable in that area had been cut deliberately. Nearly an hour passed before assistance arrived, and by then it was too late.[88] East condemned the vandalism that led to this tragedy and noted the harm it did to organized labor. Within twenty-four hours of these comments, union officials visited the *Petal Paper,* again objecting to the editorial and insisting upon a retraction. They claimed the child's death had nothing to do with the damaged cable. East rejected their explanation and angrily told the officials to go to hell. Abusive calls followed this confrontation as did subscription cancellations. On 20 May 1955, the strike finally ended, but it had been a costly one for East.[89]

The end of the strike did not relieve the economic pressure on East or the growing opposition to his views on organized labor, race, or politics. Union officials and numerous politicians charged that he sold his editorials to the highest bidder. Several candidates had asked what price he charged for his support and one wondered how much it would cost for East to come out against him. Infuriated by these questions and complaints, he decided to end all of the speculation by publishing a list of his sell-out prices. Since he had very few advertisements, he devoted an entire page to the various types of editorials available and their cost. For a "run of the mill (no animosity)" column he required $9.98; for a large company "(Hell Raisin')," $64.98; for a politician "(for or against)," $49.98; and for one involving complete honesty, no charge.[90] To drive home his point, he reemphasized his previously stated policy of printing the truth as he saw it. He recognized the problems this practice had created in the past and the probability of future difficulties, but he swore to make no changes.[91]

Events soon tested East's declaration to his word. On 31 May 1955, the Supreme Court handed down its second decision regarding school desegregation; *Brown II,* as legal scholars called it, ordered all defendants to begin desegregating their schools "with all deliberate speed."[92] Blacks needed no prompting to increase their demands for full equality. Branch offices of the National Association for the Advancement of Colored People (NAACP) petitioned more local school boards to comply with the court's ruling. More than eighty such suits were filed in the South by the fall of 1955, but only a few school officials even acknowledged receipt of the appeals. In several states, numerous spokesmen answered these legal requests with a vengeance.[93] One official in Georgia proposed a plan whereby those who advocated integration could be declared "diseased" mentally and then placed in the state's mental institutions.[94] Other less bizarre and more effective schemes involved economic and social pressure similar to that used against those seeking the right to vote.

In the summer of 1955, the most vehement reaction occurred

in Mississippi where four blacks were murdered and their assassins escaped punishment. One man, Lamar Smith, was shot in broad daylight on the courthouse lawn in Lincoln County in full view of the sheriff, but miraculously the guilty party escaped. In an even greater outrage, Emmett Till, a fourteen-year-old boy from Chicago, received a sample of southern justice when he whistled at a white woman. That night, two men kidnapped him from his grandfather's home, lynched him, and then dumped his body in the Tallahatchie River. This time the local authorities arrested the pair who admitted to the kidnapping, but an all-white jury still found them not guilty of all charges.[95] Whites who dared to show sympathy to the plight of blacks could count on similar treatment.[96] Hodding Carter, editor of the *Delta Democrat-Times*, and Hazel Brannon Smith, editor of the *Lexington Advertiser* and three other papers, spoke out against bigotry, and they felt the sharp censure of their fellow Mississippians. Unlike most whites, they survived these attacks because they operated from a position of security—a result of national reputations and diversified operations.[97] Possessing neither of these strengths, P. D. East nevertheless pressed ahead with his own assault against the rising racist fury.

The outcome of a local school board meeting drew East out of his silence, which had lasted from late April to June 1955. A group of blacks had received invitations to discuss the Supreme Court's recent implementation decree with the Hattiesburg School Board. Shortly after the meeting began, the local district attorney, Lawrence Arrington, who was running for reelection, declared that the gathering was illegal since Mississippi law forbade integrated meetings. Appalled by this obvious political gesture, the blacks walked out.[98] East believed that Arrington's intemperate action had done irreparable harm to race relations. After 31 May 1955, it seemed to East that all Mississippi politicians yelled "nigger" louder than ever before. In disgust, East wrote his second satirical editorial. He presented it in the form of a news story covering a speech by the Honorable Jefferson D. Dixiecrat, president of the Mississippi Chapter of the Professional Southerners' Club. This so-called speech advocated keeping the "nigger down."

> As professional Southerners we have kept him from voting, we have kept him fairly well ignorant and we have kept him in debt to us.... I say to you, as Professional South-

erners, we must humiliate and intimidate the Nigger every
chance we have. This is one more effective way of letting
him know to stay in his place.[99]

He went on to praise the WCC, Arrington, and all others who
had worked towards this goal. As before, several people mis-
understood East's intentions. One Petal merchant told him,
"I'm sure glad you took the stand you did. . . . I think it's about
time the black bastards learned to keep their place."[100] Judging
from additional subscription cancellations, however, a number
of readers understood his meaning.

Concerned about the economic problems this editorial
created, East once again considered whether he should continue
to take unpopular stands. He suffered from their consequences
and so did his wife and his daughter, Karen. His doubts
increased when it became obvious that old friends avoided him.
Bob Waller, the candidate for sheriff who had asked for East's
support and received it, now found the association politically
unpopular. East discovered this sad fact when he visited Waller
to give him a photography job amounting to $500. Waller did
not invite East into the house but forced him to stand on the
front porch during the entire conversation. As East lamented,
"I understood from a round-about source that he cannot afford
to associate with me because of my liberal view on the Negro
question."[101] At this crucial turning point, East received much-
needed moral support from Mark Ethridge, editor and publisher
of the *Louisville Courier-Journal* and a prominent southern
liberal. After praising the "Professional Southerner" editorial,
he closed saying, "I wish Mississippi had more voices like yours
and I hope you stay there."[102] Overjoyed with this positive
response, East remarked, "I was delighted to hear from such a
man, and my decision to write additional copy on the subject of
race was influenced by him."[103] His circle of friends was
changing slowly, keeping pace with his new attitudes on race.

Determined to speak his mind, East concluded that his
already strained relations with the Kiwanis Club would only
worsen. To avoid any personal confrontations he decided to
resign. Realizing that this decision, too, might unleash economic
havoc, he discussed the matter with Easton King. His friend
agreed that leaving the club seemed to be a morally correct
move. East wanted freedom to air his own opinions without
worrying what others might think, and he felt he could not do
this while a member of any organization. As he put it, "I'd not

be free within myself until I'd shaken all bonds. So, while I was about it, I wrote the Methodist church a letter and asked that my name be removed from the rolls. I felt as if a load had been lifted with the resignation...."[104] With no obligation to any group, he believed that he could no longer be labeled a traitor by anyone. Finally he felt free within himself.

This new-found freedom led East to state his position on civil rights more forcefully. Pulling no punches, he blamed the deplorable economic conditions of blacks as well as their low levels of education on southern whites. Although he expressed personal misgivings about the NAACP—which he considered too radical—he saw it as a necessary evil resulting from the intransigence of most whites. They had forced blacks to join by denying them their constitutional rights. For East, blacks should receive legal equality, and he felt there were good reasons to justify this action. As he put it, "I have taken seriously the teachings of Christ, and especially the teaching of 'Do Unto Others as Ye Would Have Them Do Unto You.' I have taken seriously the Bill of Rights; I am a victim of the Declaration of Independence."[105] No one, according to East, had the right to interfere with another person's pursuit of happiness. This admirable stand had only one flaw. He refused to grant blacks social equality. As he remembered, "Here I admit my own Southern prejudices, having been born and reared in Mississippi."[106] His heritage still placed a claim on him, but he had started to break its control.

This editorial, along with other attacks on racism and gubernatorial candidates,[107] led to more financial woes. One advertiser refused to do business with the *Petal Paper* because, as he said, East's ideas did not sit well with him. Viewing this as one more example of economic intimidation, East responded with a blistering editorial aimed at those trying to put him out of business. He charged that too often the press in America submitted to such pressure at the expense of the truth. As a result, he argued, injustices occurred and everyone suffered. He vowed this would never happen with his paper. "So, with the help of God, and to this we swear, as long as we can keep our heads above water we will print what we please in this paper, so long as we believe it to be right, fair, or true."[108] In a parting shot at his critics, he wrote: "In the meantime, however, we have only six words to say to those who would attempt to put economic pressure on us; the words are: GO TO HELL IN A

BUCKET!"[109] Feeling at peace with himself and unconcerned temporarily with economic realities, he refrained from any altercation for several weeks.

Pledged to print the truth as he saw it, East could not avoid being embroiled in controversy for long. He asked the local district attorney, Lawrence Arrington, why he had not kept his campaign promise to stop the bootlegging in Forrest County or to resign.[110] Since the illicit liquor traffic still flourished, East offered Arrington space in the paper to answer these and other questions. With only a week left before the primary, Arrington could not ignore East's inquiries. He responded with a strong defense of his actions, and going one step further, he applied pressure on East. For the next two days someone followed East's wife, Billie. Unnerved by the man who made no effort to conceal himself, East bought a pistol for her to carry. He believed that it was essential after the parents of Arrington's opponent had shots fired at their home. The war of nerves ended when the district attorney's wife confronted East in the post office and told him that she had half a mind to wring his neck. That evening the man tailing Billie East disappeared, but the incident proved most unsettling to the Easts.[111]

By mid-summer 1955, East's problems intensified. He lashed out at the rising tide of racial violence in Mississippi. In particular, he reacted to an editorial in the *Jackson Daily News* calling for whites to "do something" about the increasing pressure from the NAACP for school integration. East complained that this open invitation would lead to more bloodshed, and he condemned those who called implicitly for such actions. Then in an obvious appeal to the Christian values of his audience, he stated, "As for us, we pause to wonder.... and wonder we do as to what the Man who died on Calvary, in whose teachings we profess to believe, would have thought of the present situation in Mississippi."[112] In another piece, he portrayed WCC members as the new southern "redneck." Unlike their earlier counterparts, East contended, they failed to realize that they were ignorant. Because they believed that their college degrees made them brilliant, they were more arrogant and thus more dangerous than the old redneck.[113]

Remaining on the offensive for several weeks, East next posed the question, "Is it true what they say about Dixie?" He answered with a resounding yes. Quoting from statistical studies, he noted that 65 percent of Mississippi's college-educated youth left the state each year. To East, this meant that the most intelligent people migrated, leaving behind, for the most part, ignorant bigots. He believed that the state's political leaders typified those who stayed. They were "shabby, wild-eyed, rattlebrained fanatics who are half-witted, failures at every undertaking except stirring up race hatred."[114] Included in this ilk were members of the WCC whom he branded as loud mouthed, rabble rousing, and greasy fizzled. Not wanting to leave anyone out, he condemned Mississippians in general. "We have become poorer, ornerier, and meaner than a spavined, distempered mule, we, the people of Mississippi, propose to kick; we don't care a damn to build up; we wish to tear down, if it means having our 'Old Southern Customs.' "[115]

That same week, he answered those who called him "nigger lover, communist, Jew lover." He did not deny the charges, but merely asked how people could say that justice existed in Mississippi when a black man drew a sentence of death for attacking a white woman and a white man got two years in prison for attacking a black woman. In essence, he challenged the name-calling bigots to prove him incorrect when he said that blacks had few rights, if any, in Mississippi.[116] His final note to the readers concerned continued economic pressure. Noting that he had received no advertising for the dollar-day sale or the back-to-school promotion, he stated, "I kindly note, another killing has been made, US."[117]

This economic problem weighed heavily on East for several months. By fall 1955, the paper had only a few advertisers left, and the number of subscribers had dropped dramatically. Some people, not wanting even to write East, started to refuse the paper at the post office. Desperate for money, he tried to mount a subscription campaign. He offered the Baptist Church one-third of the profits if it would help him find more readers. They, and every other church in the area, refused to accept his generous offer. "I was given to understand they wouldn't touch my paper with a Bible in their hands."[118] Reflecting on the purpose of the *Petal Paper* in light of his precarious position, East wrote, "First it is hoped that the editor can make a buck out of it. Second, it is hoped that the *Petal Paper* will actually replace Scott's Tissue in the out houses of Forrest County."[119] With this said, East devoted most of his paper to subjects other than race.

He remained relatively quiet for a month. Then, in late September, his indignation was aroused once again. First, in a swipe at those who sent anonymous hate mail, he said, "I have heard jackasses bray before!"[120] He then chided the state legislature for its persistent support of prohibition. He argued that the state, by legalizing alcohol and taxing it, could finance an excellent school system. "Frankly we hold that booze is here to stay! At least on the booze let's get something out of it in taxes."[121] Next he returned to the race issue. In Hattiesburg every white school had crossing guards to help the young children, but black schools had none, even though some were situated on very busy streets. Since such discrimination violated federal law, East assumed that the problem was due to an oversight and could be rectified easily.[122] For Mississippi to regain the respect of the United States and the world, East believed that it had to begin solving its own problems; one as manageable as this would be a good place to start. Later, when the Hattiesburg school board refused to alter the circumstances, East lamented, "We have justified everything from murder on up here in Mississippi, and from all indications the situation is getting worse, not better."[123] Apparently, even simple problems had no solutions in the Magnolia State, whether for blacks or for P. D. East.

Searching for something as basic as friendship proved a difficult task for East. On the few occasions when he encountered civility, the news made page one of the *Petal Paper*. In thanking the Mississippi Power Company for inviting him to their barbecue, he opened the notice with, "I was a stranger and they took me in...."[124] From there he went on to thank everyone for their hospitality. He even praised the local postmaster for opening up after business hours so that he could mail some important letters. Needing acceptance on his own terms, he grasped at any opportunity.

Although East felt a powerful desire to be well liked, he could not subdue his criticism of Mississippi. When engaged in this exercise, he insisted, "I am not riding Mississippi to hurt it. I am riding it to help it. I ride it for the same reason I spank my four year old daughter."[125] The need to take his fellow Mississippians to the woodshed arose again by mid-October. Although he lashed out at the racist excesses of the Council, he clung, ironically, to the hope of continued segregation. He explained that if asked whether he wanted "niggers" to go to school with white children, he would answer no; but if segregation required weakening the nation, causing violence, and denying children an education, he would support integration. The preservation of America and the Constitution mattered above all else, even more than cherished southern traditions. Thus, he continued to emphasize that blacks, as citizens and human beings, deserved equal justice under the law and that segregation could not be maintained illegally. For those claiming that God had ordained the black to hold an inferior position in society, East expressed nothing but contempt. No one, he insisted, could fathom what God had intended; those who claimed otherwise used religion for their own selfish purposes, not God's.[126]

Pursuing this theme the following week, he reasoned that with brotherly love and the Golden Rule as key elements of the Christian faith, ministers and all believers should advocate love and tolerance instead of hatred and prejudice.[127] "The Christian Way of Life is not the way of ignorance, superstition, hatred, prejudice, and false witnessing. Its methods are not stirring up strife between neighbors, and rising economic pressure for selfish ends.... It is the way of the Good Samaritan—using one's goods and services to help the neighbor in need."[128]

Needless to say, East's appeal to the religious instincts of his neighbors failed to win them over. His 27 October 1955 edition bore testimony to this as he printed a wry message in the middle of a blank page: "Let's be practical about this thing. We couldn't sell this page and darned if we're going to give it away."[129]

When the *Petal Paper* completed its second year of publication, local reaction differed sharply from the previous anniversary. No congratulatory letter arrived from James Eastland, the governor's office, or other prominent state officials. No flood of advertisements appeared either. Ignoring these snubs, East ran the same thank-you note to his readers and advertisers that he had printed at the end of his first year. He expressed his appreciation to everyone for his or her kindness and support. Unfortunately, what little kindness and support he received never translated itself into money. The economic repercussions of his unpopular opinions forced him to borrow $2,000 to pay his debts for the preceding year.[130]

Despite these economic woes, East started his third year with his first substantive comment on the Emmett Till murder. In August 1955, at the time of Till's death, he had condemned racial violence without mentioning the case specifically. Although the atrocity appalled him, he believed direct comments were useless; no white man would ever be convicted of killing a black in Mississippi.[131] When the grand jury failed to indict the two men on charges of murder or kidnapping, even though they confessed to abducting the boy, East sarcastically proclaimed this another example of justice "Mississippi style." He wrote, "Maybe some of you can figure out justice, but I admit being unable to see it. . . . About the only thing left for the State Legislature to do when they meet in January is to vote a medal of merit or such to Mr. Milton and Mr. Bryant [the defendants]."[132] When he heard a rumor that the WCC planned to start a chapter in Forrest County, he remarked that they should establish their headquarters at the local zoo.[133] The following week he apologized for this caustic remark saying, "Frankly, I don't think even the skunks deserve that; after all, that a skunk should smell a bit stronger than anything else really isn't his fault. Truth is I can't find it in my heart to wish off a Council Chapter even on a skunk!"[134] After Christmas, he bemoaned Santa Claus's failure to bring badly needed money to the WCC. "Santa should be ashamed of himself! No money to spread bigotry and hate . . . just what is Christmas coming to!"[135]

Such stinging attacks nonetheless lost some of their effectiveness when East criticized racism in one breath and, in the next, suggested ways to maintain segregated public schools. In December 1955, the Hattiesburg school board proposed a bond issue that would improve schools for both black and white students. In two editorials, East supported the bond issue. He reasoned that improved facilities for blacks would equalize education and result in fewer demands for integration. Blacks, he contended, wanted a good education, as promised in the state's 1890 constitution; given this right, they might willingly acquiesce to segregation. He felt that the Supreme Court, confronted with this situation, would accept voluntary segregation. As he put it,

> We would do well to keep in mind the Supreme Court ruling. They said in effect, that segregation in school was illegal. They did not say that whites and negroes [*sic*] HAD to go to school together. . . . If segregation is voluntary, we think it would be legal, or at any rate, acceptable. . . . And one step in the right direction in that respect is to build equal schools.[136]

For all of his railing against racist excesses, he still supported segregation. Separate but equal still seemed acceptable to East.

Unmoved by East's qualified support of segregation, his advertisers and subscribers deserted the *Petal Paper* in increasing numbers. Former friends spoke to him only when forced to do so, and often, when people did speak, it was to criticize. These hostile attitudes troubled East so much that he "lay awake many nights wondering why people were so abusive and nasty because someone held an opinion different from theirs."[137] Under these circumstances self-doubts dominated his thoughts, and he began to question the motives for his behavior and his relationship to others. After much soul-searching, he decided that up until this point in his life he had acted upon instinct and not upon reason. Now, under fire, he wanted to find the explanation for his behavior if only for himself. The personal inventory that followed resulted in what he called a "true confession" column in his paper. Discussing his beliefs, East mentioned his God, who never changed but whose word was relative, his family, his friends, the United States, democracy, the Bill of Rights, and the dignity of all people. As for what he opposed, East put ignorance at the top of his list. He believed that it led to practically everything he despised—selfishness, conceit, intolerance, bigotry, and injustice. Only the cultivation of wisdom through education could eradicate ignorance. He also objected to those who tried to force their ideas on others. The right to disagree was the birthright of every American, a fact he displayed in his editorial policy of fairness to all.[138] Elsewhere in the same issue East remarked that his belief in the brotherhood of all mankind prompted him to discuss explosive issues such as race, even though such debates hurt him financially. He noted proudly, "I am my brother's brother. ... And our brother is more important to us than a dollar bill."[139]

East's public soul-searching failed to relieve his feelings of dejection. The personal snubs of old acquaintances stung him as did the increasingly vicious letters he received. As his depression deepened, he contemplated suicide for the first time in several years. To avoid further unpleasant confrontations, which would only exacerbate his condition, East withdrew. He refused to go to his office or see anyone at his home except his wife, who left him alone. From mid-January until the first of February, his mood remained the same. Finally, in desperation, he resorted to prayer. Although uncertain as to whether God answered or even listened to such supplications, he could not hold back. He needed someone to talk with, and since he felt incapable of approaching Easton King or anyone else, he turned to God. In fact, he resorted to prayer several times a day during this period.[140]

By early February, whether as a result of time or prayer, East's spirits rose and he abandoned his self-imposed seclusion. Out in public once again, he resumed his attack on racism. Senator James Eastland[141] provided him with his first target. Speaking before the White Citizens' Council of South Carolina, the senator had emphasized the righteousness of the South's cause and the need to disobey laws that ran counter to segregation. East charged that Eastland's venomous attacks on his opponents violated every tenet of the New Testament. More importantly, East noted that Eastland as a senator swore to uphold the law of the United States and yet counseled southerners and all Americans to disregard the Supreme Court's ruling on integration. To East, this demonstrated the senator's total lack of principles.[142] He then trained his critical eye on the state government. The Mississippi legislature had proposed a bill that would abridge the constitutionally guaranteed right of free speech. House Bill 34 established as legally defamatory "any word or statement, oral or written, not libel or slander, but which nonetheless, if true, would tend to expose a person to hatred, contempt, or ridicule, to degrade or disgrace him in society or to injure him in his business or occupation."[143] If passed, the bill would have forbidden all criticism of governmental actions. Legislators believed this drastic action necessary if they were to ensure continued segregation. East remarked that one would expect to find such a law in Nazi Germany or the Soviet Union, but not in the United States. He also suggested that if the legislature intended the bill to be used to keep Negroes quiet, it should use the word Negro. "Hell, we're brave here in Mississippi. Why not be honest then? Maybe we're trying to fool them 'damned yankees' some more, huh?"[144] Not satisfied with the power this bill would give the state, the legislature proposed another piece of legislation that would tax any church permitting integration. Both bills failed to pass, but, as East noted, they indicated "... the frenzy of our elected lawmakers whenever the word Negro is mentioned."[145]

East's offensive continued the following week. In one piece he returned to the artful use of satire. Tired of the constant use of religion to justify racism, he asked his readers if they knew whether heaven was segregated. Speculating on his own, he described two possible scenes at the gates of heaven. In one instance, St. Peter questioned the first prospective black entrant.

He started by saying, "Well, nigger, what's your name?" From there he asked the all-important question, "Did you ever try to vote while you lived in Mississippi?" The black answered, "No sir, your honor. Not me ... I know a nigger's place." After receiving similar replies to the other entrance questions, St. Peter declared, "Pass. You're a mighty fine nigger." The next petitioner, however, failed to measure up to St. Peter's standards. When asked her name, the woman used the term "Mrs." and failed to call St. Peter "Mr." With that the saint responded, "My name is Mr. St. Peter to you, nigger, and your name is just Lula Mae Magnolia ... Some of you niggers are getting the most outlandish notions here lately. Honest to goodness, I just don't figure it." The woman then explained that she had been killed when attempting to vote in Mississippi, and that she had been a school teacher. At that, St. Peter turned his thumb down and said, "To hell with you sister." East closed this speculative essay by cautioning his readers that if heaven did not fit this description then just possibly being a white from Mississippi might automatically condemn a person to hell.[146] Needless to say, the response to this editorial was immediate and negative. It elicited some of the most bitter letters he had ever received.[147] Practically all commented on the sacrilegious nature of the article, questioned the state of East's soul, and cancelled subscriptions. If nothing else, East found the entire episode hilariously funny.

His economic situation proved less amusing. By mid-February 1956, not one Petalite had renewed a subscription. The number of local advertisements dropped precipitously as well. January's income reflected these circumstances, falling $300 from his earnings a year earlier.[148] He recognized that if he persisted in voicing his opinions on race he could expect his situation to worsen. To disagree with the prevailing standards of the South invited social boycott, economic pressure, and a possible investigation by the State Senate.[149] Yet, when several of his readers asked how he managed to state his controversial ideas and stay in business, he responded that he could not operate in any other way.

> I say in my paper what I would like to see in other papers here in the state. By that I don't mean I would like to see more folks disagree with me ... not on your life, but I would like to see more folks with less obligation to other folks....[150]

In conclusion, he insisted that advertisers might purchase space in the *Petal Paper*, but they could never buy his soul.

To underscore this point, he printed a scathing indictment of Mississippi in his next issue. In "A Letter to a Friend," he argued that the need to feel superior had led the human race into all manner of idiocies. In Mississippi, the people acted on this innate drive by denying blacks the right to vote as well as social equality. Senator Eastland's protest aside, equal opportunity for blacks did not exist. As proof, East noted that of the twelve thousand blacks in Forrest County, only six could vote. Until January 1956, eight had been legally registered, but when two tried to pay their poll tax, they failed to find anyone who would accept their money. East also countered the White Citizens' Council's charges that the NAACP and the Communists had stirred up the racial turmoil throughout the state. He argued that while he disliked the NAACP, it was not to blame for the current unrest. Instead, that responsibility lay with the whites and no one else. He closed by saying that in a century historians would conclude, "'Niggers ain't nothing but human beings after all.' An they'll be right, too."[151] This editorial marked a significant change in P. D. East. Before he had been unwilling to grant social equality to blacks. Now this barrier had apparently fallen.

East's bold and increasingly liberal statements placed him under increasing economic and mental pressure. Not surprisingly, he developed an ulcer, but this painful discovery failed to silence him. In February 1956, a young black woman, Autherine Lucy, entered the University of Alabama by order of the Supreme Court. During her first three days of classes, mobs protesting her presence dominated the campus. State troopers, instead of dispersing the rioters, spirited Lucy away, and the trustees suspended her indefinitely for her own safety. When she charged that the trustees had conspired with the agitators, the trustees expelled her permanently.[152] East called this incident, along with the Emmett Till case, a tragedy and an affront to the dignity of the human race. On a more positive note, he held out some hope for the future.

> Inhumanity being what it is, we are not likely in a minute to reach the full light of day.... It will perhaps take years. Entrenched customs will tempt some citizens to vainly cling to the past. There may be mistakes and even tragedies

before the truths about God-given, unalienable rights are universally self-evident in the land. But the day will come.[153]

In early March 1956, East's dreams for the future seemed dashed when he learned that the White Citizens' Council planned to start a chapter in Forrest County. Most disturbing of all, the organizational meeting was to take place at the courthouse in Hattiesburg. He felt impelled to voice his objections because once the WCC denied blacks the few rights they possessed, it would try to do the same to all of its opponents.[154] At first he wrote several different editorials, but each one turned into an unacceptable, long-winded sermon. With his press deadline approaching rapidly, he scrapped the idea of writing any additional copy. Instead, he published a satirical full-page advertisement in behalf of the Council.

This was East's famous "jackass ad." It pictured a braying jackass who invited all whites to join the "Glorious Citizens' Clans." Those joining were offered guaranteed superiority, the opportunity to practice bigotry, and the chance to remain socially acceptable. Members were promised the freedom to interpret the Constitution as they saw fit; to feel superior without brain, character, or principle; and to exert economic pressure.[155] Along with the advertisement, he devoted his "East Side" column to criticizing the Citizens' Clan—as he called it. He stressed that he would not deny the WCC the right to organize, but he would deny it the right to use economic pressure against opponents. Most certainly he had himself in mind. In discussing what he dreaded the most, he remarked,

> Fear is such a force that anyone suggesting fairness to a Negro, or anyone else the mob is against, is likely to incur the wrath of the mob. Fear breeds fear, and when it's holding sway, reason and common sense and decency are forgotten things.... We all have fears. But some of us fear the loss of human rights, decency, and freedom as an American citizen. The loss of those things strikes a greater fear in me than the fear of a Negro child attending a white school.[156]

When the WCC met the following week, East's "jackass ad" and comments occupied the center stage. Wisely choosing not to attend, he sent his brother-in-law, Miles Porter, to the meeting for a first-hand report. The main speaker of the evening, Earle Wingo, held up a copy of the *Petal Paper*, displaying the full-page advertisement. In doing so, he recommended that all attending join him in cancelling their subscriptions. He concluded his speech by throwing the paper to the ground. Upon hearing this, East checked Wingo's subscription and discovered that it had been cancelled in June 1955, for nonpayment of his bill. East published this information on page one the following week. Commenting on Wingo, a Sunday school teacher and author of *The Illegal Trial of Jesus*, East wrote, "I think it's a fine thing that Christ rose from the grave, because had He not, by now Heaven only knows how many times he'd have turned over in it because of the crimes committed in His name."[157]

Further reaction to the "jackass ad" came swiftly. He received so many obscene and threatening calls that he stopped answering the telephone. One woman promised that if he showed his head outside the house, her husband would knock it off. Another woman declared angrily, "You're a nigger-loving, Jew-loving, Communist son-of-a-bitch. Somebody ought to kill you."[158] In relating this story, East remarked, "I found it to be such a pleasure to talk with ladies."[159] Heeding the warnings he received, East tried not to venture out of his house, but occasionally, he found it necessary to run errands. On one trip, while stopped at a traffic light, a man approached his car asking, "Aren't you P. D. East?" When East said yes, the man shouted, "Well, if you'll get out of that goddamned car I'll mop up the street with you." Thinking quickly, East responded with a smile, "Well, now, you don't offer a man much inducement, do you?" With that he drove away, leaving an irate man standing in the middle of the street.[160]

Although he laughed at some of the threats, he could not ignore all of them. For the second time in his life, East purchased a gun. He took it with him whenever he left his home, but he confessed, "I knew I could no more fire at a man than I could call God through the telephone company."[161] The next issue of the *Petal Paper* reflected a noticeable drop in the number of advertisements. Within a month, only three Petal merchants continued to advertise in the paper and circulation in the paper's home town dropped to less than 25. Of some consolation, for each local subscription cancelled, he received several from out of state, but they never compensated for the lost advertising revenues.[162] East suspected, but could not prove, that the WCC had organized a campaign to stop businesses from supporting the *Petal Paper*.[163]

Physically and mentally this ordeal took a heavy toll on East. His ulcer troubled him constantly. Every time he ventured into public, his stomach tightened into a knot, in anticipation of the personal snubs he would receive. He said, "I never knew whether my best friends would speak or not. Many of them didn't."[164] Mental depression plagued him as well. For several weeks he spent countless hours sitting on the edge of his bed weeping. Later, he lamented, "Why I should react in such a manner is beyond me. I was not naive as to think I could print what I had and not get by without a certain amount of abuse."[165] No matter how much he prepared himself, he never found it easy to endure the animosity of old friends and strangers. Despite all of these problems, East refused to back down. No amount of abuse would silence him. For too long, he believed, he had ignored the bitter fruits of bigotry, hatred, and intolerance. Now he had to fight back. As he told a friend at this time, "I can't look the other way when the most important issue of my life hits me smack in the face."[166] In the next issue of the paper, he declared boldly,

> I may be kidding myself, but I believe that ALL men have a friend in me—I hold an old fashioned idea that in the eyes of God, who made us all, no man is superior, nor is any man inferior. Frankly, I am a lot more concerned with how God sees me than I am with how anyone around Forrest County views me.[167]

East's good friend, James W. Silver, noted the rarity of such courage in Mississippi at this time:

> No one here can quite understand him. I think that's why he hasn't been lynched or shut up yet. "What's he getting out of this?" They ask. Not a thing they can see. Of course, what he's 'got' is his conscience and his independence. Right now, they're pretty scarce items around here—the cost is too high for most people.[168]

His rebelliousness had now led him into the fight of his life. The problems of his first thirty-five years would not compare to those that lay ahead, but then neither would the rewards.

Notes

[1] P. D. East, *The Magnolia Jungle: The Life, Times and Education of a Southern Editor* (New York: Simon and Schuster, 1960), 119.

2 Ibid.

3 Neal Peirce, *The Deep South States of America: People, Politics, and Power in the Seven Deep South States* (New York: W. W. Norton Company, 1974), 187.

4 East, *Magnolia Jungle,* 121.

5 P. D. East, *Petal* (Miss.) *Paper,* 3 December 1953, 1.

6 P. D. East, *Petal* (Miss.) *Paper,* 19 November 1953, 2.

7 Ibid., 1.

8 East, *Magnolia Jungle,* 122.

9 Ibid., 120; P. D. East, *Petal* (Miss.) *Paper,* 11 February 1954, 1.

10 Ibid.

11 East, *Magnolia Jungle,* 120, 124.

12 Ibid., 124.

13 Ibid., 125.

14 Ibid., 126. For the most informed and thorough discussion of the *Brown* decision see Richard Kluger, *Simple Justice: The History of Brown v. Board of Education and Black America's Struggle for Equality* (New York: Alfred A. Knopf, 1976).

15 Neil R. McMillen, *The Citizens' Council: Organized Resistance to the Second Reconstruction, 1954–1964* (Urbana: University of Illinois Press, 1971), 16–18; Numan V. Bartley, *The Rise of Massive Resistance: Race and Politics in the South During the 1950's* (Baton Rouge: Louisiana State University Press, 1969), 85.

16 Bartley, *Rise of Massive Resistance,* 13.

17 Walter Lord, *The Past That Would Not Die* (New York: Harper and Row, 1965), 29.

18 Quoted in McMillen, *Citizens' Council,* 163.

19 Ibid., 161–63, 180; Lord, *The Past,* 63.

20 Charles Fortenberry and F. Glenn Abney, "Mississippi: Unreconstructed and Unredeemed," in *The Changing Politics of the South,* ed. William C. Havard (Baton Rouge: Louisiana State University Press, 1972), 490.

21 Lord, *The Past,* 63.

22 McMillen, *Citizens' Council,* 16.

23 Wilma Dykeman and James Stokely, *Neither Black Nor White* (New York: Rinehart and Company, 1957), 265–69; McMillen, *Citizens' Council,* 172–73.

24 James W. Silver, *Mississippi: The Closed Society* (New York: Harcourt, Brace and World, 1966), 53–54; McMillen, *Citizens' Council,* 174–78.

25 McMillen, *Citizens' Council,* 181–83.

26 W. J. Cash, *The Mind of the South* (New York: Alfred A. Knopf, 1941), 88–89

27 Quoted in McMillen, *Citizens' Council,* 185.

28 P. D. East, "Look Back in Pain," undated text of speech given by East, 7, Box 54, East Papers, Mugar Library, Boston University.

Hereafter cited as East, "Look Back in Pain."

[29] East, *Magnolia Jungle*, 126–27; East, "Look Back in Pain," 7.

[30] P. D. East, *Petal* (Miss.) *Paper*, 11 June 1954, 1.

[31] P. D. East, *Petal* (Miss.) *Paper*, 18 June 1954, 1.

[32] P. D. East, interview with *Time Magazine*, New York, New York, February 1957, 1, Box 53, East Papers. Hereafter cited as East, interview with *Time Magazine*.

[33] P. D. East, *Petal* (Miss.) *Paper*, 1 July 1954, 1. East's comments were especially uncharitable since he already had secured the first of his three divorces. Later, Eleanor Roosevelt lent her support to East and the *Petal Paper*.

[34] P. D. East, *Petal* (Miss.) *Paper*, 8 July 1954, 1; P. D. East, *Petal* (Miss.) *Paper*, 15 July 1954, 1; *Petal* (Miss.) *Paper*, 22 July 1954, 1; P. D. East, *Petal* (Miss.) *Paper*, 12 August 1954, 2; P. D. East, *Petal* (Miss.) *Paper*, 19 August 1954, 1–2.

[35] P. D. East, *Petal* (Miss.) *Paper*, 15 July 1954. This was quoted from an article by Phil Stroupe of the Jackson *Daily News*, a Hederman paper that gave a great deal of support to the White Citizens' Council. Bob Howie, political cartoonist for the *Daily News*, also served as cartoonist for the *Citizens' Council*.

[36] P. D. East, *Petal* (Miss.) *Paper*, 5 August 1954, 2; P. D. East, *Petal* (Miss.) *Paper*, 9 September 1954, 2; P. D. East, *Petal* (Miss.) *Paper*, 23 September 1954, 2; P. D. East, *Petal* (Miss.) *Paper*, 17 February 1955, 2; P. D. East, *Petal* (Miss.) *Paper*, 4 August 1955, 1.

[37] P. D. East, *Petal* (Miss.) *Paper*, 9 September 1955, 1–2.

[38] P. D. East, *Petal* (Miss.) *Paper*, 25 June 1954, 1; P. D. East, *Petal* (Miss.) *Paper*, 5 August 1954, 2.

[39] P. D. East, *Petal* (Miss.) *Paper*, 25 June 1954, 1; P. D. East, *Petal* (Miss.) *Paper*, 1 July 1954; P. D. East, *Petal* (Miss.) *Paper*, 20 October 1954, 2.

[40] East, *Magnolia Jungle*, 127.

[41] P. D. East, *Petal* (Miss.) *Paper*, 11 November 1954, 8.

[42] East, *Magnolia Jungle*, 128.

[43] Silver, *Closed Society*, 88; Peirce, *Deep South States*, 173, 177. Had whites looked at what separate but equal really meant, this uncharacteristic action by blacks might have been anticipated. In 1950, the state spent $78.70 per year for each white student and $23.83 for each black. Salaries for white teachers averaged $1865.00 per year versus $918.00 for black teachers. Such figures could hardly be described as equal.

[44] Peirce, *Deep South States*, 176.

[45] P. D. East, *Petal* (Miss.) *Paper*, 11 November 1954, 1–2.

[46] East, *Magnolia Jungle*, 127.

[47] P. D. East, *Petal* (Miss.) *Paper*, 18 November 1954, 4; P. D. East, *Petal* (Miss.) *Paper*, 9 December 1954, 1. It should be noted that

in his autobiography East did not mention that Blass supported segregation, or that he was an officer in the Friends of Segregated Public Schools. He also failed to mention this in any of his subsequent articles on the subject.

48 East, *Magnolia Jungle*, 129.
49 Ibid.; P. D. East, "How to be a Man of Distinction," *Harper's*, January 1959, 12. Hereafter cited as East, "Man of Distinction."
50 P. D. East, *Petal* (Miss.) *Paper*, 16 December 1954, 2.
51 Ibid. An interesting point about this statement is that East left this paragraph out of his autobiography. He reprinted the rest of the editorial but omitted this damning suggestion.
52 East, interview with *Time Magazine*.
53 James O. Eastland, letter to P. D. East, *Petal* (Miss.) *Paper*, 11 November 1954, 2.
54 East, "Look Back in Pain," 10; P. D. East, application for a Nieman Fellowship at Harvard University, 2, Box 10, East Papers. Hereafter cited as East, Nieman application.
55 P. D. East, *Petal* (Miss.) *Paper*, 30 December 1954, 1.
56 Ibid., 2.
57 East, *Magnolia Jungle*, 132.
58 P. D. East, *Petal* (Miss.) *Paper*, 30 December 1954, 2.
59 Ibid.
60 East, *Magnolia Jungle*, 132.
61 Ibid., 133.
62 P. D. East, "Well, Why Not Just Form A Co-op?" *Petal* (Miss.) *Paper*, 20 January 1955, 2. The tax was levied at the source of supply and at the time of purchase. It effectively put the state of Mississippi in the illegal liquor business.
63 East, Nieman application, 2; East, *Magnolia Jungle*, 134-35.
64 East, *Magnolia Jungle*, 135.
65 Ibid., 134-35.
66 P. D. East, *Petal* (Miss.) *Paper*, 17 February 1955, 1.
67 P. D. East, *Petal* (Miss.) *Paper*, 3 March 1955, 2; East, "Man of Distinction," 12.
68 P. D. East, *Petal* (Miss.) *Paper*, 10 March 1955, 1.
69 P. D. East, *Petal* (Miss.) *Paper*, 31 March 1955, 1.
70 P. D. East, rejected pages from the *Magnolia Jungle*, 42-43, Box 11, East Papers. Hereafter cited as East, rejected pages. P. D. East, "The Band Wagon Went That-A-Way. . . .!" *Petal* (Miss.) *Paper*, 10 March 1955, 2.
71 East, rejected pages, 53; East, "Man of Distinction," 16.
72 East, *Magnolia Jungle*, 139.
73 McMillen, *Citizens' Council*, 215.
74 Lord, *The Past*, 64-67.
75 McMillen, *Citizens' Council*, 216.
76 Hodding Carter III, *The South Strikes Back* (Garden City, New

York: Doubleday and Company, 1959), 114–15.

[77] Silver, *Closed Society*, 103–9; Bartley, *Rise of Massive Resistance*, 229–30.

[78] McMillen, *Citizens' Council*, 321.

[79] East, *Magnolia Jungle*, 139.

[80] P. D. East, *Petal* (Miss.) *Paper*, 21 April 1955, 2.

[81] East, "Man of Distinction," 12.

[82] P. D. East, *Editorial Reprints from the Petal Paper and Personal Comments* (Pascagoula, Mississippi: By the Author, 1957), 2. Hereafter cited as East, *Editorial Reprints*.

[83] P. D. East, *Petal* (Miss.) *Paper*, 25 February 1955, 1.

[84] Most southerners did not share East's sympathy for labor unions. The South has long maintained open hostility to unions. For much of the post–World War II era, unionization moved slowly in this region, since liberals focused their attention on improving race relations. Right-to-work laws in ten Southern states provide ample testimony to this fact. For a thorough discussion of this topic see Ray Marshall, *Labor in the South* (Cambridge: Harvard University Press, 1967); Donald F. Roy, "Change and Resistance to Change in the Southern Labor Movement," in *The South in Continuity and Change*, ed. John C. McKinney and Edgar T. Thompson (Durham, North Carolina: Duke University Press, 1965), 225–47.

[85] P. D. East, *Petal* (Miss.) *Paper*, 28 April 1955, 1.

[86] East, Nieman application, 4.

[87] East, *Magnolia Jungle*, 145.

[88] P. D. East, *Petal* (Miss.) *Paper*, 19 May 1955, 2.

[89] P. D. East, *Petal* (Miss.) *Paper*, 2 June 1955, 2; P. D. East to Friend Crisler, 14 January 1958, Box 2, East Papers. It should also be noted that Southern Bell remembered East's support in the strike. They maintained their economic relationship with his paper long after most other area businesses had withdrawn their advertisements.

[90] P. D. East, *Petal* (Miss.) *Paper*, 2 June 1955, 3.

[91] Ibid., 1.

[92] Kluger, *Simple Justice*, 742–47.

[93] McMillen, *Citizens' Council*, 208–9.

[94] Bartley, *Rise of Massive Resistance*, 68–69.

[95] Frank E. Smith, *Congressman from Mississippi* (New York: Capricorn Books, 1964), 262–64; Lord, *The Past*, 67; Bartley, *Rise of Massive Resistance*, 82; McMillen, *Citizens' Council*, 217–18.

[96] Bartley, *Rise of Massive Resistance*, 208–12.

[97] McMillen, *Citizens' Council*, 255–56.

[98] P. D. East, text of speech given to Local Six Hotel and Club Workers, April 1959, 8–9, Box 1, East Papers. Hereafter cited as East, Local Six.

[99] P. D. East, *Petal* (Miss.) *Paper*, 9 June 1955, 2.

[100] East, *Magnolia Jungle,* 151.
[101] East, Nieman application, 3. East continued to give Waller photography jobs even after Waller ended the friendship.
[102] P. D. East, *Petal* (Miss.) *Paper,* 16 June 1955, 1.
[103] East, *Magnolia Jungle,* 151–52.
[104] Ibid., 152.
[105] P. D. East, *Petal* (Miss.) *Paper,* 16 June 1955, 2.
[106] Ibid.
[107] In the 23 June 1955 issue of the *Petal Paper* East printed what he said were his thoughts on the governor's race. They were in Chinese.
[108] P. D. East, *Petal* (Miss.) *Paper,* 14 July 1955, 1.
[109] Ibid.
[110] P. D. East, *Petal* (Miss.) *Paper,* 11 August 1955, 1.
[111] East, Nieman application, 4; East, *Magnolia Jungle,* 155; "An Editor Speaks on Civil Rights," *Hotel and Club Voice,* April 1959, 35–36. Arrington was the individual who disrupted the Hattiesburg school board meeting between white and black parents.
[112] P. D. East, *Petal* (Miss.) *Paper,* 4 August 1955, 2. East often used a religious appeal to try and convince people that bigotry had no place in modern society. He most likely persisted in this approach to avoid being attacked for opposing everything the South held dear. If this was his plan, it failed.
[113] P. D. East, *Petal* (Miss.) *Paper,* 4 August 1955, 2.
[114] P. D. East, *Petal* (Miss.) *Paper,* 25 August 1955, 2.
[115] Ibid. East never mentioned Lamar Smith or Emmett Till by name, nor did he comment that anyone had been killed. Here, as in the future, he condemned racism in general and its consequences, while rarely discussing specific examples. He also failed to credit William Allen White's editorial "What's the Matter with Kansas?" for some of the strongest and most effective language in his editorial.
[116] Ibid., 1.
[117] Ibid.
[118] East, *Magnolia Jungle,* 156.
[119] P. D. East, *Petal* (Miss.) *Paper,* 1 September 1955, 1.
[120] P. D. East, *Petal* (Miss.) *Paper,* 22 September 1955, 1.
[121] Ibid., 2.
[122] Ibid.
[123] P. D. East, "Or Conscience Salve," *Petal* (Miss.) *Paper,* 24 November 1955, 2.
[124] P. D. East, *Petal* (Miss.) *Paper,* 6 October 1955, 1.
[125] East, interview with *Time Magazine.*
[126] P. D. East, "Today This is Our View," *Petal* (Miss.) *Paper,* 13 October 1955, 2.
[127] P. D. East, "Where was Moses When the Lights Went Out?" *Petal*

(Miss.) *Paper,* 20 October 1955, 2.

[128] P. D. East, "Who Shall Stand the Gap?" *Petal* (Miss.) *Paper,* 27 October 1955, 2.

[129] Ibid., 4.

[130] East, *Magnolia Jungle,* 158.

[131] Ibid.

[132] P. D. East, *Petal* (Miss.) *Paper,* 17 November 1955, 1.

[133] P. D. East, *Petal* (Miss.) *Paper,* 1 December 1955, 1.

[134] P. D. East, *Petal* (Miss.) *Paper,* 8 December 1955, 1.

[135] P. D. East, *Petal* (Miss.) *Paper,* 29 December 1955, 1.

[136] P. D. East, "A Decision to be Rendered," *Petal* (Miss.) *Paper,* 1 December 1955, 1; P. D. East, "Answers, Unofficial, But Sincere," *Petal* (Miss.) *Paper,* 1 December 1955, 1-2.

[137] East, *Magnolia Jungle,* 160.

[138] P. D. East, *Petal* (Miss.) *Paper,* 19 January 1956, 1-2.

[139] P. D. East, "We Are Not Our Brother's Keeper," *Petal* (Miss.) *Paper,* 19 January 1956, 2.

[140] East, *Magnolia Jungle,* 163-64.

[141] To show his contempt for Senator James O. Eastland, East began to print his name in lower case letters, james o. eastland. He also began calling him "Our Senior Light" and "Our Gem."

[142] P. D. East, *Petal* (Miss.) *Paper,* 2 February 1956, 2.

[143] Ibid.

[144] P. D. East, *Petal* (Miss.) *Paper,* 9 February 1956, 2.

[145] P. D. East, "Now Ain't That a Wampus Kitty?" *Petal* (Miss.) *Paper,* 2 February 1956, 1.

[146] All of this dialogue was taken from P. D. East, *Petal* (Miss.) *Paper,* 9 February 1956, 1-2.

[147] East, *Editorial Reprints,* 15. Unfortunately, these letters and practically all of his correspondence up to 1959 have been destroyed. In 1956, Mississippi established the State Sovereignty Commission. This Commission had the duty of protecting the state's sovereignty from encroachment by the federal government. To aid in this endeavor, the Commission kept tabs on all racial liberals throughout the state. To protect himself and those who wrote him, critics as well as admirers, East burned practically all of his pre-1959 correspondence.

[148] East, *Magnolia Jungle,* 167-68.

[149] P. D. East, *Petal* (Miss.) *Paper,* 3 March 1956, 2. For a comprehensive discussion of the various types of pressure applied by the Council see McMillen, *Citizens' Council;* Bartley, *Rise of Massive Resistance;* John Ray Skates, *Mississippi: A Bicentennial History* (New York: W. W. Norton and Company, 1979), 158-59.

[150] P. D. East, *Petal* (Miss.) *Paper,* 9 February 1956, 1.

[151] P. D. East, *Petal* (Miss.) *Paper,* 16 February 1956, 1.

[152] C. Vann Woodward, *The Strange Career of Jim Crow* (New York:

Oxford University Press, 1966), 163. See also Peirce, *Deep South States*, 278–79.

[153] P. D. East, *Petal* (Miss.) *Paper*, 1 March 1956, 1.

[154] P. D. East, *Petal* (Miss.) *Paper*, 15 March 1956, 2.

[155] Ibid., 6.

[156] Ibid., 1.

[157] P. D. East, *Petal* (Miss.) *Paper*, 29 March 1956, 1.

[158] East, *Magnolia Jungle*, 180.

[159] East, "Man of Distinction," 18.

[160] East, Local Six, 11.

[161] East, *Magnolia Jungle*, 182.

[162] *Petal* (Miss.) *Paper*, 22 March 1956; *Petal* (Miss.) *Paper*, 29 March 1956; *Petal* (Miss.) *Paper*, 5 April 1956; *Petal* (Miss.) *Paper*, 12 April 1956; East, *Magnolia Jungle*, 180.

[163] P. D. East to Don Gross, 5 May 1956, Box 29, East Papers.

[164] East, *Magnolia Jungle*, 181.

[165] Ibid., 180.

[166] Albert Vorspan, "The Iconoclast of Petal, Mississippi," *The Reporter*, 21 March 1957, 35.

[167] P. D. East, *Petal* (Miss.) *Paper*, 22 March 1956, 1.

[168] Dykeman and Stokely, *Neither Black Nor White*, 208.

4

Fame But Not Fortune: The Travail of a Southern Liberal

P. D. East's "jackass ad" earned for him the enmity of many racists, but it also resulted in new friends. He discovered that there were other Mississippians, though few in number, who shared his views on race. In addition to these allies within the state, he developed friendships with like-minded people throughout the country. These national contacts started when several of East's subscribers sent his advertisement to every state and a number of foreign countries, including Germany, France, Japan, Italy, and Great Britain.[1] His reputation continued to grow as *The Reporter* carried a feature on his one-man crusade. Television and radio appearances followed this publicity, but such attention did not endear East to the majority of the people of Mississippi. The more recognition he gained, the more his economic and psychological woes increased.

In the wake of his "jackass ad," East continued his attack on the White Citizens' Council and on bigotry in general. He criticized area ministers for worrying too much about money and not enough about practicing their religion by establishing communications between the races.[2] In especially harsh words, he denounced Senator James O. Eastland. He first charged the senator with using obscenities for the public record. "On one occasion, in a Senate hearing, 'Our Jungle Gem' called a

witness a 'goddamned son-of-a-bitch.' On a number of occasions he has called a 'nigger' just what he is—a nigger."[3] Next
East accused Eastland of using his office to enhance his income.
As owner of a five-thousand-acre cotton plantation, Eastland
had become the strongest supporter of cotton farmers in the
Senate. When asked about attracting industry to Mississippi, he
responded that the state " ... needed industry like a man needed
a hole in the head. How ... can you keep labor on the farm at a
dollar a day with industry moving in and offering a dollar an
hour?"[4] Most disturbing to East was the senator's total disregard
for the law and for his oath of office. This trait was evident
when Eastland urged people to defy the Supreme Court's
ruling on desegregation. East remarked sarcastically,

> Anyone thinking that because a man of sterling character,
> golden principle, honor, intelligence, and integrity such as
> those possessed by 'Our Jungle Gem' would let a little
> thing like an oath stop him from protecting our way of life
> is not just a square, but he's downright stupid. ...[5]

Naturally, such comments increased East's unpopularity
with his fellow Mississippians, and they even caused him to
lose his wife's support. In the same issue in which he leveled
his scathing attack against Eastland, East's wife, Billie, declared:
"As a matter of public information, I would like you to know
that the opinions expressed in this paper by Editor East do not
necessarily represent the opinions of Mrs. Editor East."[6] Now
he could not even rely on the sympathy of his family. The
reality of his deteriorating economic situation struck him at the
end of May 1956. His income dropped $200 from the previous
May. Subscription figures alone bore out this depressing
situation. Total circulation dropped below the 1,000 mark for
the first time in his paper's short history. This contrasted
starkly with his previous high of 2,300. Equally disastrous, his
total list of advertisers from Petal had diminished to one.[7] If
this were not depressing enough, it now appeared that someone
systematically opened his mail. More than paranoia was at
work here. The WCC, through its contacts in local post offices,
frequently opened the letters sent to its enemies.[8]

Despite these problems, East continued his outspoken
advocacy of equality which brought him, quite naturally, into
closer association with Mississippi's black community. On one
memorable occasion, a black businessman and friend took him

into the ghetto of Hattiesburg. There, in a dilapidated home, East met a seventeen-year-old boy who had been beaten mercilessly by a group of white youths for no apparent reason. The boy and his parents remained terrified that the gang might return. The two visitors tried to calm the family's fears, and once they accomplished this task, they left. As soon as East dropped his friend off at his store, he drove around the corner, parked his car, and wept. In the midst of his tears he cried out, "God, why do you let things like this happen?"[9]

Infuriated by such brutality, he wrote one of his better columns, "A New Organization in Business—The Bigger and Better Bigots Bureau?" In this piece East held the WCC responsible for four recent acts of violence in Hattiesburg. He recalled that prior to the formation of the local Council no such episodes had occurred. Although he did not claim that members of the Hattiesburg chapter directly participated in the incidents, he maintained that the organization's rhetoric incited certain whites to take out their feelings of inferiority on blacks. He speculated that before long these thugs might begin to attack Catholics, Jews, and anyone else they considered un-American.[10]

Finding it increasingly difficult to cope with such events, East tried to leave the South for a short while. He applied for a Nieman Fellowship at Harvard University. Under this program the recipient attended Harvard for one year to undertake studies which would broaden him or her intellectually and also enable that individual to bring a greater depth of knowledge to some of the issues he or she covered. Given his poor education and the constant pressure he experienced in Mississippi, East wanted the fellowship desperately. Based on his work and recommendations from Mark Ethridge, publisher and editor of the *Louisville Courier-Journal,* and Hodding Carter, publisher and editor of the *Greenville Delta-Democrat Times,* he received an invitation from the Nieman selection committee to meet in Chicago for an interview. But a combination of nerves and sleeping pills caused East to make an extraordinarily bad impression on Louis Lyons, the foundation curator, and other committee members. They questioned his seriousness about the course work and whether he would even return to Mississippi and resume his career.[11] Under the circumstances they turned him down. As he noted, "I made a feeble effort at being unconcerned but, I admit frankly, I was crushed."[12]

East found some consolation when James W. Silver, professor of history at the University of Mississippi, and William Faulkner asked him to help them form a moderate political group in Mississippi.[13] Although such an endeavor might have seemed innocuous enough, Mississippians made the task almost impossible. The state legislature had passed a law making it a crime for any organization to institute desegregation suits in state courts. Another law banned barratry—that is, the encouragement of legal disputes. The state denied constitutional rights that people outside of Mississippi enjoyed. No form of cooperation between the races was acceptable even when it was aimed at maintaining segregation. When Erle Johnston, publicity director for the State Sovereignty Commission, expressed a willingness to work with blacks, William Simmons of the WCC snapped that Johnston "sounds like he is ready to surrender."[14] Disagreements rarely occurred. As one historian later said, "The price was simply too steep for open disagreement: lost business, insults in the press, Citizens' Council vitriol, ostracism by friends, garbage on the front lawn.... It was a brave Mississippian who dared buck the tide."[15] In light of these circumstances, and after considerable debate, the three men decided that a moderate group was impossible. Faulkner suggested, without much opposition, that such an organization would spend most of its time defending itself rather than accomplishing anything positive.[16]

Still, they wanted somehow to give courage and hope to the other moderates in the state. Silver recalled that several students at the University of Mississippi had distributed a mimeographed paper called the *Nigble Papers* (for "nigger bible") in which they lampooned Mississippi's dominant, white Scotch-Irish population, thus standing southern bigotry on its head. Finding this type of humor appealing, the three men decided to edit, rewrite, and add to this student effort and then publish the revised version as the *Southern Reposure*.[17] Faulkner and East concluded that their names could not be associated with the paper as that might reduce its effectiveness, and Silver could not claim responsibility for fear of losing his job. Thus, complete secrecy had to be maintained throughout the entire project.[18]

East volunteered to edit and publish the paper, while Silver and Faulkner were to find the financial support. He took the most difficult part of the entire project, but he received some assistance. When his printer, fearing reprisals, refused to take the job, he took it to his good friend and former printer, Easton King of the *Pascagoula Chronicle Star*. King accepted the job with enthusiasm and even helped East edit the copy. He found another ally in the Reverend Will D. Campbell, director of religious life at the University of Mississippi. Campbell provided the conspirators with five hundred stamped envelopes addressed to sympathetic clergymen in Mississippi. Also, numerous liberals and moderates on college campuses throughout the state saw to it that copies of the paper, which they received anonymously, found their way into the hands of students.[19]

In late July 1956, ten thousand copies were printed and distributed. From all reports the effort proved worthwhile. When agitated administrators at one conservative Baptist school ordered that such "trash be gathered and burned," an instant demand arose for the *Southern Reposure* and it began to sell for one dollar per copy.[20] Some readers certainly took offense at the paper's satire, but many found it most humorous. Because it resembled East's work, several people accused him of being responsible for the publication, but he denied any role whatsoever.[21] Faulkner, convinced that East had done such an excellent job with the *Southern Reposure*, sent several copies to his publisher, Random House, but nothing ever came of the gesture.[22] Nonetheless, East remained quite pleased with Faulkner's praise and the general acceptance that college students accorded the paper.

East had, in fact, done a splendid job with the *Reposure*. The banner headline read, "EASTLAND ELECTED BY NAACP AS OUTSTANDING MAN OF THE YEAR."[23] As chief writer for the paper, East created Nathan Bedford Cooclose as the alleged publisher. In his message to the readers, Cooclose discussed the need for keeping Scotch-Irish segregated from the rest of the white community. Among the reasons he noted, the most important were their habits.

> The average Scotch-Irish is a repulsive and obnoxious creature who is apt, if the notion strikes him to pull a highland fling on the main street of any one of our towns in Mississippi. In addition, they have come to expect to be served oatmeal in our finest restaurants simply because they have the required fifteen cents.[24]

Their morals were also questionable. Cooclose charged that

they bred "like turtles! In addition to their poor breeding, they are vulgar to an unbearable point. How many times have you heard one exclaim, 'Hootman,' or 'Begorrrrah!' How disgusting!"[25] He closed his column by asking, do you want your "daughter to marry a windbag, highland flinging, kilt wearing creature?"[26]

Elsewhere the paper, in an obvious swipe at those responsible for the Emmett Till tragedy, featured a news story concerning one Alexander Tell, age sixteen. This Scotch-Irish lad, it seemed, had insulted an attractive, non-Scotch-Irish woman by remarking to a friend, "What a wee bonnie lassie!" The local authorities arrested the boy and sentenced him to a long prison term—if the angry citizens did not kill him first.[27] Another item on Segregation Emphasis Month appeared on page one. It recounted the concluding rally at which Elsie Dinsmore spoke on "The Botch Made by the Scotch." Her speech "was followed by a two-hour period of quiet in which those present medi-hated and contemplated earnestly the many faceted inferiority of the Scotch-Irish race." The meeting closed after "this fruitful interlude of hate."[28] The last page carried an advertisement, a take-off on the "jackass ad," which invited people to join the Anti-Scotch-Irish Council. Its goals included keeping "the Scotch-Irish in Their Place" and keeping "The R Rolling Children Out of Our Fine Southern Schools."[29]

Silver, Faulkner, and East had hoped to publish a monthly issue of the *Southern Reposure,* but it turned out to be too much trouble. Faulkner actually did very little on the project other than provide encouragement. Moreover, it cost nearly $500 to publish the first edition. Silver managed to obtain $200 in contributions, but East had to assume the other $300.[30] It was $300 he could not afford to spend once, let alone each month.

By October 1956, East's financial condition had deteriorated so much that he raised the price of his paper from two to three dollars per year.[31] To boost his sagging income further, he contemplated putting together a booklet of his editorials and general comments on the racial situation in Mississippi. He talked with Mark Ethridge about the project, and he in turn spoke to Joseph Barnes, senior editor of Simon and Schuster. Although Barnes sympathized with East's plight and wanted to help, he believed that the booklet would not be economically feasible for a big publishing house. He also considered East's writing to be, at best, adequate. "From a purely objective point of view, these columns are, in many cases, average and it's the man himself and his courage that are fascinating."[32] Undaunted, East undertook the project on his own with Easton King as the printer.[33] At fifty cents per copy he would not get rich, but the extra income would relieve some of the economic pressure.

At the end of East's third year of publication, his paper showed a profit of $113.95. No Petal advertisers remained and local circulation rested at nine. Total circulation remained around one thousand as subscribers from across the nation continued to replace cancellations in Mississippi.[34] Even the Christmas season failed to bring its usual financial benefits. In the past, friend and foe alike had placed a Christmas greeting in the *Petal Paper*, but in 1956 East barely put together a fourteen-page edition. It was his shortest Christmas issue to date. To make matters worse, between mid-November and mid-December he lost one half of his standing weekly advertisements which constituted the backbone of his paper.[35] In trying to determine the cause of this economic disaster, East finally cornered a merchant who had been trying to avoid him. The man confessed that Citizens' Council members had made rounds of local businesses indicating that advertisement with P. D. East was financially unsound.[36]

Such retaliation was not a surprise. Ever since the "jackass ad" in March 1956, East had continued his denunciation of the WCC, or the Citizens' Council of America (CCA), as it now referred to itself.[37] To point out the inequity of the Council's "separate but equal" policy, he published the pictures of two schools, one a modern facility and the other one near collapse. He then asked his readers to decide which school was used by whites and which one was used by blacks.[38] He damned the CCA for denying equal rights to blacks on the basis of race. In a democracy, he said, whites should "do everything they can to banish forever what is left of the cruel and absurd notion that there can be any stigma attached to any human being because of race. The Creator never stigmatizes anybody."[39] He argued further that unless civil rights were equally available to all no one would feel secure. He described Judge Tom P. Brady, darling of the CCA, as an author of a book on the best-seller list for bigots, a windbag, a blabbermouth, and a professional southerner.[40] On 22 November 1956, when he did not have enough advertisements to fill a four-page paper, he devoted one entire page to all of the good things accomplished by the

Citizens' Council. He left the page blank.[41] To a group like the CCA that tolerated no deviation whatsoever from its beliefs, East's views were traitorous and deserved punishment, which it meted out in generous measure.

CCA tactics hurt East as much psychologically as financially. He seemed incapable of hardening himself to the hostility and snubs of his fellow citizens. If anything, he grew more sensitive.[42] In an attempt to escape this local censure, he started driving all over the state of Mississippi. Out of the Hattiesburg area, people failed to recognize him and would talk to him as they would any other person. In 1956 alone, he drove 25,000 miles on such sanity-preserving journeys.[43] Trips to visit Jim Silver or Easton King also figured into his mileage totals. Nevertheless, depression held East tightly in its grip. To keep the *Petal Paper* functioning in such times, he reprinted many of his past columns. On one occasion he even published an old college term paper on Shakespeare.

In an attempt to pull himself out of the depths of despair, East turned to the only other method he knew, humor. In his 10 January 1957 issue he agreed in part with what many racists were saying about Mississippi.

> A growing number of autos in the state of Mississippi are sporting tags which read: Mississippi, The Most Lied About State in the Nation. We agreed with the tags. Unfortunately, the lies are not necessarily told by persons outside the state.[44]

The same week he published an announcement for a man ostensibly running for the United States Senate seat held by "james o. eastland." The man's name was Cornpone P. Neanderthal. Accompanying this declaration of candidacy, the paper carried a picture of the potential senator. It was a photograph of the Neanderthal Man from the American Museum of Natural History. The story stated that C. P. Neanderthal was a charter member of the Ku Klux Council (as East often called the CCA), an ardent supporter of the southern way of life, and a success in his chosen profession—coon hunting. East quoted Neanderthal as saying, "I would like to point out that I got as much sense as the present representative from Mississippi."[45] The following week East noted,

> To those of you who wrote in asking if in last week's paper I had gotten the picture of Mr. Neanderthal and Senator

Eastland confused, I'd like to say that the difference in the
appearance of the two is slight.[46]

As it often did, East's humorous attacks on bigotry were
followed by serious comments as well. At the same time as he
announced Neanderthal's candidacy, he also mentioned the
Montgomery bus boycott. For over a year he had remained
silent on this issue and his remarks came only after the blacks
had achieved their momentous victory.[47] By early 1957, the
boycott, which had been modest at its inception, had assumed
immense practical and symbolic significance.[48] It had started
quite simply on 1 December 1955, when a black woman, Rosa
Parks, refused to give her seat on a Montgomery bus to a white
passenger. Her subsequent arrest sparked considerable anger
within the Negro community. Blacks had long resented the
humiliating and abusive treatment they received from white
bus drivers. This smoldering bitterness finally assumed public
form. The Women's Political Council suggested to E. D. Nixon,
Pullman porter and president of the local NAACP, that blacks
in protest should boycott the buses for one day. Nixon contacted
the Reverend Martin Luther King, Jr., and the Reverend Ralph
Abernathy, who organized the boycott for 5 December 1955.
King and Abernathy expected approximately 60 percent compliance with their wishes. Instead, they received nearly 100
percent cooperation.[49]

Elated by the response, the leaders decided to continue the
boycott until a number of black grievances had been remedied.
To better organize and direct this effort, they formed the
Montgomery Improvement Association (MIA) with King as its
president. Their demands were threefold: 1) courteous treatment,
2) passenger seating on a first-come, first-served basis, and 3)
Negro bus drivers on predominantly Negro routes.[50] Throughout
the city blacks walked to work, took cabs, or formed car pools
rather than ride segregated buses.

Whites fought back, trying to break this increasingly costly
boycott.[51] At first King and the other leaders received threatening
telephone calls. Then the homes of King and Nixon were
bombed. When these efforts failed to halt the movement, white
Montgomerians used the legal system. They enforced an old
statute that prohibited boycotts. King and eighty-eight others
were convicted under this law despite the fact that the CCA
encouraged whites to lay off their black maids for a month to
starve them into submission.[52] In a more imaginative vein,

local insurance companies cancelled the car insurance of
Montgomery blacks who, with their own touch of creativity,
turned to Lloyds of London.[53] None of these tactics, legal or
illegal, succeeded in ending the boycott. For 385 days, until the
Supreme Court ruled Montgomery's segregation law unconstitu-
tional, blacks refused to ride city buses. During the entire
ordeal, King and his followers faced violence and hostility yet
clung, though at times tenuously, to the philosophy of nonviolence. This victory marked a crucial turning point in modern
civil rights history. For the first time, blacks had used mass
action successfully against white society.[54] They could also
boast of a unifying philosophy, nonviolence, and a nationally
recognized leader, Martin Luther King, Jr. To harness this new
sense of purpose and optimism, southern blacks formed the
Southern Christian Leadership Conference, hoping to use it
throughout the South as they had used the MIA in Montgomery.

In his remarks on the boycott, East took great pleasure in
the victory and especially in its peaceful nature. He praised
Martin Luther King for his disciplined and temperate leadership
which, East felt, kept the entire project nonviolent.[55] Unable to
maintain a totally serious attitude, he took a jab at those who
used religion to justify segregation. "We gave him [the Negro]
our religion and now look what happened! Why over in
Montgomery last year the Negroes took our religious teachings
and used them against us. 'Whosoever shall smite on thy right
cheek, turn him the other also.' There ought to be a law against
that sort of thing, and we may just pass one right here in
Mississippi, too. So there!"[56]

By the end of January 1957, East's depression had run its
course and he had begun to fight more vigorously than ever to
keep the *Petal Paper* alive. The need for some relief was urgent
as the paper now lost nearly $400 per month,[57] but his personal
peculiarities made this difficult. He refused to accept any
monetary gifts. To do so, he believed, would be to profit from
the misery of others.[58] He accepted money only when it
purchased a subscription to his paper or his booklet of editorial
reprints.

With this principle established firmly, East went to Atlanta
and New York City in an attempt to promote the sale of his
booklet.[59] The Reverend Will Campbell had arranged for East
to meet with the leaders of several organizations that might
lend financial assistance. In Atlanta, he saw Harold Fleming of

the Southern Regional Council and sold him 2,000 booklets. His contacts in New York City proved equally fruitful. There he sold 1,500 booklets, and more importantly, Edwin J. Lukas, chief counsel for the American Jewish Committee, brought several groups together to discuss a subscription campaign for the *Petal Paper*.[60] Those assembled decided that East should print 15,000 promotional copies of the paper, which they would distribute throughout the country.

From this effort and an article in *The Reporter* on East, the *Petal Paper* gained over 400 new subscribers.[61] As for his booklet, he sold 3,500 on this one trip, one half of the total.[62] East's expedition proved rewarding in another way. While in Atlanta, he learned of Koinonia Farm, a cooperative operation near Americus, Georgia, and one of its leaders, Dr. Clarence Jordan. Most of the area's residents disliked Jordan and the other members of the Koinonia community because of their emphasis upon the sharing of income, pacifism, and racial equality. In 1956 and 1957 local hostility grew so intense that the farm and its occupants became targets of violence. Koinonia's enemies bombed their roadside market, burned their buildings, and fired shots from rifles and machine guns at the cooperative. Area people who tried to lend assistance found their barns burned and equipment destroyed.[63] Members of the local ministerial association condemned the barbaric harassment, and their congregations in turn condemned the resolution and told its authors that they could leave if they felt uncomfortable with southern racial patterns.[64]

Although East did not agree fully with Koinonia's concept of economic sharing or for that matter with the emphasis on religion,[65] he nonetheless had great respect and admiration for its citizens' decency. "The Koinonia Farm group is composed of pacifists who, as I understand it, are practicing to the letter the teachings of Christianity. It seems they may finish up about like the founder of the religion did."[66] To those who charged the residents of Koinonia with being "screwballs and commies," East responded, "If they are either, then I'd like to be both."[67] Commenting on the authorities' inability or unwillingness to stop the violence aimed at Koinonia Farm, he reemphasized his opinion that if the constitutional rights of one person or group could be denied, then they could be denied to anyone. As he stated quite forcefully, "Please pardon me for waving the flag, but these things for which it stands are of the utmost importance

to me—and, I think, to any person in his right mind."[68] Such
support for equal rights for all people won East few allies in
the South, but Clarence Jordan and all of those at Koinonia
Farm became his steadfast friends.

The trip was not a complete success, however. *Time
Magazine* spent a considerable amount of time and money
interviewing East in New York City and later in Mississippi,
but never actually published his story. Two points, neither very
complimentary to *Time,* led to this decision. One of the reporters who interviewed East doubted his claims of economic
distress. As he told his editor, "I am slightly dubious."[69] A
small amount of investigative work would have proven this
conclusion wrong. Of greater importance was *Time*'s reluctance
to lose any of Mississippi's advertising revenue. On one previous
occasion, *Time* had made some rather pointed criticisms of
Mississippi. The governor promptly ordered all state agencies
to cease spending money with *Time,* Incorporated. Shortly after
this decision went into effect, the magazine praised Senator
John Stennis. On the heels of this story *Time*'s editor visited
Mississippi, extolling the state's virtues throughout his stay. To
have printed an article favorable to East, and thus unfavorable
to Mississippi, *Time* would no doubt have found itself the
object of another economic boycott, and it did not want to run
this risk. East learned of these circumstances from an employee
of the Mississippi state government.[70]

Despite the success of his booklet and the subscription
drive, the *Petal Paper* failed to prosper, casting doubt on its
future. Several solutions offered themselves to East, but he
found none of them to his liking. He first thought about
reversing his stand on the race question. He dismissed this idea
as morally reprehensible. He then considered closing the paper
and moving to the West Coast, or as he put it, "as far away
from the Magnolia Jungle as I could get."[71] Although East did
not reject this alternative as readily, he eventually concluded
that even though he might leave the South, he could never
escape his rebellious nature. Trouble would follow him wher-
ever he went.

> To me such a move would be a waste of time, in view of
> the fact that no matter where I was I seemed to carry my
> own jungle with me. I saw no possible way out of the
> jungle, and I wondered if indeed the jungle were of my
> own making. I knew I could not escape me, no matter
> what my location or set of circumstances.[72]

East finally decided the least objectionable option open to him was to reduce the size of the paper and thus lower expenses. On 21 March 1957, the *Petal Paper* became a tabloid rather than a standard-size newspaper. He helped rationalize this decision by noting that the shorter paper would allow more time to work on his latest project, his autobiography.

Although lacking money, East never lacked for a sense of humor. He launched his smaller paper with an advertisement for a cross-burning kit:

> Have quantity of used lumber for making crosses. 2 X 4s well seasoned in 5-foot lengths. Kerosene furnished with orders of half dozen or more. Save on your cross burnings! "How to Build Your Own Crosskit" free with all orders. Act today ... or tonight![73]

In a subsequent issue he ran an advertisement for summer-weight sheets for members of the Ku Klux Klan.

> Don't suffer from the summer heat by using your regular uniform of a muslin bed sheet! Inquire about our complete stock of Cotton Eyelet Embroidery, designed especially for summer wear. Klanettes may enlarge the holes for arms, but your head will fit nicely through the eyelets as they are. Keep cool this summer on your rides of mercy.[74]

He further satirized the KKK as well as the cult of the southern white woman in a song entitled "The Old Fiery Cross" by John Filibuster Nightsheet. The chorus recounted the so-called good times the husband and wife of the song spent together,

> At the foot, at the foot of the old fiery cross,
> When we first went together on a real lynching spree,
> Oh, we crucified a nigger to a magnolia tree,
> And we dragged a nigger lover
> Twenty miles through the cover
> Celebrating 'round the foot of the old fiery cross![75]

The man singing the song described his wife this way:

> Your stringy blond hair's a sight to behold;
> You look as if you're a hundred years old;
> Your teeth stick out, and you drool at the mouth
> To kiss you takes all the courage I can summon
> But dammit, baby, you're a Southern White Woman![76]

East's most deadly barbs were aimed at those who used religion to support their bigotry. Building on the idea of two ministers, Will Campbell and Sam Barefield, who advocated racial equality, East published the Dixiecrat version of the Bible.[77] This translation omitted the entire Old Testament because it described the escape of Moses across the Red Sea. Use of that particular body of water made him a potential subversive and thus a danger to young minds. The New Testament remained, but portions were rewritten. John 3:16 now read, "For God so loved Mississippi that He gave it 'Our Gem.'" Luke 18:16 took on a different meaning, "But Jesus called them unto Him, and said, suffer the little WHITE children to come unto me."[78] Few Mississippians found his comments humorous; most agreed with the charge that East was a "damned heathen."[79]

East's financial crisis not only failed to stop his assaults against racism, it actually broadened the scope of his attacks. To raise extra income, he began to make public speeches on race relations. At first, he balked at the idea of speaking and taking money for the effort. He felt very uncomfortable in front of an audience, and, as he had stated previously, he did not want to profit from the misery of others. Sarah Patton Boyle, a fellow civil rights advocate and friend, helped convince him of the need to speak out and to get paid for it. As she wrote to East, "You know good and well that somebody ought to do it—and you know who that somebody is. You have in your bone and blood an awareness of a better future."[80] She noted further that any time he gave a speech he could not help but do some good. "I mean you simply cannot stand up anywhere and say your piece without casting your vote for the human family . . . and giving a witness which arouses, awakens, and encourages others."[81] As for accepting money for such appearances, Boyle emphasized that few people enriched themselves by supporting the civil rights movement. To refuse money might necessitate closing the *Petal Paper*, and in her estimation, such an action would be a great tragedy.[82] East had only recently given a speech at Dillard University in New Orleans, but he believed he had done such a poor job that he should decline any future invitations.[83] Boyle's letters persuaded him to present his message despite his oratorical limitations and to accept money for his efforts.[84]

Putting his new philosophy to work, East accepted an invitation from the National Council of Churches to appear on its nationally televised program, "Frontiers of Faith." Joining him on the 23 June 1957 program were Carl Rowan, then with the *Minneapolis Tribune,* Dr. Clarence Jordan, and Dr. Eugene C. Blake, president of the National Council of Churches. Prior to the show the men had a two-and-one-half-hour discussion as a warm-up to the show's topic, "Progress on Integration." East, though not lucid, contributed to the off-the-air debate, but when the program started, he said very little. As he put it, "My sole contribution was a few 'er, ah, umm's.' Dr. Blake tried everything he could to get the village idiot to talk. I just sat."[85] East expressed genuine dismay over his inability to make some positive contribution to the debate. Extreme stage fright apparently accounted for his poor performance, and for once he had not exaggerated his mistakes. He even failed to gain one new subscriber after his nationwide appearance. As his old friend and teacher, Dr. W. W. Stout, remarked, "Well, you didn't quite get off the ground."[86] Or as a faithful reader of the *Petal Paper* commented, "I saw you on television. I wake up screaming."[87] Although somewhat amused by such comments, East declined all speaking invitations for several months.

He remained relatively quiet throughout the summer, but the calm broke in September when he mounted a moderate attack against Orval Faubus and those fighting desegregation in Little Rock.[88] Prior to this incident, Little Rock had seemed an unlikely location for a racial disturbance. On 18 May 1954, immediately after the Supreme Court's *Brown* decision, the Little Rock school board started to prepare for desegregation. Within a year, Virgil Blossom, the school superintendent, presented the public with a workable plan. The moderate view of the state's voters and of the governor, Orval Faubus, gave practically everyone the impression that compliance with the *Brown* decision was a foregone conclusion. Few people anticipated the turmoil that erupted. Incompetent and irresponsible leadership plus racial demagoguery led to a disastrous confrontation.

By the summer of 1957, the Capital Citizens' Council (CCC) had mounted an aggressive antidesegregation crusade through newspaper advertisements, letter-writing campaigns, the use of outside speakers, and the creation of disturbances at school board meetings. Virgil Blossom's leadership faltered at this point, since he had failed to enlist the support of Little Rock's sympathetic civic leaders and to capitalize on the favorable sentiments expressed by the *Arkansas Gazette.* Politically weak city officials regarded desegregation as a matter for the educational authorities, and Faubus tried to pass the buck by claiming all decisions should be made by local authorities. Everyone knew it could be a politically explosive issue with potential losers on all sides, so no one wanted to assume responsibility.

This power vacuum allowed the CCC and a new group, the Central High School Mothers, to step in and gain the ascendency by exploiting white fears regarding the admittance of blacks to the city's schools.[89] With their power increasing, the CCC and its allies applied pressure on Governor Faubus to block forced desegregation. Faubus, with his reelection campaign under way, sensed the political winds shifting, so he took it upon himself to stop it. On 2 September 1957, the first day of school, he called out the National Guard, as he explained, "to prevent 'tumult, riot, and the breach of the peace.' "[90] In actuality it meant that blacks would be prevented from going to school with whites. Even though this was in violation of a federal court order and increased the tension in an already charged atmosphere, President Eisenhower refused to involve himself in this imbroglio. Finally, on 20 September, after considerable legal maneuvering, the federal district court ordered Faubus to remove the Guard and he complied.

At this point, Blossom pleaded with the president to help preserve the peace when desegregation occurred. Again, Eisenhower refused to act. On Monday, 23 September, when nine blacks entered Central High, a riot ensued, and Tuesday brought threats of a similar outbreak. Under such threats of chaos, the president federalized the National Guard which escorted the blacks to school instead of blocking the entrance. Only token desegregation had taken place but hard-line southern racists compared this action with Reconstruction and occupation by federal troops.[91] One Mississippi community, Forest, was so outraged that they ordered the high school band to stop playing the "Star-Spangled Banner" before football games and to play "Dixie" instead.[92] Although East never gave the Little Rock episode in-depth treatment, he was appalled by what had taken place.[93] He pointed out that Faubus seemed ignorant of the North's victory in the Civil War which ended any claim a states' righter might have made regarding the superiority of state law over federal law.[94] Three weeks later he noted rather fatalistically, "faubus flubbed. ABOUT GOVERNOR FAUBUS IT IS SAID HE'S GOT LITTLE ROCKS IN HIS HEAD. And that's about the size of the situation in Arkansas, so why write more?"[95] For the next nine months, however, he did write more. In October 1957, after Eisenhower had finally enforced the federal court order for desegregation, East condemned the Baptist ministers who called on God to remove the blacks from Central High School. Sarcastically, he commented that God "must have an especially soft spot in His heart for Baptist preachers like those in Little Rock of which there seems to be more than there are Christians."[96]

Later, in a more reflective mood, he contemplated the damage that Faubus and other racists had done to the reputation of the United States throughout the world. Americans, he believed, must have appeared utterly hypocritical, preaching the superiority of democracy to black nations, while denying constitutional rights to its own black citizens. Such actions, he concluded, undermined America's foreign policy and caused more damage than the spies who gave the atomic bomb secrets to the Soviet Union.[97] To reverse this trend, he believed the country needed "some calm, intelligent leadership, while I don't know who would fill the need, I have some ideas about who won't fill the need. But, alas, impeachment is such an unpleasant and messy business, but it is sometimes a necessity."[98] He reasoned that Eisenhower through his vacillation shared as much responsibility as Faubus. In spite of the gravity of the situation, he could not resist a little humor. He wrote that 1957 had been a year of questions and one of the better ones asked was, "DO YOU WANT YOUR DAUGHTER TO MARRY A FAUBUS?"[99]

Try as he might, East could find little humor in his own economic condition. As the *Petal Paper* drew near to completing its fourth year of operation, he asked himself, as he had done in the spring, whether he could continue to afford his publishing enterprise. In the past year he had gone $4,000 in debt, and future prospects seemed bleak.[100] The number of Petalites taking the paper stood at two, and like the preceding year, no Petal merchants advertised with him. Thanks to national publicity, circulation outside Mississippi had grown, but it failed to provide the necessary funds to keep the paper alive. Finances were so bad that in late October when his old ulcer hemorrhaged or a new one developed, he could not afford to see a physician for the necessary treatment.

After much soul-searching and with a great deal of reluctance, he decided to go on the lecture tour. He disliked

public speaking intensely, but could see no other option that
would allow him to continue publishing the paper. Both
Easton King and Will Campbell urged him to seize this
opportunity because, in their opinion, the paper should not be
allowed to die. As King put it,

> The *Petal Paper* is lousy, P. D., but it's a beacon of hope in
> an otherwise dark area. If you can take the stand for
> moderation you have and survive, others will take hope
> and eventually may speak out in behalf of sanity. If you
> fail, if you are forced out of business, the bigots will take
> full credit for it and other voices will not be heard for a
> long, long time. If for no other reason, the *Petal Paper* is
> important as a symbol.[101]

Needing assistance on this new endeavor, East wrote to an
"esteemed Southern editor,"[102] as he called him, asking for
advice about approaching a speakers' bureau or agent. The
editor responded by listing the advantages and disadvantages of
the tour, and he volunteered to write his agent in New York
City to help him line up lectures. Before making any final
decision, East sought the counsel of his New York City friends.
Feeling face-to-face contact superior to telephone conversation,
he went to New York. Upon arrival, he went to the agent the
southern editor friend had promised to contact in his behalf.
Not only had the agent never heard of East, he had not heard
from the editor for two years. The blatant lie of a friend struck
East a hard blow. He could not fathom why anyone would treat
a person in such a manner.

To make matters worse, East received similar treatment
from the head of a New York City "do good" organization, as
he dubbed it.[103] Through this man he also made an appointment
to talk with the editor of a national news magazine. When the
time came for him to meet with these individuals, both were
too busy to see him.[104] Out of pride, East refused to associate
with either of these men in the future. He nonetheless had
better luck with people he had met on his previous trip to New
York. Roy Wilkins, Edwin Lukas, Albert Vorspan, Rabbi
Eugene Lipman, Irving J. Fain, Oscar Lee, and others concurred
with King and Campbell. They helped him sell 300 new
subscriptions and gave him several possibilities for group sales.

On this more pleasant note, East returned to Mississippi
determined to keep the *Petal Paper* alive. As he remarked, "Of
course, it was better to be a conforming Kiwanian, but even in

that state of mind I knew such a fate would be worse for me than the one which I suffered."[105] In explaining to his readers why he would continue to fight for the rights of blacks, he wrote,

> I have concluded that if "They can do it to them, then they can do it to me." And I don't want it done to me; thus, my rights are connected directly with the rights of every single person in the Nation. In short, I do not feel that I'm a free man so long as a single slave exists. When I make an effort in behalf of the rights of the Negro, I'm making an effort in behalf of myself, my daughter, and her children. That's about as simple as I know how to make it.[106]

East received further encouragement for his efforts when a radio station in Hamburg, West Germany, contacted him shortly after his trip to New York City. The station had done an hour-long play on East and William Faulkner entitled *Das Lachen in Der Magnolia,* translated as "The Laughter in the Magnolia." He received a copy of the script, but since it was in German, he never read it. Shortly thereafter, a newspaper in Sweden did a feature story on the paper.[107] Again, he never had it translated. Most significantly, his story appeared in a book by Wilma Dykeman and James Stokely, *Neither Black Nor White,* which dealt with the effects of the *Brown* decision upon the South. The husband and wife writing team gave him very high marks for courage and decency.[108] His growing fame failed to have an impact on local merchants, and his 1957 Christmas issue was the shortest such edition in the paper's history. Fame clearly had its price.

Notes

[1] P. D. East, *The Magnolia Jungle: The Life, Times and Education of a Southern Editor* (New York: Simon and Schuster, 1960), 179. Hodding Carter of the *Delta-Democrat Times,* Mark Ethridge of the *Louisville Courier-Journal,* and Jim Silver helped distribute the ad.

[2] P. D. East, "Mr. Morse Had a Code," *Petal* (Miss.) *Paper,* 19 April 1956, 1; P. D. East, "In Hoc Signo $ $ $ In the Sign," *Petal* (Miss.) Paper, 26 April 1956, 1.

[3] P. D. East, " 'Our Gem,' He's Real Gone, Man, Real Gone—Now Ain't He a Real Cool Cat, Man!" *Petal* (Miss.) *Paper,* 31 May 1956, 1.

[4] Ibid.

[5] Ibid.

[6] P. D. East, *Petal* (Miss.) *Paper*, 31 May 1956, 2.

[7] East, *Magnolia Jungle*, 187.

[8] P. D. East to Don Gross, 25 May 1956, Box 29, P. D. East Papers, Mugar Memorial Library, Boston University. Hereafter cited as East Papers. East noted to Gross, of *Time Magazine*, that a letter he had received from Gross had been opened and that this occurred frequently.

[9] East, *Magnolia Jungle*, 188.

[10] P. D. East, "A New Organization in Business—The Bigger and Better Bigots Bureau?" *Petal* (Miss.) *Paper*, 7 June 1956, 1.

[11] Louis Lyons to Tim Seldes, 10 April 1958, Box 10, East Papers; P. D. East, *Petal* (Miss.) *Paper*, 31 May 1956, 1-3; P. D. East, *Petal* (Miss.) *Paper*, 14 June 1956, 1; East, *Magnolia Jungle*, 173-75. At this time East had been nominated for a Pulitzer Prize by Hodding Carter and a Hattiesburg resident, Margaret Olsen.

[12] East, *Magnolia Jungle*, 174; P. D. East, *Petal* (Miss.) *Paper*, 14 June 1956, 1.

[13] To protect Jim Silver from the WCC and others who had tried unsuccessfully to have him fired from his position at the University of Mississippi, East never used his friend's name when relating this episode in his autobiography. He referred to Silver as Dr. Josh Brass. To avoid any connection with the *Southern Reposure*, Silver destroyed East's letters to him, and he urged East to do the same with his letters. James W. Silver to P. D. East, 2 August 1956, Box 25, East Papers.

[14] Walter Lord, *The Past That Would Not Die* (New York: Harper and Row, 1965), 79; John Ray Skates, *Mississippi: A Bicentennial History* (New York: W. W. Norton and Company, 1979), 158-59.

[15] Lord, *The Past*, 79-80.

[16] East, *Magnolia Jungle*, 194.

[17] Letter to the author from James W. Silver, 28 June 1977.

[18] Faulkner feared the project would be written off as one produced by a couple of cranks. He also was concerned that physical reprisals might occur. James W. Silver to P. D. East, 4 July 1956, Box 25, East Papers.

[19] James W. Silver to P. D. East, 2 August 1956, Box 25, East Papers.

[20] East, *Magnolia Jungle*, 196.

[21] P. D. East, *Petal* (Miss.) *Paper*, 2 August 1956, 1.

[22] James W. Silver to P. D. East, 3 August 1956, Box 25, East Papers.

[23] *Southern Reposure*, Summer 1956, 1. A copy of this paper was supplied to the author by James W. Silver.

[24] Ibid.

[25] Ibid.

26 Ibid. East wrote this column with a minor assist from William Faulkner and Easton King.

27 Ibid., 2.

28 Ibid., 1.

29 Ibid., 4.

30 Letter to the author from James W. Silver, 28 June 1977.

31 P. D. East, *Petal* (Miss.) *Paper*, 18 October 1956, 1.

32 Joseph Barnes to Albert Vorspan, 14 September 1957, Box 4, East Papers. Barnes, however, later encouraged East to write an autobiography, and he helped ensure its publication.

33 P. D. East, *Petal* (Miss.) *Paper*, 10 October 1956, 1. East also noted that so many requests came in for some of his past editorials that his supply of extra papers had long since been exhausted. The booklet solved this problem nicely.

34 East began to receive some national publicity at this time. Albert Vorspan mentioned East's battles in his article, "The South, Segregation, and the Jew," *Jewish Frontier*, November 1956, 17. East received even more generous treatment from the Fellowship of Reconciliation in Alfred Hassler's "South by East," *Fellowship*, November 1956, 14–15. He was mentioned in *Harper's* and the *Los Angeles Times-Mirror*.

35 P. D. East, "Look Back in Pain," undated text of speech given by East, 7, Box 54, East Papers. Hereafter cited as East, "Look Back in Pain." East, *Magnolia Jungle*, 209–11.

36 *Magnolia Jungle*, 211.

37 The Citizens' Council had gone national by the summer of 1956, trying to gain strength from unity. State chapters formed a national committee, but they encountered difficulties from the beginning. The various state chapters, even in bigotry, resented any type of centralized control. Neil R. McMillen, *The Citizens' Council: Organized Resistance to the Second Reconstruction, 1954–1964* (Urbana: University of Illinois Press, 1971), 116–20.

38 P. D. East, *Petal* (Miss.) *Paper*, 26 August 1956, 1.

39 P. D. East, "Do Negroes Have Rights? Almost Another American Myth," *Petal* (Miss.) *Paper*, 11 October 1956, 1.

40 Ibid.

41 P. D. East, *Petal* (Miss.) *Paper*, 22 November 1956, 2.

42 John Howard Griffin to Maxwell Geismar, 16 November 1959, Box 93, Maxwell Geismar Papers, Mugar Memorial Library, Boston University. Hereafter cited as Geismar Papers.

43 East, *Magnolia Jungle*, 208. When East's second wife, Billie, filed for divorce, she complained that her husband would leave without advising her where he was going or when he would return. Such habits apparently started at this time and grew increasingly abusive by 1961. *Billie Porter East* v. *P. D. East*, Chancery Court of Lamar County, Mississippi, June 1961, 2, Box 45, East Papers.

[44] P. D. East, *Petal* (Miss.) *Paper,* 10 January 1957, 1.

[45] Ibid.

[46] P. D. East, *Petal* (Miss.) *Paper,* 17 January 1957, 1.

[47] This trait in East has been noted before, but it bears repeating. On numerous occasions he failed to mention some very important events regarding the civil rights movement, e.g., Ross Barnett's election in 1960. This habit remained with him throughout the rest of his career. As to why this pattern persisted, one can only speculate. One charge was that, despite his great courage, East was lazy and that the effort required to collect background information and to uncover the facts of each development proved too difficult. East himself suggested that the actions of racists violated human decency so much that his comments seemed useless.

[48] For the best account of the boycott see Martin Luther King, Jr., *Stride Toward Freedom: The Montgomery Story* (New York: Harper and Row, 1958).

[49] Ibid., 39–40.

[50] Ibid., 49.

[51] Dominic J. Capeci, Jr., "From Harlem to Montgomery: The Bus Boycotts and the Leadership of Adam Clayton Powell, Jr., and Martin Luther King, Jr.," *Historian* 41 (August 1979): 730–31. It was estimated that the city bus line lost over $250,000 in fares, the city several thousand in taxes, and downtown merchants several million dollars in business.

[52] Preston Valien, "The Montgomery Bus Protest as a Social Movement," in *Race Relations: Problems and Theory,* ed. Preston Valien and Jitsuich Masuoka (Chapel Hill: University of North Carolina Press, 1961), 123.

[53] Lord, *The Past,* 71.

[54] Carl M. Brauer, *John F. Kennedy and the Second Reconstruction* (New York: Columbia University Press, 1977), 6; C. Vann Woodward, *The Strange Career of Jim Crow* (New York: Oxford University Press, 1966), 169; William H. Chafe, *Civilities and Civil Rights: Greensboro, North Carolina, and the Black Struggle for Freedom* (New York: Oxford University Press, 1980), 113; Howard Zinn, *SNCC: The New Abolitionists* (Boston: Beacon Press, 1964), 18.

[55] P. D. East, "The $ Is Noted: Wise Decisions Have Been Made," *Petal* (Miss.) *Paper,* 3 January 1957, 1.

[56] P. D. East, *Petal* (Miss.) *Paper,* 24 January 1957, 1.

[57] P. D. East to Mr. Yarrow, 30 May 1958, Box 29, East Papers.

[58] Sarah Patton Boyle to P. D. East, 5 May 1957, Box 1, East Papers; Harry Fleischman to James B. Carey, 29 November 1957, Box 2, East Papers. Sarah Patton Boyle tried to convince East of the necessity of accepting gifts of money.

59 It should be noted that when East went to New York City and Atlanta he did not tell his wife why he was making the trip. East, *Magnolia Jungle*, 6.

60 East, *Magnolia Jungle*, 211–13; Edwin J. Lukas to P. D. East, 4 January 1957, Box 3, East Papers. The groups meeting with East were the American Jewish Committee, the NAACP, the AFL-CIO, and the Fellowship of Reconciliation.

61 P. D. East, *Petal* (Miss.) *Paper,* 26 December 1957, 1; East, *Magnolia Jungle*, 212–13; Albert Vorspan, "The Iconoclast of Petal, Mississippi," *The Reporter*, 21 March 1957, 33–35. For another perspective on East's work at this time see "White Mississippi Editor Pokes Fun at Jim Crow," *Jet*, 14 March 1957, 12–15.

62 Regarding the final sales distribution of the editorial booklet, none went to people in Petal, only 30 to people in Hattiesburg, with the remaining 6,970 going throughout the rest of the country. Of further interest, Easton King had a cross burned in his yard for printing the booklet. East, *Magnolia Jungle*, 213.

63 Clarence Jordan, *Petal* (Miss.) *Paper,* 21 February 1957, 1–2.

64 Kenneth K. Bailey, *Southern White Protestantism in the Twentieth Century* (New York: Harper and Row, 1964), 150.

65 P. D. East to Tim Seldes, 3 March 1958, Box 4, East Papers.

66 P. D. East, *Petal* (Miss.) *Paper,* 21 February 1957, 1.

67 P. D. East to Tim Seldes, 3 March 1958, Box 4, East Papers.

68 P. D. East, *Petal* (Miss.) *Paper,* 21 February 1957, 1.

69 P. D. East, interview with *Time Magazine,* New York, New York, February 1957, 6, 8, Box 53, East Papers. Hereafter cited as East, interview with *Time Magazine.*

70 Lawrence to P. D. East, no date, Box 29, East Papers. Although undated, Lawrence's letter was in the folder labeled 1954–1957. This time span fits with East's interview, and the dates on these prove to be quite accurate when compared with the dated letters they contain.

71 East, *Magnolia Jungle*, 224.

72 Ibid.

73 P. D. East, *Petal* (Miss.) *Paper,* 28 March 1957, 1.

74 P. D. East, *Petal* (Miss.) *Paper,* 2 May 1957, 1.

75 Ibid., 7.

76 Ibid.

77 P. D. East, *Petal* (Miss.) *Paper,* 18 April 1957, 1.

78 East, *Magnolia Jungle*, 226.

79 Ibid., 227.

80 Sarah Patton Boyle to P. D. East, 7 April 1957, Box 1, East Papers.

81 Ibid.

82 Sarah Patton Boyle to P. D. East, 5 April 1957, Box 1, East Papers.

83 Despite East's doubts about his ability as a public speaker, the magazine *Vital Speeches* reprinted his talk at Dillard University.

P. D. East, "The South, Collectively, Is a Patient Most Ill: An Obligation That Cannot be Ignored," *Vital Speeches*, 15 May 1957, 476–79. Since Dillard University was an all-black school, several people asked East when he intended to speak to whites. To this he responded, "Their sneers, I am frank to confess, fail to bother me. I'm just sorry for the dumb bastards."

[84] P. D. East, *Petal* (Miss.) *Paper*, 28 March 1957, 1.

[85] P. D. East, *Petal* (Miss.) *Paper*, 18 July 1957, 1.

[86] Ibid.

[87] Ibid.

[88] The bulk of this discussion of Little Rock was taken from the following sources: Numan V. Bartley, *The Rise of Massive Resistance: Race and Politics in the South During the 1950's* (Baton Rouge: Louisiana State University Press, 1969), 251–69; McMillen, *Citizens' Council*, 269–85. Numerous other accounts have been written on this topic. Among the best of these works are, Daisy Bates, *The Long Shadow of Little Rock: A Memoir* (New York: McKay, 1962); Corrine Silverman, *The Little Rock Story* (Tuscaloosa: University of Alabama Press, 1959); Virgil Blossom, *It Has Happened Here* (New York: Harper and Row, 1959); Elizabeth Huckaby, *Crisis at Central High: Little Rock, 1957-1959* (Baton Rouge: Louisiana State University Press, 1980).

[89] McMillen, *Citizens' Council*, 271–72. Of special concern was the fear that black boys would be allowed to dance with white girls or act out love scenes in school plays with whites. Also, the CCC and its allies never failed to mention that the white working class and not the white upper class would be forced to send their children to desegregated schools.

[90] Quoted in McMillen, *Citizens' Council*, 274.

[91] Lord, *The Past*, 73.

[92] P. D. East, *Petal* (Miss.) *Paper*, 10 October 1957, 1.

[93] East apparently did not consider his treatment of the Little Rock situation to be important enough to include in his autobiography.

[94] P. D. East, *Petal* (Miss.) *Paper*, 12 September 1957, 1.

[95] P. D. East, *Petal* (Miss.) *Paper*, 3 October 1957, 1.

[96] P. D. East, *Petal* (Miss.) *Paper*, 17 October 1957, 1.

[97] P. D. East, "Them Furriners—How Much Cotton Do They Buy?" *Petal* (Miss.) *Paper*, 2 January 1958, 1.

[98] Ibid.

[99] P. D. East, "1957: A Year for Questions—And One of the Best Was," *Petal* (Miss.) *Paper*, 2 January 1958, 1.

[100] "East Publications Operating Statement Year 1957," Box 45, East Papers.

[101] East, *Magnolia Jungle*, 240.

[102] East never stated in his autobiography to whom he was referring. Out of the few letters that exist from this period, however, there are several between East and Hodding Carter. The questions and answers East discussed in his book are almost identical with those contained in this correspondence. P. D. East to Hodding Carter, 20 October 1957, Box 1, East Papers; Hodding Carter to P. D. East, 29 October 1957, Box 1, East Papers; Hodding Carter to P. D. East, no date, Box 1, East Papers.

[103] East never mentioned the man's name or the organization, or for that matter, anyone involved in the episode.

[104] The magazine in question was probably *Newsweek*. Although East never mentioned the publication in his autobiography, he did mention contacting *Newsweek* in the *Petal Paper*. P. D. East, *Petal* (Miss.) *Paper*, 26 December 1957, 1.

[105] East, *Magnolia Jungle*, 237.

[106] P. D. East, *Petal* (Miss.) *Paper*, 7 November 1957, 1.

[107] P. D. East, *Petal* (Miss.) *Paper*, 14 November 1957, 1. East never bothered to have the script translated, and he apparently did not keep his copy because it was not in his papers in Boston. P. D. East, *Petal (Miss.) Paper*, 26 December 1957, 1. The Swedish newspaper article was also missing.

[108] Wilma Dykeman and James Stokely, *Neither Black Nor White* (New York: Rinehart and Company, 1957), 205-8.

5

Misfortune Continues

Despite the problems that P. D. East's reputation caused him, he did not retreat into obscurity. He believed that he had to bring his message on racial equality to as many people as possible. In 1959, in line with this policy, he accepted an offer from *Harper's* magazine to write a guest editorial. Ironically, national attention such as this merely exacerbated his economic woes. With his paper on the verge of collapse, various groups outside Mississippi solicited contributions to help pay his mounting debts. This money kept the paper alive, but it did not bring prosperity. His financial and psychological problems continued unabated. In spite of these difficulties and the added burden of a failing marriage, he managed to write his auto-biography. The book won new supporters for him, but it added to his misery as well. At best, fame for P. D. East remained a two-edged sword.

East opened 1958 as if he were determined to court disaster. He plunged into a candid discussion of his religion. Over the years, so many letters had arrived regarding his lack of formal church membership that he felt the matter required a detailed discussion. Realizing the sensitive nature of the subject, he commented that "I know many ways of committing suicide, one of the most effective is a discussion of one's views on religion. This, then, is a suicide note."[1] He began by admitting that he thought about God a great deal. This did not mean, however, that he thought about religion, which, he argued, was often far removed from God.[2] He then denied being a Christian at any time in his life and expressed doubts about ever becoming one, owing to his weak moral character. His nominal Christianity as a youth had been forced on him by his mother. In rejecting the formal church, he said that it reminded him of a country club without the golf course and bar. Although some people needed such an institution, he never felt that he did. He regarded the idea of life after death as a product of man's immature, egotistical nature. Immortality existed, but through one's children or work, not through the soul. He denied the divinity of Christ, calling him a great and good man, nothing more. God, he believed, was evident in all individuals, with none being more important than any other. God was a part of everything. East closed by stating,

> I think each of us had to take those parts of religion which we need as individuals and mold our own religion from the whole. It would, I feel, be foolish to try to justify any single concept of religion. What I call my religion can be stated in one word, FAIRNESS. If you wish to consider me an idiot, please feel free to do so.[3]

Reaction to East's religious views were mixed, running from complete agreement to total disagreement, but surprisingly no one sent an angry or nasty letter. Critics stated their differences of opinion with grace and genuine concern. One of the more perceptive and amusing notes came from Jim Silver:

> Your last "editorial" proves beyond a shadow of a doubt that you are nothing more than a God damned atheist. Why the hell you don't leave God out of all this and get down to real brass tacks I don't know. Anyway, you have more guts than brains and that is certainly priceless these days, especially in the Magnolia state.[4]

The Reverend Will Campbell also questioned East's intelligence, good naturedly. While driving through the state with East, Campbell informed him of his theological stupidity, especially concerning the gospel of Jesus. East, quick to respond, agreed to his dull-wittedness, and then asked Campbell, since he seemed to think he was so smart, to give him a simple definition of the gospel and the Christian faith in ten words. Campbell, in a flash of brilliance, replied, "We're all bastards but God loves us anyway."[5] Upon hearing this, East swung the car off the road and asked his passenger to repeat what he said.

East then sat in silence, counted the number of words on his fingers, and then informed his friend he had two words left if he wished to try again. Writing later about the incident, he commented, "Before I sign up again with the Methodists, I think I'll wait and see if that little Baptist brother survives. If he does, I might join with him."[6]

East's editorial generated numerous exchanges with his readers for months. His disbelief aside, religion and religious people remained important to him throughout his life. He had great respect for those who appeared totally committed to their faith and to justice for all. His best friend, John Howard Griffin, noted that many of the people East considered his closest allies came from the ranks of the deeply religious, e.g., Griffin, Thomas Merton, Jacques Maritain, Clarence Jordan, and Will Campbell. Griffin also remarked that East rarely developed intimate ties with those who failed to meet his standards.[7]

Although he kept his theological discussion serious, he turned his humor loose on other topics. When several readers asked why Mississippi had apparently fallen behind Arkansas as the most bigoted state, East admitted that his state had slipped in the race for "Total assdom." He expressed the firm belief that Mississippi would regain the lead as soon as the state legislature reconvened. To support his position he asked: "Is it not true that the Lord and the U.S. Constitution giveth . . . and the State Legislature taketh away?"[8] In a swipe at the CCA, he noted that in the last four years the mule population showed a marked decline. As for what happened to the animals, he quoted a fictitious expert as saying, "This figure representing the total loss of mules is close to the figure given by the citizens' councils as being their total membership. Citizens' council members denied flatly that they are the lost jackasses."[9] Several weeks later he announced a new breakthrough in winter apparel for members of the KKK: electric sheets "for unfinished missions on these cold nights."[10]

East also wrote to Roy Wilkins concerning snow in Mississippi. Since snowfall in Hattiesburg was rare, he told Wilkins that such an event carried special meaning. For him the significance was in the snow's color—white. "Now hear me! The snow was WHITE! And if God didn't have something very special in mind, He'd have made the WHITE snow some other color. When WHITE snow falls from God's heaven, need more be said?"[11] Wilkins responded in kind, "I guess that will 'learn' me that the Lord meant white to be white and black to be black, and that if He had wanted the two to mix, He would have sent gray snow to Mississippi."[12]

In March 1958, one of East's friends, Aubrey Williams, tried to convince him to use his wit in a genuine money-making enterprise. Williams wrote to Drew Pearson regarding East, whom he compared to Will Rogers. Pearson, in turn, forwarded Williams's letter along with his own recommendation to Bell Syndicate Newspaper Features, the national distributor of his column, suggesting East as a possible client. The president of the Bell Syndicate, John Wheeler, asked East if he wanted to write a daily humorous piece for national distribution. The column would be relatively short, no more than 300 words. If East agreed, he and Bell would split the syndicate fee equally.[13] Mildly intrigued by the possibility, East wrote to Joe Barnes, senior editor at Simon and Schuster and the person working with him on his autobiography. Barnes was enthusiastic about the opportunity. He told East to send Wheeler edited versions of several of his more humorous stories already published in the *Petal Paper*. Wheeler had never read the paper and thus East could make the effort with a minimum of work.[14]

The more East thought about this undertaking the less he relished the idea. What little enthusiasm he had mustered originally he soon lost. Although he expressed his thanks to Williams, Pearson, and Wheeler, and told them he would do as they asked, he never followed through on his promise. Finally, he wrote to Wheeler and stated that work on his autobiography prevented him from accepting the offer.[15] That was not the actual reason, however. As he put it, "Stated simply, I just wasn't interested!"[16] Here he had the opportunity to increase his income, and he walked away with no detailed explanation. Prior to the proposal from Wheeler, he had sunk into one of his periods of depression; once he rejected the column, he was consumed with guilt. To escape, he began sleeping for long periods of time. Work on his book practically stopped. He wrote very little copy for the paper, and the material he produced was poor.[17]

By May 1958, East had not shaken his deep depression, but the daily movement of Mississippi toward a genuine police state offended him so much that he regained some of his old enthusiasm for the fight against bigotry. The Citizens' Council in Mississippi attempted successfully to abridge academic freedom when it led to criticism of segregation. The CCA kept files on the social views of every college educator in the state. When suspected of wrong thinking, the Council placed spies in offenders' classrooms hoping to obtain proof that these people were brainwashing students into accepting desegregation.[18] On state-supported campuses, the Council screened every out-of-state speaker and, although lacking official power, it had virtual control over who gained final approval. Since the CCA possessed less authority over private schools, it turned to desperate acts.

In the spring of 1958, Millsaps College, a small Methodist school in Jackson, announced an upcoming forum on Christianity and race relations. As part of the program, the college invited an integrationist to speak to the students. In an angrily worded letter to the administration at Millsaps, the president of the Jackson CCA affiliate, Ellis Wright, stated his strong opposition to the appearance of anyone challenging the validity of segregation. The South, he declared, found itself in a life and death struggle to preserve its way of life, and in such a battle compromise, however meager, could not be tolerated. Millsaps, he warned, must take a firm position either for or against segregation. Wright ignored the fact that the college practiced segregation and had no intentions of changing. For him the matter was closed to discussion without exception.

Ellis Finger, president of Millsaps, and the school's trustees refused to be intimidated by the Council. Echoing East's beliefs, Finger responded that denial of one school's freedom opened all others to similar intrusions. He closed his letter pledging Millsaps's intention to preserve "a climate where freedom may prosper and where intimidation, fear and bondage are doomed. The only alternative is dreaded thought control."[19] The trustees provided additional support for academic freedom when they stated, "The purpose of a college is not to tell people what to think but teach them how to think."[20] Undeterred, the Council charged the school's administration with obscuring the issue with a "'thick smokescreen of academic freedom.'"[21]

Resorting to his powerful sense of ridicule, East called those associated with the college "the Methodist misfits of Millsaps." As to their defense of academic freedom, he labeled it flimsy.[22] He then likened Jackson Citizens' Council president and prominent undertaker, Ellis Wright, to God. "Now everyone who knows anything knows that God is a Jackson planter (undertaker). He'll plant anyone, for a fee, except Negroes. Everyone knows that God is a solid citizen." He went on to declare that "academic freedom should exist, provided no one is so foolish as to try to exercise it."[23] In his last comment on the issue East noted, "For one, I'm mighty glad we have free speech here behind the cornpone curtain, but I sometimes feel the supply exceeds the demands."[24] Undoubtedly to East's delight, the people at Millsaps College persisted in their demands for freedom of speech on campus. The race relations seminar went on as scheduled with the prointegrationist speaker on the program, although at the last minute, the Council managed to have its voice heard when one of its members addressed the meeting.[25]

With the episode closed, East continued his offensive against CCA intrusion into education. The Citizens' Council, along with the American Legion, the Daughters of the American Revolution, and the United Daughters of the Confederacy, initiated a racial indoctrination program aimed at high-school students. Sara McCorkle, head of the Council's youth league, led the effort to censor textbooks, library materials, and educational films that might prompt youths to oppose segregation. Shunning the role of passive leadership, McCorkle spoke to nearly every high school in the state about the need for racial purity. To encourage student participation, she organized a Mississippi essay contest centered on the theme of racial integrity. For source materials, participants had to use books the CCA provided to each high school by such authors as Judge Tom Brady, Herman Talmadge, and the late Theodore Bilbo. The winning essay reflected the lessons learned well: "We in the South do not intend to obey men, however exalted their seats or black their robes and hearts. As long as we live, so long shall we be segregated."[26] The Council's efforts at thought control reached down to the third and fourth grades with the publication of its "Manual for Southerners." Under headings such as "God Put Each Race By Itself," "White Men Built America," "Race Mixers Help Communists," "Mixing Races Will Make America Weak," and "Segregation is Christian," the Citizens' Council presented its views to the very young.[27]

Repulsed by such activities, East lamented that while the United States was based on some very noble precepts, such as democracy and equality, "a few idiots with closed minds" seemed bent on destroying the very foundations of American life.

> Abe Lincoln said something about the failure of this government; in effect, it was that if this nation fails it will not be from without, but from within. One luxury a free

people cannot afford is a closed mind. But Mississippi is not only breeding them, we're educating them. We confess that the realization of such abounding stupidity sends us to our knees. In such moments of hopelessness we find no other place to go.[28]

East also reprinted sections of the "Manual for Southerners" in his paper on several occasions to give his readers an idea of the type of propaganda disseminated to white southerners.

Another tactic employed by the Council, even more threatening to freedom of thought, came from the Jackson, Mississippi, chapter's decision to conduct a door-to-door survey on the racial views of every white resident of the capital city. As United States Representative Frank E. Smith of Greenville, Mississippi, charged, "It was a skillful plan to search out anyone who deviated in the slightest and to bludgeon into silence those who had any differing ideas."[29] Those conducting this "Freedom of Choice" survey wanted to know how many people opposed integration and would support and possibly join the CCA to maintain segregration. To no one's surprise, the Citizens' Council announced that 98 percent of the white people in Jackson backed school segregation and pledged to aid the Council in any crisis. The canvas had a chilling effect upon anyone contemplating dissent from CCA doctrine. As one observer commented, the Council had "created a climate of fear that has strait-jacketed the white community in a thought control enforced by economic sanctions."[30] Another Mississippian wrote to the now defunct *Jackson State Times,*

If a group of serious-minded individuals, armed with pencils and a known philosophy of "you're either with us or against us," comes around to your door, demands to know your personal views and applies the pressure, only a Mongolian idiot would fail to give the right answers and pay the $5.00.[31]

Although not a Mongolian idiot, East could not resist such a challenge. He made his position clear, as if he needed to, by publishing an exchange between the president of the Jackson Council and a very brave Methodist minister. Ellis Wright, or God as East called him, sent a letter to all city residents alerting them to the NAACP's attempts to integrate southern society. He then proceeded to explain the reason for the house-to-house canvas and noted the prominent role played by Ross Barnett. Outraged by this plan, the Reverend John E. Sutphin fired back a controlled but indignant response to Wright. He explained that since no one had as yet interviewed him, he wanted to inform the Council of his opinions. Giving his unqualified support to integration, Sutphin said he especially favored what he called kneeling integration. "I will welcome any opportunity to kneel in prayer with anyone to seek a solution to our current dilemma."[32] He closed by expressing amazement over Wright's practice of not allowing blacks to lie in state at his funeral home. He claimed he could not comprehend such a position since Wright's attitude suggested that he would like "to bury a lot of colored folk."[33] East commented, "And me? Hell, I'm on the preacher's side!"[34]

Although East lavished few such compliments upon his fellow Mississippians, he managed very positive comments about his supporters outside the South. In June 1958, he mentioned Steve Allen for the first time. Allen had subscribed to the paper the previous month, and now East urged his readers to give up Ed Sullivan's show for Allen's.[35] As advocates of social justice, East and Allen developed a fairly close friendship, which lasted until East's death. Later that summer, East discussed another of his friends, Irving J. Fain. The two men had met sometime in 1957 during one of East's trips to New York City.[36] Fain was a millionaire business executive, civil rights activist, and philanthropist. In East, he saw a man fighting for similar goals, and a man who needed economic assistance. With considerable financial reserves at his disposal, Fain added the *Petal Paper* to his already long list of aid recipients. In 1958 alone, East received $1,050 from Fain, and the gifts continued to arrive until Fain's death in 1970.[37] East appreciated the friendship and help so much that he dedicated his autobiography to Fain, along with Easton King and his old friend and teacher, W. W. Stout of Mississippi Southern College in Hattiesburg.

East's Northern friends also tried to help him in other ways. One such intimate revealed that Professor Allen K. Chalmers, of the Boston University school of theology, sought a person to contact ministers throughout Mississippi and enlist their aid in support of desegregation. In his first letter to East, Chalmers noted the racist position taken by the vast majority of Protestant leaders in Mississippi. According to Chalmers, only East's friends, Rabbi Charles Mantinband of Hattiesburg and Bishop Brunin in Jackson, appeared openly sympathetic.[38]

This analysis described accurately the condition of religion in Mississippi. National church leaders supported the Supreme Court's decision on desegregation but many congregations in the South, especially in Mississippi, ignored the official stance of their denominational authorities. As one prominent southern historian remarked, "Many southern congregations harbored some of the bitterest prejudices and hatred. The church in the South . . . failed to meet the challenge of the age."[39] To be sure, some ministers opposed bigotry and such efforts no doubt had a sobering effect on the extremists, but such men were exceptions—and often unemployed.[40] Under these circumstances, many potentially supportive ministers kept quiet on the subject of race.

Chalmers wanted to let racial moderates know that they had allies, and he hoped that such support would encourage them to speak out. He regarded their efforts in behalf of desegregation, as absolutely essential. Being realistic, he warned East that the job would be difficult, frustrating, and worst of all a project that would provide few immediate and measurable results.[41] On 30 September 1958, Chalmers, eager to begin, sent East a check for $100 to begin making contacts. Several weeks after receiving this commission, East flew to Boston after a speaking engagement at Wake Forest University. There he and Chalmers mapped out East's travels for the next several months.[42]

East's first reports to Chalmers revealed the uneven rewards of the job and possibly some of the editor's marital problems as well. For his first stop, he chose Millsaps College in Jackson. The faculty and administration gave him a warm welcome along with a promise to help in whatever way they could. He next visited Tougaloo College where he received a similar reception. East turned down an offer by one faculty member to hold meetings at the university because he felt that the contacts should be made before adopting a program of action. While in Jackson, he also met with Medgar Evers. Evers praised East's work and asked him to speak to the local NAACP chapter the following spring. Even though these contacts were all favorable, East made no approaches outside the university community and civil rights groups.[43] His late November trip proved less rewarding. Traveling for an entire week to different cities, he discovered only four ministers he considered moderates and two of those favored segregation. In writing to Chalmers concerning this adventure, he closed dejectedly by stating, "It was depressing and I feel dreadful because of my failure."[44] On a personal basis, East's November trip revealed the existence of serious marital problems. Supposedly devoted to his wife and child, he failed to return home for Thanksgiving, although he was only fifty miles from home. He even remarked in his letter to Chalmers that the day was a poor one on which to make calls, but he made no effort to return to Hattiesburg.[45] He did remain at home for Christmas, however.

While searching for moderate ministers, East continued to seek additional sources of income. He spent a considerable amount of time giving speeches to raise extra money. As usual, he belittled his speaking ability. After one talk to a Unitarian group, he reported that the following Sunday they all joined the local Baptist church.[46] Someone must have disagreed with East's assessment because he secured numerous engagements. Thereafter, in the fall of 1958, he lectured at Tuskegee Institute, Wake Forest University, and for the third time, Dillard University. In late November, he received valuable national exposure on radio. Station WIP in Philadelphia broadcast and syndicated a show produced by the Pacific Foundation called "Search for Peace." When host Marvin Reubin questioned him on his concept of peace, East based his response on the Ten Commandments and the Golden Rule. This was a position East believed in firmly and one that attracted numerous supporters.[47] Further publicity came his way when James McBride Dabbs, former head of the Southern Regional Council, author, and prominent southern liberal, told host Mike Wallace on an ABC television program that East was one of a select group that could save the South from racism.[48]

At times, though, the efforts of East and his friends represented nothing more than an economic holding action. He no longer had any local subscribers to the paper. In fact, he received so many abusive telephone calls that he secured an unlisted number. He observed wryly that he owned the only newspaper in the country with an unlisted number.[49] His financial statement for 1958 reflected his lack of local popularity as he lost nearly $3,000 and had to borrow $4,000 to keep from going bankrupt.[50]

At times, he could not even count on his friends for their full support. When Wilma Dykeman and James Stokely's book *Neither Black Nor White* appeared, East had Professor W. W. Stout write a review. Stout produced a mean-spirited critique which rarely if ever touched upon the book's main theme and showed Stout's increasing disenchantment with East's position on race. The professor had put East in a difficult situation. Dykeman and Stokely rightfully protested the feeble effort as did a more recent acquaintance, literary critic Maxwell Geismar. He called the review "coarse, vulgar, and stupid,"[51] and questioned East's commitment to civil rights. For East to criticize Stout's work would have been a direct affront to an old friend, but to ignore the objections raised by his newest friends would have been equally insulting. To extricate himself from the dilemma, East asked Geismar to write a review under the guise of seeking a northern opinion of the book.[52] All parties seemed satisfied with the solution, and the friendship between East and Geismar grew stronger. A potentially disastrous confrontation had been avoided.

East's prospects seemed to brighten somewhat when John Fischer of *Harper's* magazine gave him an opportunity to write a guest editorial for the January 1959 issue. In alerting his readers to the good news, East related that in December 1956, when Fischer had voiced his support for the *Petal Paper*, *Harper's* received four cancellations from irate readers. Now with a 2,500-word piece by the *Petal Paper's* editor, East speculated that the January issue might be the last in *Harper's* illustrious history.[53] The article, entitled "How to Be a Man of Distinction," gave the paper a much-needed boost. By early February 1959, over 200 letters arrived. The writers commended him for his fight against bigotry and occasionally requested a subscription.[54] In East's opinion, the most important consequence of the guest column was the friendship and support he received from Senator Paul Douglas.[55]

Although the *Harper's* article seemed to get the new year off to a good start, within a week deep depression returned. This time East's emotional turmoil had nothing to do with the paper or his stand on racial equality. His father, James East, had suffered a severe heart attack. Although East had never felt any deep love for his mother, Bertie East, he had strong ties of affection with his father. East regarded his adoptive father as a kind and decent man. Writing to his good friend Maxwell Geismar, he told of the agony he endured while visiting his gravely ill father:

> Max, you'll never know what an experience that was. I stood by his bed and watched him in such severe pain, and

> I was unable to do a damned thing to help him. God! I
> recalled the hardness of his life and the goodness of his
> nature, and I wondered about the values of so many things.
> I guess I'll never grow up. Some things I just can't accept.[56]

On 18 January 1959, after lingering for quite some time, James
East died. The strain on P. D. was so great that his ulcer
hemorrhaged and he could not attend the funeral.[57]

The despair he felt became quite apparent in his work. For
over a month he failed to make any trips to locate moderate
ministers for Professor Chalmers; and his writing, when he did
not run reprints of past editions, grew very acerbic. The humor
remained, but it was mean-spirited. In one column, he devoted
considerable space to various ways a person could commit
suicide, and using graphic detail, he explained the virtues and
drawbacks of each method. He closed by stating, "If you prefer
to commit suicide and suffer, you know, prolong the agony and
really suffer like hell, you may want to be a liberal in Mississippi."[58] Even his comments on the men running for the
governor's seat in Mississippi lacked their usual sense of the
absurd and instead carried a bitter flavor. He suggested that
each candidate submit to brain surgery to determine if he had a
brain. If one were found, the individual would be forced to
withdraw from the race because "Anyone with an ounce of
brain would be out of character in the race which is always
filled with idiots and grade A morons."[59] Rather than a brain,
he believed those running for office needed an extra set of vocal
cords because "It's going to be the damndest 'Nigger!' shouting
contest the state has ever had."[60] He grew so angry and depressed
that he turned down an offer from the *Nation* to write a report
on the racial situation in Mississippi. He sat down at the
typewriter and tried to relate his experiences, but the words
refused to come.

East's despair faded somewhat by late January. At that
time he met John Howard Griffin through their mutual friend,
Maxwell Geismar. The two men took an instant liking to one
another, and over the next thirteen years, East grew closer to
Griffin than to any of his other friends. The depth of their
relationship made Griffin an invaluable ally.

East's spirits rose further when some of his financial
burdens lifted. Thanks to the efforts of Geismar, Alfred Hassler
of the Fellowship of Reconciliation (FOR), and several other
FOR members, a group calling itself "The Friends of P. D.

East," organized to solicit money to keep the *Petal Paper* alive. Hassler, unsure of East's willingness to accept such assistance, told him that some of the most important liberal publications, like the *Nation* and the *Progressive,* required special subsidies to maintain their operations.[61] East, in view of his precarious financial circumstances, agreed with Hassler's proposal.[62]

Only one obstacle remained. Lillian Smith, one of the group's early sponsors, expressed reservations about the project. She feared that if southerners discovered East's northern base of support, he might lose what effectiveness he had in the South. Despite her doubts, she pledged to lend help if East wished to go through with the plan. He immediately brushed aside her theory. In a letter to Geismar, he wrote, "Well, hell, daddyo, no one could do more to me than I've already done to myself. Let's be fairly honest about this thing . . . I'll take anyone's money."[63] With their question settled, "The Friends of P. D. East" went into action and brought together a very impressive array of supporters including such notables as Eleanor Roosevelt, Harry Golden, Carl Rowan, Dr. Martin Luther King, Jr., Steve Allen, Van Wyck Brooks, and Harry Belafonte. To get the effort started immediately, Steve Allen contributed $350.[64] Within two months East received approximately $1,000, and by the end of the year nearly $5,000.[65] This money certainly eased East's burden, but his economic condition had deteriorated so much that he had to raise his subscription rate from $3.00 to $5.00 per year.

More financial help came East's way and, with it, increased national recognition of his efforts in behalf of racial equality. Local Six of the Hotel and Club Employees' Union in New York City gave him its sixth annual Better Race Relations Award and a $500 check. The 27,000-member union bestowed this honor on the person they believed had done the most in 1958 to further the civil rights of all people. East no doubt came to the union's attention through his friends in New York. Harry Fleischman, director of the National Labor Service and a long-time supporter, pleaded his cause, as did Roy Wilkins of the NAACP. Wilkins, a member of the union's civil rights award nominating board, voiced his pleasure at Local Six's choice when he spoke to the convention audience:

> Your Union deserves to be congratulated on selecting for honor and presentation of the Better Race Relations Award a man who rightly deserves such honors. You are all

probably aware of the Biblical question: "Can any good
come out of Nazareth?" Well, Jesus came out of Nazareth
and your guest of honor today came out of a place where
few people expect any good to come from. For this he
deserves double congratulations.[66]

When East rose to accept the award and give his acceptance
speech, he received a standing ovation from the audience. He
received another when he concluded his remarks.[67] The award
boosted his sometime sagging spirits, and provided additional
and much needed cash.[68]

East's good fortune continued. On 27 April 1959, owing to
the efforts of several of his readers in California, Paul Coates, a
Los Angeles newspaper columnist and television personality,
interviewed East on his KTTV television program and devoted
one of his columns in the *Los Angeles Times* to the *Petal
Paper*. Coates asked both his readers and viewers to lend whatever support they could to P. D. East and his cause. "Normally,
I don't go around hawking newpapers. Especially other people's
newpapers. But today, I make an exception. It'll cost you five
bucks a year, which seems a small price to pay for somebody
else's courage."[69] In addition to the television appearance, East
had one other exciting and important meeting. Two of his
friends, Earl and Mary Myers, took him to meet Upton Sinclair
and his wife. East remained friends with Sinclair until the
novelist's death in 1968.[70]

The response to Coates's plea was overwhelming. Within a
month, East received 613 letters and $2,207.[71] The mail came
from a cross section of society. Many correspondents told him
that they could not afford the $5.00 price of a subscription, but
would send one or two dollars to help. No matter how little
these people contributed, East still gave them a year of the
paper. Commenting on the decency of those responding to his
television interview, he remarked that he made every possible
effort to avoid being a sentimental slob, to avoid being touched
or moved by anything:

> I admit frankly that many of the letters received penetrated
> my thick, crusty hide; many of them moved me to mutter
> "Thank you for such wonderful people." Such warm and
> wonderful letters almost bring tears to my eyes. It's impos-
> sible to express the gratitude I feel and owe to Paul Coates
> and his friends who wrote me.[72]

On 3 June 1959, the Coates show was broadcast in New York City, and by late June, East had received another $600.[73]

East informed Paul Coates that practically no one had sent an unpleasant letter.[74] Only five negative responses appeared out of over six hundred. One anonymous writer charged that East and Coates were part Negro.[75] One woman even went to the trouble of putting her nasty comments in a poem:

> You do not guess or think
> How greatly your expressions stink
> In your devilish eyes you show
> How your degraded feelings go
> You are the kind who'd delight any morn
> To hear a half and half had been born.[76]

Accustomed to the intolerant attitudes of Mississippians, East expressed surprise that he had not received more negative opinions.

East's joy was short-lived because by late June many irate letters started to arrive, but not from those who opposed his ideas on race This time the indignant mail came from his original California supporters. Their hostility stemmed from East's ignoring their paid requests for subscriptions to the *Petal Paper*. Paul Coates had so many complaints concerning East's failure to respond that he himself grew impatient. One letter informed Coates that the writer would never again allow her "sympathies to be aroused by an appeal of this kind, no matter how well founded and sincere it may seem."[77] The woman also threatened to publicize the matter if she did not have her money returned or her subscription started. Coates sent the letter to his top assistant, Irwin Moskowicz, with the notation "I am continually getting mail like this—even at home. What the hell is the matter with East?"[78] Informed of the seriousness of the problem, East apologized in his paper for the inordinate delay. In explaining his actions, he said that he was not prepared for the overwhelming response and that, with no one to help him, the work of adding new subscribers took a long time.[79]

East failed to give his readers the full story behind his inaction. He was a very private person and did not like to air his most serious personal problems in public. In early March an old kidney ailment returned, causing his testicles to swell to twice their normal size. His doctor ordered him to bed for two weeks with a gradual return to normal activity.[80] East refused to remain inactive and the problem persisted. Before he had left for California to appear on the Paul Coates show, Geismar had told him to see a good doctor in Los Angeles; the Friends of P. D. East would pay the bill. "Please oblige, seriously, before your goddamned testicles drop off," Geismar had urged.[81] But East had disregarded Geismar's advice. After completing the California trip, the editor thus once again found himself flat on his back for several weeks.

Fear also interfered with East's working schedule. On 26 April 1959, the day he left for the Coates interview, Mack Parker, a black arrested for raping a white woman in Poplarville, Mississippi, was dragged from his jail cell by a howling mob and lynched. With Poplarville only thirty miles from Hattiesburg and racist violence spreading, Billie East, afraid for her daughter and herself, fled from their home and spent the night with a friend.[82] When East returned from California, his family felt secure enough to move back into their home, but East refrained from commenting on the case for nearly a month. Only the blatant abuse of justice by the grand jury investigating the murder prompted East to speak out. The Federal Bureau of Investigation had compiled a massive amount of evidence on the case, including the names of those involved. The grand jury, however, refused to look at the material because it considered the FBI's actions to be outside interference. As a result, the murderers went free once again, proving that in Mississippi whites would not be punished for killing blacks.[83] An anxious East contended that

> The act committed against Mack Parker represents a very real threat to the safety and security of every individual citizen of the nation. Who can feel safe and secure in his own house, no matter where he lives so long as a man can be taken from the law and murdered?[84]

Lamenting the deplorable situation and how it saddened him, East wrote to Maxwell Geismar, "I knock my ass off preaching to these red neck bastards and we have a thing like Mack Parker. It is a bit depressing at times, I'd say."[85]

Of all the problems that East faced in the spring and summer of 1959, the most aggravating and time consuming was his court appearance for child neglect. Since his 1952 divorce from his first wife, Katherine, he had been paying $50 per month in child support for his son, Byron. In 1958, his financial condition had deteriorated so much that he failed to make the payments. He could barely feed his own family, and with Katherine remarried, he reasoned that Billie and Karen's needs exceeded hers.[86] In late spring 1959, his ex-wife took him to court for child neglect. Upon receiving the subpoena, he wrote to Geismar complaining, "My ex-wife is hauling me into court for non-support of child. That god damned baptist bitch! I don't especially care for her, you know."[87] With East sick much of the spring, the judge postponed the hearing until mid-July. To help relieve some of the legal pressure, East wrote Joseph Barnes at Simon and Schuster requesting him to pay Byron 50 percent of all the royalties up to $5,000 after the publication of his autobiography.[88] Once in court, the judge ordered him to resume his child support payments. At the conclusion of the hearing, East lost his temper when speaking to his ex-wife's lawyer. He called the man several obscene names and then added, "If you god damned Baptist bastards will leave me alone, I'll agree."[89] Later he confessed that he would be back in court soon because he could not pay the $50 per month. Deeply depressed over these circumstances, he still mustered some humor when he told Maxwell Geismar,

> I'm so god damned depressed and upset right now . . .
> Max, I may take a sock, if I can find one without a hole,
> and go out on the front porch and shit in it, then whenever
> anyone, just any goddamned one, passes, I'll fling a sock
> full of shit at them.[90]

With the help of the Friends of P. D. East, he managed to make the payments.

Even when he finally put all of the California and New York people on his subscription list, his troubles did not end. A number of them disliked his views on religion intensely. Criticism became so great that he again commented on the subject. He asked his readers to tolerate his views just as he tolerated theirs. He reemphasized his belief in God, and to make clear his exact convictions, he reprinted the 1958 column in which he expressed his religious beliefs.[91] Instead of helping, the piece served to infuriate many of his new readers, who cancelled their subscriptions. East seemed unable to avoid trouble in any section of the country.

He tried to fight the despondency that such episodes brought on by concentrating on positive stories. He devoted one issue of the paper to Steve Allen and how their relationship had developed.[92] Another edition featured Harry Golden.[93] Such efforts failed to boost his morale, and renewed despair surfaced in his writing once again. In one piece he suggested raising black children as a cheap source of food for whites.[94] At other times, his spirits sank so low that he could not even produce bitter satire. On these occasions, he ran articles from back issues, calling them "Notes from the Past."

The gubernatorial election depressed him even more. The contest proved to be the "nigger shouting" affair he had predicted earlier. Four candidates had entered the field and the eventual winner, Ross Barnett, was the most virulent racist of the group. Barnett had joined the White Citizens' Council very early and had been an active member. He told one campaign rally, "I am proud that I have been a Citizens' Council member since the Council's early days. I hope that every white Mississippian will join with me in becoming a member of this fine organization. They are fighting your fight."[95] To show his solidarity with segregationists everywhere, he went to Knoxville, Tennessee, to act as counsel for six men who had dynamited a school in Clinton, Tennessee, to prevent desegregation. Barnett claimed that his many years as a Sunday School teacher impressed upon him the belief that God was the original segregator. Although many politicians used the segregation issue to ensure victory, Barnett embraced white supremacy as the truth. He was a true believer.[96] One of his campaign songs said in part, "He's for segregation 100 percent. He's not a mod'rate like some other gent."[97] Such convictions earned him the enthusiastic backing of the Citizens' Councils of America, and this support was not given lightly. It had regarded the previous governor, J. P. Coleman, as disloyal because he failed to back Orval Faubus, called interposition legal poppycock, and did not attend a key CCA convention meeting.[98] After this so-called debacle, the Council vowed to support only fully trustworthy individuals, and Barnett qualified easily.

East feared that Barnett's election would set race relations back "a few years beyond the Dark Ages."[99] With Barnett as governor, East speculated that the men who killed Mack Parker would never be caught, and, even if they were, the governor would award them the "Magnolia Medal with a Pine Tree cluster."[100] East's fears were well founded. Once in office, Barnett continued his close alliance with the CCA. For the first time the Council had a man in office who granted their every wish. Senator James O. Eastland and Representative John Bell Williams had made government recording studios available which enabled the CCA to make a weekly fifteen-minute telecast devoted to racist propaganda, but such aid seemed stingy when compared to the largesse of Barnett. By 1964, the state of Mississippi, through the State Sovereignty Commission, had donated $193,000 to the CCA.[101] All matters of race were turned over to the Council leadership rather than to state government officials. As James W. Silver remarked, the new governor created "what amounted to an office of prime minister for racial integrity and conferred it upon Bill Simmons,"[102] administrator and chief spokesman for the CCA.

Equally disturbing to East, but not unexpected, was the harsh treatment meted out to a young black, Clyde Kennard, who tried to enter all-white Mississippi Southern College in Hattiesburg. Kennard was turned down for admittance by the college's president because of unspecified irregularities and questionable moral character. This judgment came despite an excellent record in the army and three successful years at the University of Chicago. When Kennard tried to leave the campus, the police arrested him for speeding and having liquor in his car.[103] Practically everyone present said that the alcohol had been planted. East visited the campus the next day, and faculty and students alike assured him that Kennard had been framed.[104] The Mississippi Supreme Court eventually agreed with this conclusion, but by that time Kennard had been framed for stealing chicken feed from his mother's farm. Actually, the farm's hired hand did the stealing, but the prosecution argued that Kennard had told him to commit the crime. For this theft, which totaled $10.71, Kennard received three years in prison. While there, he developed cancer and, because of the negligent attitude of the officials, his surgery came too late. He died before finishing his sentence.[105]

East's mental state got little help from John Fischer and *Harper's*. He had submitted a short section of his autobiography for possible publication in the magazine. The appearance of this piece, he hoped, would boost the sales of his forthcoming book. Fischer rejected the material:

> The difficulty, I think, is that we have done all that we feel we should—for the present—on race relations and related topics—and we think we ought to call a halt for a little while. I think we ought to wait for something else from you.[106]

The rejection threw East into a terrible fit of depression. He wrote Maxwell Geismar that he had lost all confidence in the merits of his book. Acknowledging the positive comments made by Geismar and Van Wyck Brooks, he still could not endure rejection from his friends. He had enough of that from his all too numerous enemies. In total despair, he wrote, "That bastard, Fischer! He was the only hope I had."[107]

With the quality of his writing suffering and with his increased use of old articles, East's readers began to comment that the *Petal Paper* had lost much of its spark. Some charged that East was either lazy or unconcerned or possibly both. Defending himself, East declared that, far from being unconcerned, he was too concerned:

> I find it more and more difficult to be a happy, light-hearted, crusading soul when every time I pick up the newspaper or listen to a newscast I learn of something new in the field of bigotry and assdom. It is most depressing to me after six years of flinging my head against the wall of stupidity, I look around to see what has been accomplished and what I see is Senator Eastland and Governor-elect Barnett. I sort of ask myself one question over and over again—what the hell's the use? I don't know what the use is.[108]

He then apologized for the paper's poor quality, but he cautioned that he could not guarantee any immediate improvement under the circumstances. Several weeks later, on the completion of his sixth year of publication, he noted with equal chagrin, "What a helluva way to spend six years!"[109]

The only break in this gloomy atmosphere came when John Howard Griffin spent a few days during mid-November in the Easts' home while traveling through the South as a black. Griffin felt particularly threatened in Hattiesburg, so he asked the Easts if he could stay with them. Billie East agreed to his visit as long as he refrained from investigating the racial situation in the immediate area. She feared that further reprisals might come their way if Griffin used their home as a base of operations. Griffin promised to abide by Billie's wishes. East drove into the black quarters and picked up his friend. The evening darkness allowed the two to enter the East home without the neighbors' knowledge. What struck Griffin more than anything else about the Easts was their isolation from the white community. Only two families invited them into their homes, the local rabbi, Charles Mantinband, and Milton Fine, another member of the local synagogue. East spent his time working on his book and his newspaper; his wife, as Griffin related, spent "much of her time fishing in a nearby tank in the afternoon—a lonely existence."[110] Griffin's visit was a pleasant diversion for all, but after two days of almost non-stop conversation, Griffin asked East to drive him to New Orleans so that he could resume his black odyssey.

With Griffin's departure, East concentrated once again on completing his book and lampooning the racial excesses of his fellow Mississippians. In late November a splendid opportunity for criticism presented itself when the CCA's newspaper, the *Citizens' Council*, printed a list of seventy-four organizations that it considered enemies of the Council and the South. As expected, the American Civil Liberties Union, the NAACP, the Anti-Defamation League, and the Southern Regional Council appeared on the roster, but some rather unlikely candidates found the Council's wrath heaped on them. Prominent in this category were groups such as the Benevolent and Protective Order of the Elks, the YWCA, the leadership of the Methodist Church, the Episcopal Church, and various United States government agencies—including the Air Force and the Labor and Treasury departments. A note at the end of the list encouraged everyone to file it away for future reference.[111] When he reprinted this article, East observed, "It is good to note God and the Baptist church aren't against the WCCs."[112] The following week, he published a letter from a friend to William Simmons of the CCA demanding that the United Church of Christ appear on the enemies list. The Reverend Richard Ellerbrake wanted immediate recognition for his church's devotion to Christian love rather than racial hatred. After Ellerbrake's plea, East added, "We lose more preachers that way."[113] Obliging the good reverend, CCA added to the number of their enemies and by the summer of 1960 they totaled nearly one hundred.

East delighted in attacking not only the CCA, but the Mississippi chapter of the Daughters of the American Revolution (DAR) as well. In early 1960, the DAR started a campaign to censor textbooks for all Mississippi schools. The women investigated the backgrounds of all textbook authors, of people featured as subject matter in the books, and of those whose works were recommended as supplementary and reference reading. Among those found suspect, the most offensive were Mary McLeod Bethune, Archibald MacLeish, and Henry Steele

Commager. Miss Bethune allegedly belonged to seventy-one organizations that the DAR recognized as un-American. Her sponsorship of the American Committee for the Protection of the Foreign Born drew special criticism as did the fact that she received a birthday card from the Congress of American Women. East joked that this card proved again that women should not have birthdays.[114] MacLeish offended the DAR by supporting the Friends of Abraham Lincoln's Brigade and the International Labor Defense. Commager committed the unforgivable sin of backing the National Committee for a Sane Nuclear Policy. "Now, please," East countered, "for just a second consider the man, Commager. Why, hell, he doesn't want to blow up the world! Yes, Sir, if ever I saw anything pro-Communist and simply, downright, plain UN, that's it."[115]

When the women displayed the unacceptable textbooks at the headquarters of the CCA in Jackson, Mississippi, East ran a banner headline in the *Petal Paper:* "Witches Mount Brooms Today in Jackson."[116] East concluded by predicting that one day when historians assessed the accomplishments of the DAR, it would rank right beside, if not above, the CCA and the KKK.[117]

To show that he was not against everything, East discussed those organizations he considered worthwhile. He still held firmly that to ally himself with any group meant a loss of personal freedom, so he eschewed any memberships except that of the human race. Even here he said he had given serious thought to dropping out.[118] The groups whose principles and aims he shared were the Fellowship of Reconciliation, the Americans for Democratic Action, the SANE Nuclear Policy Group, and the American Civil Liberties Union. He expressed a firm belief that other organizations existed that attempted to enlighten America, but these four most closely reflected his views. He especially singled out the ACLU for defending the rights of everyone, even those with whom it disagreed. Undoubtedly his own situation had much to do with this opinion.[119]

The administration of Governor Ross Barnett, and its extremely close ties with the CCA, made an already intolerant atmosphere even more repressive. At the urging of Barnett the legislature, during the first ten weeks of his administration, introduced twenty-four new segregation bills. One piece of legislation struck a blow for international bigotry when the legislature resolved to support the Union of South Africa's policy of apartheid.

Other laws appointed the governor as sole judge of text-books used in Mississippi schools, advised circuit clerks to refuse the Justice Department voter registration information, and, most intimidating of all, promised to prosecute anyone who testified "falsely" before the FBI and the Civil Rights Commission. No proof was necessary to show that the testimony was false.[120] The State Sovereignty Commission increased its activities under Barnett. In the past, Governor Coleman had used it primarily to spread propaganda concerning Mississippi's fair treatment of blacks. The investigative arm of the agency remained weak, if nonexistent. Now extensive secret probes were conducted and dossiers compiled on subversives through-out the state. Also, it was at this point that the Sovereignty Commission began donating money to the CCA.[121] One bill that failed to pass would have encouraged anyone dissatisfied with their economic and social status in Mississippi to become a resident of another state. East said that if it had become law, he and Easton King would have been the first to leave.[122] Petalites certainly embraced the new level of intolerance. When a group from the Mennonite Biblical Seminary visited Petal to talk with East, it could not get proper directions to his home. Those with whom the students talked became angry. One man said that East would not be able to walk one block before someone killed him.[123]

Undeterred by such attitudes and laws, East maintained his onslaught against bigotry, especially that of the increasingly powerful CCA. When the Council published its next installment of the "Manual for Southerners," East dutifully reprinted it with his own editorial comments. He said he presented it "in the true, humble, honest, forth right spirit in which it was written for our children—to close and warp their little—oops, heavens! Now if you please, bow your head and give thanks for a TRUE picture of our Southern history."[124] One particularly ludicrous section of the "Manual" used chickens to illustrate the rightness of segregation. It explained how a farmer observed his white and red chickens refusing to mix and living apart in the same coop. The moral was that segregation was obviously God's and nature's plan.[125] To highlight this absurdity, East added that he had seen black chickens walking on the sidewalks, and when a white one approached, the black chickens stepped into the street and waited, hats in hands, until the white chickens passed. Only once, East claimed, had he seen this behavior pattern broken and then the white roosters lynched the "uppity" black rooster.[126] Two weeks later when East presented yet another segment of the "Manual," he gave a new rationale for carrying this "educational information." He said that the state legislature had reportedly earmarked a considerable amount of money for distribution to those promoting the southern point of view, and he wanted to be on the payroll. If such funds went to the CCA, he felt certain it would dispense a sizeable sum to him since his paper entered so many northern homes.[127] Many Mississippians, in addition to East, found the "Manual for Southerners" unsatisfactory and no further issues appeared.[128]

Although East's major focus was always on Mississippi, he did not remain totally silent on national civil rights developments. While his comments were never extensive, he backed the sit-in demonstrations and the 1960 Civil Rights Act. On 1 February 1960, the use of sit-in demonstrations as an effective weapon in the drive for civil rights started in Greensboro, North Carolina. Four college students at North Carolina A & T College sat down at the lunch counter of the F. W. Woolworth store and asked for coffee. The store manager refused to serve the young men at the white counter but said he would gladly wait on them at the black counter downstairs. The youths declined his offer and said they would stay until they were served coffee or until the store closed. They promised to return each day until the store met their demands, and they kept their promise, coming back day after day in increasingly larger numbers. As in the Montgomery bus boycott, blacks in Greensboro had taken the initiative instead of responding to white actions, and in the spirit of Montgomery the demonstrators adhered to a policy of nonviolence. Within a few days, similar sit-ins occurred in other North Carolina cities and during the next two weeks sit-ins, wade-ins at pools, kneel-ins at churches, and read-ins at libraries spread to fifteen cities and five states. With blacks resisting segregation, and the federal government and some sympathetic southern whites giving aid, racial barriers began to fall slowly. The sit-ins proved so successful that they spawned a new civil rights organization, the Student Nonviolent Coordinating Committee (SNCC), and rejuvenated an old one, the Congress of Racial Equality (CORE).[129]

It took East until June 1960 to state his support of the sit-ins. He believed that the national publicity given to the sit-ins would expose southern prejudice and make its tragic consequences unacceptable. Who would not be appalled, he wondered, by the unreasonable and brutal reactions of southern authorities to the nonviolent black protest? Even his seven-year-old daughter Karen understood the injustice of such actions.[130] When she saw police ordering blacks out of the Woolworth lunch counter, she asked her father, "Daddy, why can't the colored people eat just like everybody?"[131] East liked the fact that his daughter had developed this concern, but he also found the question difficult to answer. As he noted, "How do you explain bigotry and prejudice without causing it?"[132] He finally told her that some people fail to respect the rights of others.

East's answer did not satisfy him, but he could not at that time think of a better one. The question and answer continued to trouble him. In late June he wrote, "I've thought of the matter many, many times since. I've wondered how many children in the Nation asked their parents the same question and I've wondered what sort of answers were given to the children."[133] Unable to resolve the problem in his own mind, he reprinted an article by Lillian Smith that had appeared earlier in the magazine of the Fellowship of Reconciliation, *Fellowship.* She described the long history of black debasement by white society and argued that it was necessary to halt this practice for the good of everyone, black and white. Blacks, she argued, somehow had to demonstrate to white society the need for legal and social equality. A loving attitude, not hatred, would be the only way the change would occur.[134]

East also voiced his approval of the 1960 Civil Rights Act which Congress hoped would increase the number of black voters. From the beginning of his crusade he had been critical of southerners who denied blacks the right to vote, and his complaints grew louder each year. During the 1959 governor's race, one candidate had actually suggested separate ballot boxes for whites and blacks. East pointed out that with so few blacks able to vote there was no need for such a system.[135] He mentioned frequently that of the 12,000 blacks living in his home county, Forrest, none were able to vote, and statewide only 6.8 percent of the black population went to the polls.[136] Those southern politicians who claimed that blacks were able to cast a ballot were simply liars. East hoped that the new act would reverse this situation. In part, the act succeeded. It corrected a flaw in the 1957 Civil Rights Act that allowed the federal government to initiate legal action against individual registrars who discriminated against blacks. When confronted with such suits, the registrars resigned. With no one to prosecute, this legal remedy proved worthless. The 1960 act permitted the federal government to proceed against the state government and not just the registrars. It also provided for the appointment of a federal referee to register black voters if a federal judge found a pattern of discrimination in any area. Armed with this added legal power, the federal government increased its legal actions on behalf of blacks, but one problem remained. Few southern federal judges were willing to declare any locality as habitually discriminatory.[137] Although he recognized the law's short-comings, East believed that the legislation represented a step in the right direction. He also applauded Senator Paul Douglas's futile efforts to strengthen the act. He said nothing further, though, about the 1960 Civil Rights Act.[138]

East's relative silence on it and on the sit-ins derived in part from the growing difficulties in his marriage. As his behavior grew more erratic (leaving home, refusing to speak to his wife, and throwing temper tantrums), his wife, Billie, understandably lashed back. She began drinking heavily and made life as miserable as possible for her husband.[139] During the spring of 1960, East began dating a woman from Georgia.[140] As the relationship between the two grew closer, they had sexual relations on several occasions. East believed that these intimate contacts should be more frequent if she had as much love for him as he had for her. The woman, in a long, sad letter, responded that they were about as close as they could ever be because she was a lesbian. She expressed her love and affection for him but emphasized that their sexual contacts had arisen from her occasional need for a man, any man, and her concern for his loneliness. Since her roommate and lover disapproved of these casual encounters, the woman decided that she and East could be friends and nothing more.[141] East's distress was so great that he pursued this woman for another month before giving up the relationship as hopeless. Crushed, he nonetheless managed to joke about it. In a letter to Maxwell Geismar, he discussed his dilemma. "I was coming along pretty well, and I learned she was a lesbian, which, per se, I give not a damned; however, I stopped the chase when it struck me that damned if I was going to have a mistress who had a mistress!"[142]

By the time this affair had run its unnatural course, East's attention turned again to the publication of his autobiography, *The Magnolia Jungle*. He had worked on the project for two years with the editorial help of Joseph Barnes, Maxwell Geismar, and John Howard Griffin. The book received very favorable reviews throughout most of the country. At one point, it appeared the book would become a motion picture, but the offer never materialized.[143] East did receive a great deal of publicity, however. A New York City radio station, WOR, carried a forty-five-minute program that featured *The Magnolia Jungle* as the major point of discussion.[144] In late August, he appeared on the "Today Show" with Arlene Francis to discuss the book and to boost sales.[145]

His friends were especially kind in their remarks. Upton Sinclair praised East's work and declared, "If some foundation does not subsidize this man it will be said of them: 'Eyes have they but they see not!' "[146] Van Wyck Brooks told him, "Your book makes me feel better about Mississippi. You are a born civilizer and a first-rate American."[147] Harvard Professor Frank Freidel, who had met East through James Silver, expressed his pleasure with the book as did another friend, Aubrey Williams, who commented, "I say without reservation that that guy is hitting the hardest licks being dealt bigotry and prejudice in the South."[148] He received similar comments from James McBride Dabbs and Sarah Patton Boyle. Virginia Durr, another friend and southern liberal, revealed her thoughts to East:

> You proved that you know better than any of us what it is to be poor in the South. And how the lack of money has forced us to swallow our pride. It is this helplessness rather than poverty that makes us so mean, and makes us take it out on the "Nigger." Unless some rare and special and precious man comes along like you and refuses to look down and looks up instead.[149]

One response that he treasured more than most came from Lillian Smith. In praising the book, she emphasized East's strength of character and his courage. To underscore this point, she recounted their first meeting. They had discussed their childhoods over lunch. She had described her very comfortable life, telling East of her father and his huge lumber mills and the segregated milltowns, and of his moral and cultural confusion and how his humanity became tangled up with segregation and the social and economic gap between the mill owner and millworkers.

> And then P. D. had said quietly, "My father could have been one of your father's millhands." I almost cried, I hurt so terribly for Dad and me and hardly at all for P. D. who had risen above it so completely. P. D. and I stared at each other a long time, then smiled, then ate our lunch and enjoyed it. It was a beautiful and terrible moment and I hope, someday, to write about it.[150]

Not all of the reactions to the book were positive. Norman Vincent Peale remarked that East showed a regrettably negative attitude. "After all, going against one's fellow man is not the positive way for a democracy such as ours. We are praying for him."[151] One reviewer, Jay Milner of the *New York Herald-Tribune*, who had worked previously for Hodding Carter, attacked not the book but East's methods of fighting bigotry. He argued that they were totally ineffective. Instead of using humor and ridicule, he felt that East should adopt Carter's technique of relentlessly appealing to reason with an occasional sharp jab but only when provoked. Milner resented the fact that the book received any positive reviews and described those who rendered them as "hothouse" liberals.[152] Shortly after the book's release, a Baptist minister in Hattiesburg delivered a sermon in which he viciously attacked East as anti-Christ, antireligious, anti-Mississippi, anti-everything.[153]

More serious were the death threats East received. On one occasion, just as he prepared to leave a gas station, a very angry man walked over to him and stared directly into his eyes. He then bellowed, "Somebody ought to kill you, you son-of-a-bitch." East climbed quickly into his car, but the man stuck his head into the window and repeated his threat, adding, "You're a god-damned traitor." Unable to hold his temper, East responded, "And a communist, too, and let's not forget that I'm a nigger-lover." The man shouted back, "Somebody's going to kill you. Somebody ought to kill you." Then, as East pulled his car out of the station, the man spit, hitting the car's rear window.[154]

The most absurd reaction came from Easton King's partner in the *Chronicle Star*. East dedicated his autobiography to his old friend King, to W. W. Stout, and to Irving J. Fain. King's business colleague, the major shareholder in the paper, believed that he should have been mentioned in the book, especially on the dedication page. To show his displeasure, he went over King's head and ordered the *Chronicle Star* print shop to cease printing the *Petal Paper*. King was frustrated and upset, but he could do nothing about the situation. East, in desperation, turned to Aubrey Williams in Alabama, who agreed to print the paper. The extra cost and the distance between Hattiesburg and Montgomery made this a poor alternative, but the only one available. Williams told East not to worry about the charges. This bothered East so much that in August he reduced the paper's frequency from weekly to biweekly to reduce Williams's economic losses.[155]

To make matters worse, East's book failed to produce any substantial income. His profits barely paid for copies of the book that he sent to friends or for his son Byron's child support payments.[156] As he observed, the critics loved the book but the people did not dash out and buy it. With this expected revenue absent and outside contributions down, he suffered his worst financial year since the paper's inception. He lost $4,300 for fiscal 1960,[157] and his prospects for the future looked dim. Economic security continued to elude his grasp despite his rising popularity outside the South and with southern liberals.

Notes

[1] P. D. East, *Petal* (Miss.) *Paper*, 16 January 1958, 1.

[2] East tended to dwell on God and religion a great deal. Both the paper and his autobiography are filled with such references.

[3] P. D. East, *Petal* (Miss.) *Paper*, 16 January 1958, 1.

[4] James W. Silver to P. D. East, no date, Box 25, P. D. East Papers, Mugar Memorial Library, Boston University. Hereafter cited as East Papers.

[5] P. D. East, *Petal* (Miss.) *Paper*, 3 April 1958, 2; Will D. Campbell, *Brother to a Dragonfly* (New York: Seabury Press, 1977), 220.

[6] P. D. East, *Petal* (Miss.) *Paper*, 3 April 1958, 2.

[7] John Howard Griffin, taped response to questions submitted by the author, Fort Worth, Texas, 6 December 1976. Hereafter cited as Griffin, taped response.

[8] P. D. East, "Of Our Critics We Ask—Just Give Us Five More Days," *Petal* (Miss.) *Paper*, 2 January 1958, 1.

[9] P. D. East, *Petal* (Miss.) *Paper*, 23 January 1958, 1.

[10] P. D. East, *Petal* (Miss.) *Paper*, 6 February 1958, 1.

[11] P. D. East, *Petal* (Miss.) *Paper*, 27 February 1958, 1.

[12] P. D. East, *Petal* (Miss.) *Paper*, 13 March 1958, 1.

13 P. D. East, rejected pages from the *Magnolia Jungle*, 439–40, Box 11, East Papers. Hereafter cited as East, rejected pages.

14 Joseph Barnes to P. D. East, 27 March 1958, Box 4, East Papers.

15 P. D. East to John Wheeler, 25 June 1958, Box 4, East Papers.

16 East, rejected pages, 440.

17 Ibid., 440–41.

18 James W. Silver to P. D. East, 6 November 1956, Box 25, East Papers. Silver wrote to East that he had a copy of one letter that a spy in his class sent to Robert Patterson of the Citizens' Council of Mississippi. After informing East about his difficulties, Silver admonished him that "it would be foolish as hell for any part of this nonsense to appear in the Petal monstrosity. I'm sure the boys scrutinize your paper carefully and attention to me in it might conceivably be the kiss of death." Also, see Numan V. Bartley, *The Rise of Massive Resistance: Race and Politics in the South During the 1950's* (Baton Rouge: Louisiana State University Press, 1969), 229; Neil R. McMillen, *The Citizens' Council: Organized Resistance to the Second Reconstruction, 1954–1964* (Urbana: University of Illinois Press, 1971), 244.

19 P. D. East, "Academic Freedom, or Methodist Misfits?" *Petal* (Miss.) *Paper,* 17 April 1958, 1.

20 Ibid.

21 McMillen, *Citizens' Council,* 245. For the most detailed discussion of this issue see Hodding Carter III, *The South Strikes Back* (Garden City, New York: Doubleday and Company, 1959), 180–84.

22 East, *Petal* (Miss.) *Paper,* 17 April 1958, 1.

23 Ibid.

24 P. D. East, *Petal* (Miss.) *Paper,* 22 May 1958, 1.

25 McMillen, *Citizens' Council,* 245–46; Carter, *South Strikes Back,* 180–84.

26 Quoted in James W. Silver, *Mississippi: The Closed Society* (New York: Harcourt, Brace and World, 1966), 69.

27 McMillen, *Citizens' Council,* 240–42.

28 P. D. East, "WCC's New Approach—Close the Young Minds Now?" *Petal* (Miss.) *Paper,* 22 May 1958, 1.

29 Frank E. Smith, *Congressman from Mississippi* (New York: Capricorn Books, 1964), 272.

30 Silver, *Closed Society,* 41.

31 Ibid.; McMillen, *Citizens' Council,* 125, 252.

32 P. D. East, *Petal* (Miss.) *Paper,* 1 May 1958, 1.

33 Ibid.

34 Ibid.

35 P. D. East, *Petal* (Miss.) *Paper,* 19 June 1958, 1.

36 East never mentioned the precise date that he met Fain. An examina-

tion of his autobiography and his financial records makes it clear that he knew Fain by 1957, but not before. A cursory examination of the Irving J. Fain Papers at Rhode Island College in Providence, Rhode Island, provided no insights into the matter. Sally Wilson, assistant archivist, and Professor Stanley Lemons, both of Rhode Island College, gave the author valuable assistance in this search.

37 Statement of Loans Received by P. D. East, 1958, Box 45, East Papers. Since East's financial records are practically nonexistent, the author has been unable to determine the exact extent of loans made to East by Fain. Most likely the amount was considerable.

38 Allan Knight Chalmers to P. D. East, 29 April 1958, Box 1, East Papers.

39 Thomas D. Clark, *The Emerging South* (New York: Oxford University Press, 1968), 14; Kenneth K. Bailey, *Southern White Protestantism in the Twentieth Century* (New York: Harper and Row, 1964), 142–49.

40 Clark, *Emerging South,* 264.

41 Allan Knight Chalmers to P. D. East, 30 September 1958, Box 1, East Papers; P. D. East to Maxwell Geismar, 10 February 1959, Geismar Papers.

42 P. D. East to Allan Knight Chalmers, 29 October 1958, Box 1, East Papers.

43 Ibid.

44 P. D. East to Allan Knight Chalmers, 28 November 1958, Box 1, East Papers.

45 Ibid. This incident may mean nothing, but again it must be emphasized that Billie East's divorce decree stressed her husband's long absences with no mention of destination or return time, and his disregard for his family. *Billie Porter East vs. P. D. East,* Chancery Court of Lamar County, Mississippi, June 1961, 1–2, Box 29, East Papers.

46 P. D. East, *Petal* (Miss.) *Paper,* 28 August 1958, 1.

47 P. D. East and Marvin Reubin, Script from "Search for Peace," Radio Station WIP, Philadelphia, Pennsylvania, 30 November 1958, 3.

48 James McBride Dabbs to P. D. East, 15 September 1958, Box 1, East Papers; P. D. East, *Petal* (Miss.) *Paper,* 10 October 1958, 1–2.

49 P. D. East, *Petal* (Miss.) *Paper,* 25 September 1958, 1; P. D. East, "How to be a Man of Distinction," *Harper's,* January 1959, 12–18. Hereafter cited as East, "Man of Distinction."

50 "East Publications Operating Statement Year 1958," Box 45, East Papers.

51 P. D. East, *Petal* (Miss.) *Paper,* 26 June 1958, 1.

52 Maxwell Geismar, "The Stokelys and the South," *Petal* (Miss.)

Paper, 16 October 1958, 1.

53 P. D. East, *Petal* (Miss.) *Paper*, 11 December 1958, 1.

54 P. D. East, *Petal* (Miss.) *Paper*, 5 February 1959, 1.

55 P. D. East, *Petal* (Miss.) *Paper*, 15 January 1959, 1.

56 P. D. East to Maxwell Geismar, no date, Box 93, Geismar Papers.

57 P. D. East to Maxwell Geismar, no date, Box 92, Geismar Papers.

58 P. D. East, *Petal* (Miss.) *Paper*, 8 January 1959, 1.

59 P. D. East, *Petal* (Miss.) *Paper*, 15 January 1959, 1.

60 Ibid.

61 Alfred Hassler to P. D. East, 29 January 1959, Box 93, Geismar Papers.

62 P. D. East to Maxwell Geismar, 10 February 1959, Box 93, Geismar Papers.

63 Ibid. P. D. East to John Howard Griffin, 10 February 1959, Box 93, Geismar Papers.

64 Alfred Hassler to P. D. East, 16 March 1959, Box 26, East Papers.

65 Maxwell Geismar to P. D. East, 21 April 1959, Box 28, East Papers; Alfred Hassler to P. D. East, 5 May 1959, Box 26, East Papers; Alfred Hassler to Friends of P. D. East, no date, Box 26, East Papers.

66 "A Session on Civil Rights," *Voice: Hotel and Club*, April 1959, 13.

67 Ibid.

68 P. D. East, *Petal* (Miss.) *Paper*, 26 March 1959, 1.

69 Paul Coates, "A Fellow to Whom We Should Subscribe," *Los Angeles Times*, Sec. 1, 28 April 1959, 24.

70 P. D. East, *Petal* (Miss.) *Paper*, 18 June 1959, 2.

71 P. D. East to Irwin Moskowicz, 28 May 1959, Box 45, East Papers.

72 P. D. East, *Petal* (Miss.) *Paper*, 28 May 1959, 1.

73 P. D. East to Maxwell Geismar, no date, Box 93, Geismar Papers.

74 P. D. East to Paul Coates, 9 May 1959, Box 45, East Papers.

75 Anonymous to P. D. East, no date, Box 5, East Papers.

76 Jean de Desley to P. D. East, no date, Box 5, East Papers.

77 Grace Williams to Paul Coates, no date, Box 26, East Papers.

78 Ibid.

79 P. D. East, *Petal* (Miss.) *Paper*, 7 July 1959, 1. His wife, Billie, seemed to have provided less and less help to her husband at this time. She did not support his stance on race, and as East noted to Paul Coates, "She just wished the whole thing was over and done with. That everybody, including me, would shut up." Paul Coates, *Los Angeles Times*, 24.

80 P. D. East to Maxwell Geismar, no date, Box 93, Geismar Papers; P. D. East to Allan K. Chalmers, 17 March 1959, Box 28, East Papers.

81 Maxwell Geismar to P. D. East, 21 April 1959, Box 28, East Papers.

82 Richard Ellerbrake, "Prophet in a Magnolia Jungle," *Youth*, 14 February 1960, 14.

83 John Howard Griffin, *Black Like Me* (New York: New American

Library, 1976), 49; Clark, *Emerging South,* 209. Several years later, when an official of the Mississippi State Sovereignty Commission was asked if he thought Parker's murderers would ever be caught, he replied, no, and "Besides, three of them are already dead." Silver, *Closed Society,* 8.

84 P. D. East, *Petal* (Miss.) *Paper,* 28 May 1959, 1.

85 P. D. East to Maxwell Geismar, no date, Box 93, Geismar Papers.

86 Receipts for child support payments were found from 1952 until 1958 in Box 45, East Papers.

87 P. D. East to Maxwell Geismar, no date, Box 93, Geismar Papers.

88 P. D. East to Joseph Barnes, 4 June 1959, Box 45, East Papers.

89 P. D. East to Maxwell Geismar, no date, Box 93, Geismar Papers.

90 Ibid.

91 P. D. East, *Petal* (Miss.) *Paper,* 9 July 1959, 1.

92 P. D. East, *Petal* (Miss.) *Paper,* 2 July 1959, 1–4.

93 P. D. East, *Petal* (Miss.) *Paper,* 9 September 1959, 1–4.

94 P. D. East, *Petal* (Miss.) *Paper,* 30 July 1959, 1–3.

95 McMillen, *Citizens' Council,* 226.

96 Silver, *Closed Society,* 43.

97 Neal Peirce, *The Deep South States of America: People, Politics, and Power in the Seven Deep South States* (New York: W. W. Norton and Company, 1974), 177.

98 Walter Lord, *The Past That Would Not Die* (New York: Harper and Row, 1965), 77.

99 P. D. East, *Petal* (Miss.) *Paper,* 17 September 1959, 1.

100 P. D. East, *Petal* (Miss.) *Paper,* 3 September 1959, 1–2.

101 McMillen, *Citizens' Council,* 38–39, 337.

102 Silver, *Closed Society,* 43.

103 Ibid., 93–94. Liquor was prohibited in Mississippi at this time and possession was a criminal offense. In most cases the law looked the other way, but the courts used it when they wanted to convict those they considered to be troublemakers.

104 P. D. East, *Petal* (Miss.) *Paper,* 8 October 1959, 1.

105 Silver, *Closed Society,* 94.

106 John Fischer to P. D. East, 16 October 1959, Box 4, East Papers. In a letter to the author, Fischer gave a different reason for the rejection. He said the material was little more than a rewrite of the "Man of Distinction" article. He stated further that *Harper's* had printed many other pieces on race relations and welcomed controversial material. John Fischer to the author, 29 June 1977.

107 P. D. East to Maxwell Geismar, no date, Box 93, Geismar Papers.

108 P. D. East, *Petal* (Miss.) *Paper,* 29 October 1959, 2.

109 P. D. East, *Petal* (Miss.) *Paper,* 12 November 1959. With the help of the Friends of P. D. East and the money from the Paul Coates Show, approximately $8,000 came to East, but he still lost $1,000 in 1959. East Publications Operating Statement Year 1959, Box 45, East Papers.

[110] Griffin, *Black Like Me*, 77. Details of Griffin's visit with the Easts are found in his book on 71–79.

[111] P. D. East, *Petal* (Miss.) *Paper*, 31 December 1959, 1–2.

[112] Ibid., 1.

[113] P. D. East, *Petal* (Miss.) *Paper*, 7 January 1960, 1.

[114] P. D. East, *Petal* (Miss.) *Paper*, 14 January 1960, 2.

[115] P. D. East, *Petal* (Miss.) *Paper*, 25 February 1960, 2.

[116] Ibid., 1.

[117] Ibid.

[118] P. D. East, *Petal* (Miss.) *Paper*, 28 January 1960, 1.

[119] Ibid., 1–2.

[120] Lord, *The Past*, 77–78.

[121] McMillen, *Citizens' Council*, 336–37.

[122] P. D. East, *Petal* (Miss.) *Paper*, 30 June 1960, 1.

[123] Harold Regier to P. D. East, 7 March 1960, Box 24, East Papers.

[124] P. D. East, *Petal* (Miss.) *Paper*, 24 March 1960, 1–2.

[125] Ibid., 2.

[126] Ibid. The pattern of blacks walking in the streets rather than the sidewalk when whites approached persisted well into the 1960s.

[127] P. D. East, *Petal* (Miss.) *Paper*, 7 April 1960, 1.

[128] McMillen, *Citizens' Council*, 240.

[129] The best discussion of this significant development can be found in William H. Chafe, *Civilities and Civil Rights: Greensboro, North Carolina, and the Black Struggle for Freedom* (New York: Oxford University Press, 1980). See also Howard Zinn, *SNCC: The New Abolitionist* (Boston: Beacon Press, 1964); August Meier and Elliot Rudwick, *CORE: A Study in the Civil Rights Movement, 1942–1968* (New York: Oxford University Press, 1973), 104–31; Arthur I. Waskow, *From Race Riot to Sit-In, 1919 to the 1960s: A Study in the Connection Between Conflict and Violence* (Garden City, New York: Doubleday and Company, 1966), 242–43; Pat Watters, *Down to Now: Reflections on the Southern Civil Rights Movement* (New York: Pantheon Books, 1971), 72–78; Benjamin Muse, *The American Negro Revolution: From Nonviolence to Black Power* (New York: Citadel Press, 1960), 4–6.

[130] P. D. East, *Petal* (Miss.) *Paper*, 2 June 1960, 1.

[131] P. D. East, *Petal* (Miss.) *Paper*, 23 June 1960, 1.

[132] Ibid.

[133] Ibid.

[134] P. D. East, *Petal* (Miss.) *Paper*, 25 August 1960, 1.

[135] P. D. East, *Petal* (Miss.) *Paper*, 28 May 1959, 1.

[136] P. D. East, *Petal* (Miss.) *Paper*, 5 May 1960, 1.

[137] Steven F. Lawson, *Black Ballots: Voting Rights in the South, 1944–1969* (New York: Columbia University Press, 1976), 203–49. See also Pat Watters and Reese Cleghorn, *Climbing Jacob's*

Ladder: The Arrival of Negroes in Southern Politics (New York: Harcourt, Brace and World, 1967), 211–12.

138 P. D. East, *Petal* (Miss.) *Paper*, 21 April 1960, 1.

139 P. D. East to anonymous, 1 July 1960, Box 42, East Papers.

140 He apparently visited this woman on his speaking tours and also whenever he felt the need to leave his home. Such trips no doubt account for some of the unexplained absences Billie East complained about in the divorce decree.

141 Anonymous to P. D. East, 24 February 1960, Box 42, East Papers.

142 P. D. East to Maxwell Geismar, no date, Box 30, Geismar Papers.

143 P. D. East to Joseph Barnes, 4 June 1960, Box 45, East Papers.

144 Ed Fitzgerald and Pegeen Fitzgerald, Transcription of Broadcast, Radio Station WOR, 15 July 1960, East Papers.

145 P. D. East, *Petal* (Miss.) *Paper*, 29 December 1960, 1.

146 Upton Sinclair to Joseph Barnes, 21 July 1960, Box 6, East Papers.

147 Van Wyck Brooks to P. D. East, 6 September 1960, Box 6, East Papers.

148 Aubrey Williams to Joseph Barnes, 29 June 1960, Box 6, East Papers; Frank Freidel to Joseph Barnes, 21 July 1960, Box 6, East Papers.

149 Virginia Durr to P. D. East, 5 August 1960, Box 6, East Papers.

150 Lillian Smith to Joseph Barnes, 8 July 1960, Box 6, East Papers.

151 Norman Vincent Peale to John Howard Griffin, no date, Box 2, East Papers.

152 Jay Milner to P. D. East, 22 August 1960, Box 6, East Papers.

153 P. D. East, "Look Back in Pain," undated text of speech, Box 54, East Papers.

154 P. D. East, "Letter from a Southern Editor," *The Independent*, April 1964, 5.

155 P. D. East to Maxwell Geismar, no date, Box 28, Geismar Papers; P. D. East to Peter Charleton, 20 July 1960, Box 6, East Papers.

156 P. D. East to Byron East, 10 August 1960, Box 29, East Papers.

157 Operating Statement Year 1960, East Papers.

6

The Slow and Painful Return to Obscurity

P. D. East's prominence as a civil rights advocate was short lived. In February 1962, when he received his last national award for his efforts on behalf of racial justice, he was so involved in marital problems that he failed to publish the *Petal Paper* for the next six months. In a three-year period from 1961 through 1963, he went through two devastating divorces. Local bigots added to his problems by hurling lies, legal prosecution, and death threats at him until he finally fled Mississippi in 1963, fearing for his life. He never returned to his native state. Laboring under tremendous emotional strain, East began to suffer from serious health problems. Only his remarkable courage, the help of loyal friends, and the support of his fourth wife, Mary Cameron Plummer, enabled him to carry on his crusade, albeit a less vigorous one, until his death in 1971.

East's huge debt for 1960, despite revenues from *The Magnolia Jungle* and $5,000 from the Friends of P. D. East, prompted him to seek additional income.[1] With great reluctance, he resumed his public speaking career. His hatred of this work was rarely reflected in the audiences' reactions. After addressing 200 journalists at the University of Michigan, he received an ovation that exceeded that given to any other outside lecturer in the Department of Journalism's twelve-year program.[2] He met with similar success elsewhere, but always remained an unwilling orator. Not all of his options proved so fruitful. Senators Paul Douglas of Illinois and Pat McNamara of Michigan tried to relieve some of East's financial distress by obtaining tax-exempt status for the *Petal Paper*. Douglas's warning that the venture had little hope for success proved accurate.[3]

Trying to make light of his calamitous economic situation, East wrote to Maxwell Geismar that for him to have all of his bills paid "would probably be bad, because I'm arrogant enough being broke; if I had 25 cents in my pocket and I didn't owe, I'd have to be shot, I'm sure."[4] Much of the humor began to subside when he fell further behind in his mortgage payments and his utility bills. As he remarked to Geismar at this time, "I'm so god damned depressed. Nothing helps. I'm so fucking tired of living—but I'm scared of dying—quite a mess, I'm sure."[5]

Early 1961 brought no relief to East as his second marriage verged on collapse. Billie East could no longer tolerate her husband's absences from home nor could she continue to bear the brunt of his fits of depression. His mental state not only caused him to leave home without telling her, but it also led to violent temper outbursts during which he threw food and dishes against the walls and kicked and tore up furniture. At other times, he subjected her to long periods of silence, and when he finally spoke, he ridiculed her behavior and appearance.[6] When she in turn threatened East with physical violence, he expressed genuine fear for his safety. On 23 March 1961, after she had run up large bills at various local department stores,[7] East moved to an apartment, leaving the house for his wife and daughter. After he paid his first month's rent his total assets dropped to $2.56.[8] Predictably, no psychological sense of relief followed the break from his family. The experience was too traumatic. As he told Geismar, "The whole of my self-made mess pretty well caught up to me and I feel a bit depressed, to state it mildly."[9]

The entire episode deepened his already strong sense of insecurity. Feeling responsible for his marital problems, he sought someone to whom he could confess. He chose his dearest friends at this time, Max and Anne Geismar. In the course of one conversation, East asked them, "Why don't you adopt me?" Max Geismar replied, "I think we have."[10] Not meant to be malicious or critical, the remark nonetheless troubled East. He finally sat down and wrote an apology to the

Geismars for leaning on them too much and thereby jeopardizing the relationship. He explained that his dependence on them stemmed from the fact that he had so few truly close friends. He went on,

> Now, take into account my background, my almost innate insecurity and loneliness [*sic*], my warm and deep regards for you, and you have it—the reason I've imposed on you to the degree I have. For my imposition, Max, I'm so very sorry.[11]

The apology provided some relief, but the need to discuss his culpability still existed. In his friend, Sarah Patton Boyle, he found a ready listener and excellent counselor. Her advice seemed especially appropriate because her marriage had experienced similar difficulties on account of her commitment to civil rights. She told East to accept all responsibility for the marriage's failure, but to do it privately, only to himself. Otherwise, she cautioned, he would continue to try and assess a certain amount of blame to each partner while never reaching any satisfactory conclusions. "As long as you keep asking yourself if this, that or the other thing was the other person's fault or your own, you're really running away from blame. When you run from things, they only pursue, I've found."[12] Boyle added that neither she nor East were normal people because they stood and fought against the established practices in southern life. As misfits, they made poor marriage partners.[13] This dialogue helped restore East's spirits, at least temporarily, as he began to joke about his fate. He remarked to Geismar, "Been plagued recently by what to give up for Lent, but now I've decided: my god damned wife."[14] Even after the divorce was granted in June 1961, he used humor to combat his strong feelings of guilt. He commented to Maxwell Geismar, "Well, I must go now and marry No. 3; I've lost all their names, so I just keep up with the numbers."[15]

Such humor did not alter the fact that his economic situation had become more desperate than ever before. In addition to the child support he had to pay for his son, Byron, he now had the extra burden of $80 per month for his daughter, Karen, plus the mortgage payment on the family's home.[16] East had anticipated this financial disaster and tried unsuccessfully to find a solution prior to the divorce. He asked several generous contributors to the *Petal Paper* for $500 per month for one year.

To repay each person he proposed using the future royalties from a novel he hoped to have published by Random House entitled *A Cock for Asclepius*. The book, he claimed, was near completion, and since he had started a second draft, he predicted a publication date of early 1962. He intended to pay 6 percent interest on the money plus 10 percent of all income beyond the amount of the loan.[17] For references he listed Maxwell Geismar and Mary Heathcoate, an editor for his publisher. He also enclosed a brief synopsis of the book. The work basically was East's autobiography retold in a novel, with enough changes to make it different from *The Magnolia Jungle*.[18] To East's great disappointment, no one wanted to risk their money on this venture; so he had to seek relief elsewhere.

He turned to Harry Golden, an old friend and the publisher of the *Carolina Israelite*. Through Alfred Hassler, East understood that Golden was willing to loan him $1,500. Until his other possibilities had failed, he resisted asking Golden, not wanting to impose on their friendship. Circumstances, however, left him no alternative. He explained that the pressure of worrying about money to pay his bills made it nearly impossible to finish the second draft of his novel.[19] Golden responded that Hassler must have misunderstood him because he could not make a loan that large. He offered to write a letter, however, like those authored by the Friends of P. D. East, asking for contributions to East and the *Petal Paper*. To start the campaign, he would donate $150.[20] East accepted this proposal gladly because Hassler, treasurer of the Friends, was in Europe at the time and unable to lend immediate help.[21] By late August 1961, Golden mailed out the appeal. Many people responded positively and close to $1,500 poured in to ease East's financial difficulties temporarily.[22]

Occupied by his personal problems, East paid scant attention to civil rights developments throughout the spring and summer. He devoted only a few columns to the CCA and its activities in the South. His most interesting revelation concerned a letter from William Simmons, CCA official and advisor to Governor Ross Barnett, to the Mississippi State Sovereignty Commission which stated that the Citizens' Council had a large file on East's anti-Mississippi activities and would make it available if needed. [23] East had always suspected the existence of this information, but never had proof until he received a copy of the letter from an anonymous friend. Beyond these few comments, he said very little. He practically ignored the Freedom Rides that had started in May 1961.

This was a rather startling omission considering the impact of this tactic on southern society and the civil rights movement. Under the leadership of CORE and its dynamic new director, James Farmer, proponents of integration sought to force the desegregation of lunch counters, restrooms, and waiting rooms at bus terminals throughout the South. Starting from Washington, D.C., the Freedom Riders had a relatively calm trip until they reached Anniston, Alabama. There a white mob attacked the bus and its occupants and eventually destroyed the vehicle. Only the intervention of an Alabama highway patrolman, Eli Cowley, saved the civil rights advocates from further harm. With a new bus, they proceeded to Birmingham where they received no police protection whatsoever. The chief of police, Eugene "Bull" Connor, claimed that he was short-handed since it was Mother's Day and most of his men had gone to visit their mothers. Even more violence awaited the Freedom Riders in Montgomery. There angry segregationists not only clubbed the riders but also the press and a representative from the Justice Department. With this, John F. Kennedy, on the advice of his brother Robert, ordered federal marshals into the city to provide the protection that local authorities seemed unable or unwilling to give. Shortly thereafter the governor reluctantly called out the National Guard to maintain order.

Undaunted by the violence and heartened by federal assistance, another group decided to push into Mississippi. Once the riders tried to use the terminal facilities, local authorities charged them with disturbing the peace and other minor crimes. The NAACP alone paid over $300,000 for bail, fines, and legal fees. The Freedom Rides nonetheless finally paid off when Attorney General Robert F. Kennedy asked the Interstate Commerce Commission to enact more stringent rules for desegregation of interstate transportation terminals. By the end of 1962, CORE felt certain that its struggle had been won.[24] This victory and the large number of crusading blacks who entered the state inspired many Mississippi blacks to seek equality.[25]

East mentioned these significant developments only when describing a conversation at the Geismars' with attorney William Kuntsler. Kuntsler, who had tried unsuccessfully to intercede on behalf of the Freedom Riders in various Mississippi jails, had met with Ross Barnett. The governor had asked, "What would you think if your daughter married a dirty, kinky-haired, field-hand nigger?" Barnett then lectured the lawyer on the danger of racial intermarriage and the inferiority of blacks, and closed by warning Kuntsler to keep his racial theories to himself: "I don't want you lynched here in the state capitol."[26] Kuntsler left in disbelief that a governor in the United States had threatened him in this manner. This story represented all of East's public remarks on the Freedom Rides. In his 24 August 1961 issue he apologized for the paper's rather bland nature for the past several months, and explained that his lack of ranting and raving resulted from his falling "victim to high living and low thinking."[27] He promised to rectify the situation with the next issue.

East failed to keep his promise. He said very little about racism or the civil rights movement for the rest of the year, and he relied almost totally on articles by others and reruns of his favorite columns. His attention had been diverted elsewhere. Friends of his, A. I. and Faye Botnick, who worked for the Anti-Defamation League, introduced him to Elizabeth,[28] a psychologist and divorcée with two children. Less than one week after they met, he had fallen in love with her. He told her that he had never felt this way about any other woman. As he put it, she had made his life worth living and helped restore his flagging self-confidence. She was the wife he had been looking for all of his life. He remarked to his old friend, Maxwell Geismar, "Truly, for the first time in my life, I'm in love—*in* love, Max."[29] When Geismar asked East if he could financially afford a third marriage, he responded, "No, I can't afford it, not financially; but emotionally, for the sake of my very soul, I can't afford otherwise."[30]

To convince his new love of his sincerity, he sent her numerous letters and telephoned her frequently. The courtship was a long distance affair because Elizabeth was employed as director of testing and guidance at a Texas university. The separation seemed of little consequence to East, whose ardor remained strong. Within a few weeks, Elizabeth began to express her deep love for East. She was especially impressed that her son and daughter accepted him so readily and with so much affection. As she noted, "I love you so completely. Please know how proud I'll be to be your wife."[31] One month after meeting they decided to marry. Elizabeth wished to delay the ceremony until she had completed her doctoral dissertation.[32] East agreed to her request, stating that he wanted her to finish since her work made her so happy.[33] He told Geismar that the wedding would take place in May 1962, but both partners decided to act sooner. On 6 October 1961, one-and-a-half months after they met, they married.

After a brief honeymoon, East moved to Texas. The publication of his newspaper did not depend upon his continued residence in Mississippi, but his wife's job necessitated her presence at the university. For East the most troubling aspect of this departure was the prolonged separation it caused from his daughter, Karen. Unlike his relationship with his son, Byron, he always felt very close to Karen. Both he and his new wife wrote to Billie East asking if Karen could spend at least one-half of her time with them.[34] In his letter, East asked permission to visit Karen at Christmas and stated his desire to take her back to Texas for the spring and summer. Billie agreed to the Christmas reunion and subsequent short stays but balked at the idea of Karen's leaving for any extended period of time. She feared that her daughter would see her father and his new family at their best and find life in Mississippi wanting by comparison. As a result, Karen remained with her mother and maternal grandmother, Tressie Porter.[35]

Although East's marriage brought him much joy, one nagging problem remained. He continued to go further into debt. Each month he made two child support payments and one mortgage payment plus covering his own liabilities. Added to this was the expense incurred for the move to Texas. His burden grew even heavier when Billie East had difficulty finding employment. She told her ex-husband that her lack of experience and his "communistic reputation" made it almost impossible for her to locate a suitable position.[36] She was without income and unable to pay Karen's rather large doctors' bills. Under the circumstances, East volunteered to assume responsibility for all of Karen's medical services.[37] His only problem was finding the necessary money.

To raise the funds, he sought loans from two friends. He turned first to Milton Fine, owner of Fine Brothers Matison Company, a department store in Hattiesburg. Fine had loaned money to East in the past and had advertised in the *Petal Paper*. On this occasion, East borrowed $500 with the promise to have Random House repay this sum from the profits he would earn once his novel was published.[38] In late November, when this amount proved insufficient for his needs, he returned to Irving J. Fain. He asked Fain to loan him $2,000 over the next four months. Again, he promised to assign royalties from his book to cover the $2,000. East warned Fain about the uncertain nature of this repayment plan but emphasized his desperate need.[39] Fain brushed aside East's word of caution. He told him never to be shy or sensitive about asking for help, and to forget about giving him the royalties from the novel. "If you don't get the money, then you can't pay me back. That's the chance that I'm willing to take."[40] The first check arrived the week before Christmas, brightening East's holiday season.[41]

Further good news came when the New York Civil Liberties Union (NYCLU) gave him the Florina Lasker Civil Rights Award along with a check for $1,000. Each year the NYCLU conducted a nationwide search for the individual or organization that displayed the most consistent and outstanding courage in the defense of civil liberties.[42] East was overjoyed at this honor, especially when he learned that past recipients of the award included Roger Baldwin, founder of the American Civil Liberties Union, the black students at Central High School in Little Rock, Arkansas, and Herbert Block, editorial cartoonist for the *Washington Post*.[43] The award ceremonies were to take place on 22 February 1962, and the selection committee would provide an all-expense-paid trip to New York City for him and his wife.

East had little time to savor this rare distinction because serious trouble began to jeopardize his marriage. In early January 1962, Elizabeth went to the hospital for treatment of an infection. After numerous tests, the doctors found nothing wrong and dismissed her. On 12 January, the following day, she demanded to be readmitted and the physicians complied. They finally concluded that her illness was psychosomatic, but she remained in the hospital for the rest of the month for therapy. While undergoing this treatment, she revealed to her husband for the first time that she had a long history of emotional problems dating back to high school. Her mother told East that Elizabeth had been committed to a state mental institution because of drug addiction. East was shocked at this revelation and angry that he had not been informed of this situation before their marriage. His love for his wife helped him overcome the pain that he felt, and he spent practically every waking moment at her bedside. He tried as best he could to continue publishing the *Petal Paper* by relying more than ever on the work of others. He even tried to make the revisions requested by Random House on his novel while staying with his wife.[44]

When Elizabeth began to respond to the treatment, she blamed her husband for her latest relapse. She argued that his volatile nature upset her greatly. Equally troubling to her was his inability to show constant progress on his novel and the newspaper. In short, she accused him of laziness. In an effort to help the Easts resolve their marital problems, John Howard Griffin acted as a counselor. He explained to Elizabeth that practically all creative writers have unproductive days when they become impatient and short-tempered with those closest to them. In an act of true friendship, Griffin spent several weeks at the Easts' trying to help as best he could.[45]

By late February, Elizabeth felt well enough to accompany her husband to New York City to watch him receive the Florina Lasker Award. The trip proved less than enjoyable. When Maxwell and Anne Geismar gave a party for the Easts, Elizabeth's instability revealed itself once again. The Geismars invited several blacks to this celebration and Mrs. East could not cope with their presence. Shortly after the party began she fainted, and after she regained consciousness she left the house for the remainder of the evening.[46] Her emotional state deteriorated rapidly thereafter and East's life grew more complicated than ever.

Within two weeks after returning from New York City, Elizabeth East tried to kill herself. She had attempted this several times before. Considering this history, East believed he could not leave her alone. He stayed with her twenty-four hours a day.[47] After several weeks the strain became so great that he called his mother-in-law, asking for her help. As soon as she arrived he entered the hospital for treatment of his ulcer and a thorough physical examination.[48] His mental state grew even worse when he learned that his daughter, Karen, needed surgery.[49] The time he had spent watching his wife, recuperating from his own illness, and worrying about Karen interrupted all of his other work. From mid-March until August 1962, the *Petal Paper* failed to appear, and East was too absorbed in personal problems to care.

Medical expenses from hospital visits and drug and doctors' bills dealt him a staggering blow. He spent the $1,000 from the Lasker Award before he received the check, and advertising

revenue for the months his paper was published amounted to
$63 for January and February and $25 for March.[50] For assistance
he turned again to Harry Golden, thanking him for his past aid
and remarking that he might have done something foolish, like
committing suicide, had this help not arrived. East closed his
plea by apologizing, "Oh, hell, Harry, forgive me. My cross is
dragging all over Texas right now."[51] Golden, responding to
this not so subtle hint, sent out an appeal for contributions to
the P. D. East Fund. The money received did not even cover
half of the debts. Still financially pressed, East asked Steve
Allen for a $2,500 loan. This time he did not promise to use the
profits from his prospective novel, *A Cock for Asclepius*, as
repayment. He stated that he had planned a new novel, *If No
Kingdom Come*, and would use money from it if there was
any.[52] Allen agreed to the arrangement but could send only
$1,000. Additionally, however, Allen paid for two full-page
advertisements in the *Petal Paper* for his autobiography, *Mark
It and Strike It*, and two more for the National Committee for a
Sane Nuclear Policy. He also asked the publishers of his latest
book to take advertising space in the *Petal Paper*.[53]

Allen's assistance relieved temporarily some of East's economic pressure, but a new problem arose which no amount of
money could solve. Four doctors had found East's wife profoundly disturbed. Two said she was highly neurotic and the
other two labeled her psychotic. All recommended placing her
in an institution for specialized treatment,[54] but she refused to
go. East felt that he could not sign the commitment papers. To
do so would violate a pledge he had given his wife when she
first agreed to visit a doctor.[55] East's mother-in-law reinforced
her daughter's decision by claiming that the source of the
problem was P. D. himself. Accepting this theory, in early June
Elizabeth East asked her husband for a temporary separation.
After some heated words, East left and went to John Howard
Griffin's home in Mansfield, Texas.[56]

While staying with Griffin, East's health broke once again,
and he entered the hospital. Medical tests conducted during his
second stay revealed a serious affliction. He suffered from
acromegaly, a disease in which the bones of the head, hands,
and feet become enlarged permanently. Triggered by an over-
active pituitary gland, the ailment was fatal unless treated. In
East's case, the disease was not in an advanced stage and had
gone into remission, but the doctor urged frequent examinations
to monitor possible changes.[57]

Learning of her husband's problem, Elizabeth East asked him to return to their home; together they would try to solve their marital difficulties. In less than a week, however, she demanded a permanent separation and ordered him to leave. Her mother readily seconded her daughter's command, adding again that East had caused all of the problems. After a fierce argument he acquiesced, but he had no place to go. He refused to impose on John Griffin anymore. To make matters worse, Elizabeth threatened to get an injunction preventing him from removing his possessions until he paid the medical bills and over $400 for the mortgage. With only $70 to his name, he left, wandering around for ten days until he decided to return to Hattiesburg. Soon after returning, he borrowed enough money from the bank to move his possessions from Texas to his new home before his wife could legally intervene.[58]

In the depth of depression, East had to find a solution to his monetary ills. He believed that he could not ask for additional funds from Milton Fine, Irving Fain, or Steve Allen, since he was already deeply in debt to all of them. His old friend, John Griffin, offered him anything he had—time, money, or a sympathetic ear. East accepted the moral support, but refused the money that he knew Griffin could ill afford to give.[59] He turned instead to a rather wealthy woman from New York City, Ethel Clyde. In the past, she had made generous contributions to the paper, and he thought she might come to his aid with a $1,000 loan.[60] He hoped in vain. Mrs. Clyde told him to seek help from those who understood him better than she.[61] In desperation he turned to his publisher, Random House, asking for an additional $500 advance on his as yet unfinished novel. The company turned him down.[62] As a last resort, he pleaded with Harry Golden for another appeal on his behalf. He noted the short time that had passed since the last mailing but stated his great need. "No sob story, but I say frankly, honestly, and with great sorrow, never in my life have I been so desperate."[63] Without hesitation, Golden acted to raise money, although his efforts were not as successful as those earlier in the year.

East's monetary burdens were lifted momentarily, but the trauma of his failing marriage left him distraught. He felt very guilty because he could not hold his temper and be patient with his wife. After much soul searching, he found no excuse for becoming so angry with someone so ill, especially since he still loved her. As he remarked to Irving Fain, "I believe these are the most depressing days of my life. To see someone so ill, whom you love, and to be unable to help is hard to cope with."[64] His mood grew worse when he learned from his wife's psychologist that her condition had deteriorated further. She had reportedly lost touch with reality, had a fixed grin on her face, and experienced numerous hallucinations. Her mother finally admitted that Elizabeth might need some help, but never pressed her to obtain the intensive therapy essential to full recovery. In a letter to John Griffin, P. D. echoed his statement to Fain, "John, I think this is the lowest point in my life, and I've had some low ones."[65] These agonies caused his ulcer to start bleeding once again.

Despite the overwhelming tension and despair, he decided that he must resume publication of the *Petal Paper*. In late August 1962, he started the process of catching up with his schedule. In the second issue to appear he gave an explanation for the paper's long hiatus. He noted his and his wife's numerous hospital visits, seven between the two, but he never mentioned their separation. He promised to do what he could to make his paper current and cautioned his readers that incidents discussed in each issue would not coincide with dates on the paper.[66]

East's comments on racial tensions in the South remained subdued even when violence erupted on the campus of the University of Mississippi with enrollment of the school's first black, James Meredith. This confrontation between the federal government and Mississippi revealed to the nation the irrational, uncompromising, and violent nature of the state's white supremacists. When the United States Fifth Circuit Court of Appeals ordered Ole Miss to accept Meredith, Governor Ross Barnett stated he would rot in jail before submitting to this demand. On statewide television, he encouraged his audience to help him oppose the federal government's policy of racial genocide.[67] He dragged out the old idea of interposition in which a state could protect its citizens by placing itself between them and federal law.[68] To bolster the courage of all white Mississippians, he declared, "We must either submit to the unlawful dictates of the federal government or stand up like men and tell them 'NEVER!'"[69] A man of his word, Barnett blocked Meredith's first attempt to register. Under other circumstances, his performance would have been amusing. As the governor stood in the university doorway, Meredith and a sea of federal marshals approached him. Even though there was only one black person in sight, Barnett asked, "Which of you is James Meredith?"[70]

Barnett and Lieutenant Governor Paul B. Johnson stopped several subsequent attempts by Meredith to enroll. Emboldened by each denial, Mississippi racists grew more hostile towards the federal government and Meredith. Violence seemed inevitable. Such a possibility worried Barnett. He had incited his supporters to this fever pitch, but he shrank from physical brutality. At the same time, he was even more fearful of backing down and losing face with his constituents. Attorney General Robert F. Kennedy discovered this stubbornness and indecision when he tried to persuade Barnett to comply with the court order by reminding him that Mississippi was, after all, part of the United States. Barnett replied, "We have been a part of the United States, but I don't know whether we are or not."[71]

The governor retreated from his hard-line position only after the Fifth Circuit Court found him in contempt and ordered him to admit Meredith or face a jail sentence and a $10,000 per day fine. Confronted with overwhelming force, Barnett, on television, asked the people of Mississippi to accept desegregation. By this time federal marshals had escorted James Meredith to the campus and placed him under guard in one of the dormitories. But while an unsuspecting President Kennedy assured a national television audience that the University of Mississippi was desegregating peacefully, violence exploded in Oxford. An angry mob of several thousand students and outsiders attacked the marshals and state police. Once the marshals fired tear gas at the crowd, the police withdrew, claiming that their gas masks failed to protect them. This left 300 federal marshals to hold off the rioters, who now started firing weapons. It took the federal troops, called in by Kennedy, until 2:15 A.M. to arrive from Memphis, and before they quelled the disturbance, 2 people lay dead and another 375 others were injured. The next morning Meredith registered for classes and under the protection of the marshals remained until he graduated the following June. Meredith's tenure at the school was never easy. Although guarded constantly, he still faced death threats. One short poem illustrated the pressure he dealt with on a daily basis, "Roses are red, violets are blue; I've killed one nigger and might as well make it two."[72]

In a short paragraph, East expressed his sorrow over those killed and injured. In the same column, he printed a letter he wrote to Arthur Schlesinger, Jr., advisor to John Kennedy and subscriber to the *Petal Paper*.[73] Displaying gallows humor, East asked Schlesinger to support a federal grant to Mississippi in an amount equal to the fines imposed on Barnett by the Fifth Circuit Court of Appeals. He then demanded money to restore the grass on the University of Mississippi campus which had been trampled by uninvited federal troops. "This is a serious matter to us, the citizens of Mississippi. Sir, that trampled grass was WHITE!"[74] Schlesinger replied, joking, that he had referred the matter to the Justice Department.[75]

One issue after he made these remarks on the Meredith case, East fell silent once again. Renewed racist harassment put him on the defensive. When he returned to Hattiesburg in July, he thought that enough time had passed since his departure for people to have forgotten about him and leave him alone. He saw no need to request an unlisted telephone number, but in less than a week threatening phone calls started again. More serious trouble arose when the federal court charged Theron Lynd, the local voting registrar, with discriminating against blacks. The morning the hearings began a large crowd gathered outside the federal building. As the people milled about, they began condemning the Kennedys, the federal government, and finally East. Someone shouted, "If it weren't for that bastard P. D. East ole Theron wouldn't be in that court house right now! Did you know East has been off somewhere going to a NAACP school learning how to register niggers to vote?"[76] During his hearing, Lynd continued the attack on East. Later, speaking to a local Methodist men's club, Lynd stated, "There is one known communist in Hattiesburg, and that's P. D. East."[77] He went on to note that "He's a friend of some Jews we've got our eye on too."[78]

Disgusted by such charges and frightened by their possible consequences, East decided to see his lawyer, Harold Cubley. He asked him if he could sue Lynd for libel. Cubley advised that it would be a waste of time and money, but East did not want to let the accusation go unchallenged.[79] He wrote to Lynd requesting that he exercise one of two options: apologize or prove his statement. East then questioned the voting registrar's motives and added, "Such a statement can do and does great damage to the person against whom it's directed."[80] Lynd never responded.

Hostility aimed at East intensified after Lynd's attack. At a grocery store, a man shouted at him loudly, "Hello, Mr. NAACP."[81] East laughed in the man's face. Shortly after this incident, a man walked up beside him on a Hattiesburg sidewalk and said, "You bastard."[82] East did not argue with the gentleman, but he did not laugh this time. The situation became more frightening when Milton Fine told East that a local law enforcement official had heard, "They are out to get East."[83] Fine said the officer claimed that "They have an extensive file on him, that he's the leader of it all, that he gets $425 each month from some organization, possibly the NAACP."[84] No one knew who "they" were, but East guessed that either the CCA or the KKK was involved.

On 18 October 1962, he received a call from his wife. She told him immediately that he could return to Texas and live in the work room if he wished. When he asked why, she replied, "Things in Hattiesburg are much worse than you think."[85] She noted that when she had talked to her lawyer in Hattiesburg about a divorce, he had mentioned that a segregationist group in Jackson was ready to spend $25,000 to "get P. D. East one way or another."[86] East asked her to have her lawyer inform the organization that if they gave him $20,000 he would leave the state. This way everyone would profit. He would have $20,000 and the unknown group would save $5,000.[87]

East discounted his wife's story, suspecting that it might be her way of getting him to return on her terms.[88] It took him only one day to change his mind. His ex-brother-in-law, Miles Porter, warned him, "They are going to kill you."[89] Again, "they" could not be identified, but for East it made no difference. Fear held him in its grip. A friend of Porter's in Moselle, Mississippi, about fifteen miles north of Hattiesburg, described rumors that East was responsible for the integration problems throughout the state and that he would pay for the troubles he had caused. On the way to Hattiesburg, East overheard the same story in a cafe. Porter urged him either to leave or carry a gun.[90] Even Maxwell Geismar pleaded with his friend to arm himself and make known his willingness to fight back. "I am not kidding, and I have lost patience to a degree with the idea of pacifism in situations like this, when you can be a sitting duck for racist hoods."[91]

East rejected the idea of carrying a weapon, but he accepted the advice of his lawyer. Cubley instructed his client to keep his car locked at all times and check it thoroughly, under the hood and seats and in the trunk, before driving anywhere. Racists frequently planted alcohol in the automobiles of their enemies (Clyde Kennard was a prime example). Since possession of liquor was illegal in Mississippi, the individual faced arrest and jail. East knew a man who, like Kennard, had been sentenced to seven years in prison even though it was common knowledge that he had been convicted falsely.[92]

A legal frame of this type especially worried East. He wrote to Geismar, "I don't mind telling you, Max, right now I'm scared shitless; these bastards are experts at framing people."[93] Under intense pressure, East's ulcer hemorrhaged and he developed severe, almost unbearable headaches. His friends begged him to leave for a few weeks, but he could not afford to go.

On 20 October 1962, East's worst fears were realized: local authorities opened legal actions to put him in jail. He was charged with civil contempt for having failed to make child support payments to his son, Byron. In March 1962, when Byron reached the age of nineteen, East stopped sending the money. His lawyer, Harold Cubley, told him that he could do this and the law could not touch him as long as he stayed out of Mississippi.[94] When East returned to the state in July, no suits were filed against him, but within two weeks of Lynd's accusations, he received a citation demanding $450 plus lawyer's fees. At the 9 November hearing he asked his first wife, Katherine, if she had initiated the proceedings. She replied that she had not, and her attorney, William Harelson, had informed her that it was out of her hands.[95]

In 1959, Harelson had attempted unsuccessfully to inject the race issue into East's previous trial for failure to pay child support. Now he saw the opportunity for revenge. In a conference with Judge Tom Ott and Cubley, Harelson stated that he did not care if East paid the money—he wanted him sent to jail. The judge refused the request and the three men entered the courtroom. When East told the court that he could not pay $450, Harelson jumped from his seat and started shouting. He said that he had been too generous to East and now he intended to have him punished to the fullest extent of the law. As he spoke, Harelson clutched the arms of his chair so tightly, the color drained from his face, and his body trembled. Alarmed at this performance, East whispered to his lawyer, "That man is sick."[96] Cubley agreed and added that it was also "a matter of a difference in principles."[97] The judge ruled that East must pay $450 in child support and a $50 attorney's fee by 9 December 1962.

A very depressed East called John Griffin to report the outcome of his hearing. In desperation he asked Griffin to pray for him. Griffin agreed, saying that he and his whole family would make a novena to St. Jude, helper of the helpless. About three days later he telephoned Griffin to inquire if he had kept his promise to pray for him. Griffin replied that he and his family had remembered him every day. East snapped back, "Well, would you mind cutting it out. Things have gotten worse."[98] He could not resist a joke even at this low point.

East had not been exaggerating when he said that his situation had deteriorated. He discovered that a local detective agency had been hired to investigate him. For two months people had told him about the agency, but he refused to believe them until he learned that the woman living across the street from him had been employed to record the license numbers of all cars stopping at his home. Who had paid for the service and why remained a mystery, but he intended to stop this intrusion into his life. Angrily he offered the Risk Detective Agency and its client the opportunity to interview him and look at his files. He said that he saw no point in keeping people uninformed who expressed a genuine interest in his activities. Sarcastically, he requested them to call on him in the morning. "You see, as a general rule I take a nap in the afternoon."[99]

Problems with the United States Postal Service caused even more concern on his part. On 14 November 1962, he received notification that, owing to the irregular publishing schedule of his paper, the Post Office had decided to revoke his second-class mailing privileges unless he filed a petition for a hearing or resumed regular issuance.[100] East had until 15 December to comply with the government's order or face final withdrawal of his second-class permit. At this point, East believed that there was no end to his problems. He faced a possible jail sentence and continued legal harassment. A $25,000 reward was reportedly available to anyone willing to take care of him one way or the other. He owed his friends thousands of dollars. His health had deteriorated under all of this pressure. His third marriage had turned out to be a disaster. Now the Postal Service threatened to do what the racists had as yet not achieved: stop publication of the *Petal Paper*. It had not been a good year.

Considering his multifaceted predicament, East concluded that he must first deal with his financial problems. Prior to his court appearance, he wrote to Alfred Hassler, treasurer of the

Friends of P. D. East, asking for further assistance. Some help came within a few weeks.[101] To raise money he returned to public speaking. For most of 1962 he had rejected offers for such appearances because of his preoccupation with more pressing matters, but now he had to go despite physical and psychological ailments. The money from his speeches and the aid from Hassler enabled him to pay the $500 before the court's 9 December deadline.

After one speech at Vassar in early December, he stopped in Washington, D.C., on his way home. There he informed Arthur Schlesinger, Jr., of his numerous problems and his continued fear of being framed. Concerned for East's safety, Schlesinger sent him to talk with Burke Marshall, assistant attorney general for civil rights. Marshall had played an important role in the Meredith case and understood the situation in Mississippi quite well. He offered the swift assistance of the Justice Department should East be caught in a legal frame within federal jurisdiction.[102] Reassured somewhat, East returned to Hattiesburg.

With the prospects of jail reduced, East turned to his troubled newspaper. From August through early October 1962, he had tried to publish all back issues of the paper, but his legal problems brought this project to a halt. Since the Postal Service required him to resume regular publishing, he discontinued his futile catch-up effort and concentrated on the current numbers. The long overdue June through October issues never appeared as he skipped to November 1962. For reasons of economy the paper at this time became a monthly. He owed printer Aubrey Williams $1,800,[103] and he wanted to reduce that indebtedness if possible. In a letter to his subscribers, he apologized for the paper's sporadic appearance, explaining that his and his wife's constant illnesses had made work nearly impossible. Moreover, the money generally used to support the paper had gone toward medical bills. Not once did he mention his marital or legal problems. With the approval of his readers, East said he wanted to keep the *Petal Paper* alive for one very important reason. "The *Petal Paper*, however bad the journalism, however infrequently it appears, however [*sic*] all its faults, is a symbol of moderation (even sanity, sometimes) in an area where such symbols are all too limited."[104] Readers of the paper responded warmly to the letter and sent their encouragement to his efforts.

Although East now breathed a little easier, he knew that further difficulties lay ahead. Shortly after Christmas he journeyed to Texas to encourage his wife to file for divorce. She had stated quite clearly on numerous occasions that they could not live together as husband and wife. As a result, he wanted the marriage ended. He said that if she declined to take action he would do so in July 1963, under Mississippi law. On hearing his proposal, she indicated that she would turn the divorce proceedings into an ugly affair by filing a countersuit. East begged her not to do this because they and their children would be hurt terribly by the charges and countercharges. Elizabeth remained firm in her determination to fight a divorce despite her dislike for her husband. When East returned home, he wrote her that he was determined to file for divorce in July.[105]

As East noted to Geismar, it was a very strange situation. "She doesn't seem to want a divorce, just my ass out of the house, but she demanded I send money, so I just laugh and laugh."[106] Increasingly petty, Elizabeth declined to return his Lasker Civil Rights Award. East had requested it, and even promised to return it because Karen wanted to see what her father had won. Elizabeth nonetheless refused even to acknowledge his requests.[107]

To add to his woes, the charge of Communist affiliation arose once more. This time Roger Miller, the editor of the *Petal-Harvey Dispatch*, a small but virulently racist newspaper, made the accusation. Miller, noting that the ACLU had given East the Lasker Award and $1,000, claimed that the organization was a well-known Communist front. As evidence he quoted J. Edgar Hoover, the California Joint Fact-Finding Committee on Un-American Activities, and other unspecified legislative committees.[108] The implication was that East's association with the ACLU made him a Communist. The following week, Miller said the response to the "exposé" of East had been so resounding that he decided to carry a follow-up story. This time he accused Steve Allen of Communist leanings. East had reviewed Allen's latest book in his December issue and this provided sufficient reason for Miller's attack. According to the *Petal-Harvey Dispatch*, not only had Allen established a friendship with East, but he had also become a leading supporter of the National Committee for a Sane Nuclear Policy, another Communist front organization, according to Miller. For his proof, Miller relied on Myron Fagan's book, *Documentation of the Red and*

Fellow-Travelers in Hollywood and TV.[109]

When East read these two articles, paranoia gripped him as before. Such allegations of communism, he felt, invited a legal frame from the area's superpatriots. Anxiously, he corresponded with George Rundquist of the ACLU, John Griffin, Lillian Smith, Senator Paul Douglas, Aubrey Williams, Easton King, Maxwell Geismar, Burke Marshall, Arthur Schlesinger, Jr., and others. The ACLU asked Miller for equal space to defend itself, but he used the request as an opportunity to expand his attack. Schlesinger told East to have the *Petal-Harvey Dispatch* check with the Justice Department about the status of the ACLU.[110] East knew, however, that Miller would not bother to make this effort and, even if he did, he would not believe the government. In a letter to Max Geismar, East repeated his oft-expressed concern. "Frankly, I [*sic*] scared shitless of a legal frame—look at Clyde Kennard, or Bill Higgs. So who's next?"[111] His fears did not diminish for several months. Not until late March 1963 was he able to turn again to more immediate concerns.[112]

At that time East had to act quickly if the *Petal Paper* was to survive. Past efforts by financial supporters had kept the paper alive but never provided a firm economic basis. East hoped to remedy this problem by attracting new subscribers. He had obtained the mailing lists of two liberal magazines and intended to send promotional copies of the *Petal Paper* to all 2,000 addressees. The only stumbling block was a lack of money. His bank account totaled $37.33. To acquire the needed cash, he first contacted Milton Fine, a long-time supporter, and explained that he wanted a loan for $750. Of this sum, East earmarked $500 for bills and $250 for the promotional issue.[113] He promised to repay Fine with money received from the subscription drive, and if it failed to produce sufficient revenue, he hoped to use funds from speaking engagements. Thanks to the help of John Howard Griffin, he had signed with the Redpath Speakers Bureau. With its professional assistance, he believed he could raise his income substantially.[114] Fine trusted East, but did not have $750 to loan at this time.[115] Ethel Clyde ultimately provided East with the much-needed loan,[116] and the March 1963 promotional issue appeared as planned. In his plea for new readers, East combined humor with economic reality when he stated, "This promotional issue is being mailed to about 2,500 persons—those in addition to our regular 17, who get the paper each month. If the *Petal Paper* doesn't get additional subscribers, the editor will be dead."[117]

This special edition succeeded to a point. Money came in but far too slowly to be of immediate help. With this, East asked John Howard Griffin to write an appeal similar to the ones from Alfred Hassler and Harry Golden. He told his old friend, "It seems to me that if something doesn't break, I will."[118] Griffin, as usual, lent his assistance. In his letter, he emphasized the need to respond quickly: "The sad fact is that P. D. is living in his 'wall to wall' poverty physically ill and saddled with more problems than any man I know, and is about at the end of his tether."[119] Griffin asked each recipient of the appeal to support freedom of speech by contributing to East and the *Petal Paper*. Responses to Griffin's plea eased the pressure somewhat, allowing East to split the money between living expenses and his printer, Aubrey Williams, to whom he owed $2,500.[120]

With his financial worries relieved momentarily, East directed his attention to racist-inspired violence in Alabama. In April 1963, Martin Luther King and the Southern Christian Leadership Conference (SCLC) began a campaign in Birmingham to desegregate all public facilities, not just those involved with interstate trade, and to stop discrimination in hiring and promotion practices. The city was reputedly the most segregated in the nation. Blacks had practically no political power and little communication with the white community. To remedy this situation, the SCLC launched a series of sit-in demonstrations but local officials obtained an injunction to halt the protest. Since the order came from a state court, King decided to ignore its message. To emphasize his determination to disobey unjust laws, he participated in the next day's demonstration and was arrested. Upon his release a week later, local business leaders, concerned about the economic repercussions of the protests, met secretly with King and representatives from the black community in an effort to resolve the problems. When the negotiations proved fruitless, King decided to increase the pressure. He turned to young blacks to swell the ranks of those willing to go to jail.

Police Commissioner Eugene "Bull" Connor responded by having his men viciously attack the marchers. Using police dogs, cattle prods, high-pressure fire hoses, and nightsticks, local law enforcement officials sought to weaken the resolve of the demonstrators. In early May, with the crisis growing worse, business leaders promised substantial changes if the blacks would resume talking and suspend their activities. The SCLC agreed and the meetings began once more. After four days of discussion, blacks gained every goal they had sought. Angry white extremists, reputedly the KKK, tried to sabotage the agreement by bombing the home of King's brother and the motel used as the movement's headquarters. In response, blacks rioted throughout the night, but King managed to calm his followers and the plan went into operation. The policy of direct confrontation had succeeded.[121]

Pleased over the victories, East nonetheless decried the treatment meted out to black Americans. He felt shame and horror that members of his race had brutalized blacks as if they were the lowest form of life. "It is a sad thing, indeed, a pathetic thing, to see men, women, and children, all with guaranteed equal rights under the law of the land, have dogs turned loose on them for wanting to attempt to attain their rights."[122]

The violence in Alabama hit East on a personal level as well. At the height of the Birmingham turmoil, a friend of his, Bill Moore, intended to walk from Baltimore to Jackson, Mississippi, to ask Ross Barnett to ensure freedom for the state's blacks. To draw attention to his march, Moore wore signs protesting segregation. But he never made it to Mississippi. On 23 April 1963, outside of Altalla, Alabama, he was murdered. Members of CORE, the organization to which Moore belonged, and SNCC tried to complete the walk but failed when Alabama officials arrested them for breach of the peace.[123]

East expressed shock and anger over Moore's death. "Will there be any point in the death of others who may die before we come to our senses? The answer again is the same; there is no point in the death of anyone, except as God chooses—not man."[124] Responsibility for this tragedy, East believed, belonged to everyone who had not spoken out boldly on behalf of equal rights before this incident. The bulk of the blame, however, lay with Governor George Wallace. His inflammatory rhetoric condemning the federal government for trying to assure constitutional rights to everyone incited racists to take violent actions against the "enemies."[125]

As East grieved over the death of his friend, another of his allies was struck down. On 12 June 1963, Medgar Evers, Gulf

States field secretary of the NAACP, was murdered outside his home in Jackson, Mississippi. East opened his comments on the slaying by recalling that the first human lung transplant in the United States had occurred at the University of Mississippi Medical School in Jackson. He contrasted this remarkable breakthrough with Evers's death. Such events, he argued, represented one of Mississippi's paradoxes. Expanding on this theme, he quoted Senators Eastland and Stennis, Jackson's mayor, and the state's leading paper, the *Jackson Clarion-Leader*. All had expressed grief over the deplorable killing and voiced the wish that justice be done. East did not doubt the sincerity of these remarks, but he believed beyond any doubt that the past actions and statements of those cited led to Evers's murder. They might not have pulled the trigger, but they had certainly helped load the rifle. Both Stennis and Eastland had joined a group of eighteen southern senators who denounced President Kennedy's call for civil rights legislation. Mayor Allen Thompson had refused to establish a biracial committee to discuss racial discrimination and had not acted on numerous charges of police brutality against blacks and their allies. The *Clarion-Leader* had printed a piece on Evers's association with the left-wing American Veterans' Committee which had raised money to help him fight for equality. Declarations such as these fueled racial hatreds and implicitly sanctioned brutal actions on the part of white Mississippians to block efforts at integration. "This kind of blindness has loaded, does, and will load guns. The last one was aimed at Medgar Evers. That's true, but who can say where the next one will be aimed? At you? At me?"[126]

Reiterating the point he made on Bill Moore's death, East charged that although certain people carried more guilt than others, all Americans had to bear partial responsibility for this tragedy. For too long, he contended, people had remained complacent about the battle for equality. "In a very real sense it doesn't matter who pulled the trigger that took a human life on June 12th in Jackson—all of us share the blame, the guilt is that of us all."[127] He also remained pessimistic about the future. The bloodshed, in his opinion, would continue as long as whites felt that blacks demanded "special rights." Somehow, whites had to understand that blacks sought only what was rightfully theirs under the Constitution. "Before God, I cannot see that the Negro citizen wants anything more than equal rights—his rights under the law—his dignity as a human being, created in the image of His maker."[128]

East not only grieved for his friend, but became fearful once again for his own safety. As soon as he heard of Evers's slaying, he left Mississippi. He spent a week hiding in Louisiana and returned only when he ran out of money.[129] Griffin urged East to stay away longer and suggested that he visit Father Thomas Merton at the Abbey of Gethsemani in Trappist, Kentucky. The monks would provide him with room and board and moral support. East wrote Merton about this possibility. Merton encouraged him to come and promised to provide a "spiritual band-aid" for his troubled soul.[130] When East asked permission from the Father Abbot he joked that he was considering joining the Trappist order at Gethsemani but would do so only if he could have his weekends free. The abbot did not know whether to take East seriously or not, so he asked Griffin to explain this most unusual request.[131] Although East did not make the trip to Kentucky due to the distance, he remained good friends with Merton.

The summer brought other problems to East. In early July 1963, East again pleaded with his wife to initiate divorce proceedings and promised to do so himself if she failed to act. When she did not reply, he filed for divorce, charging her with desertion. When she learned of East's actions, she decided to extract financial satisfaction for what she considered abusive treatment.[132] East wanted to treat her fairly and asked John Griffin what he thought would be reasonable compensation. Griffin, with great delight, suggested, "I would send the lady about 50¢ each for the last three lays, and send her mother a quarter for each of them which I believe is the standard pimping fee."[133] The court, more generous than Griffin, ordered East to pay $1,000.[134] Max Geismar tried to comfort East after the divorce, but East rebuffed the effort. He told Geismar, "As long as I go around marrying sick wimmin [*sic*], I think I deserve what I get. I'm thinking of setting up a Marriage Bureau aimed at finding wives for enemies. I sure can pick 'em."[135] He added that the next time he contemplated marriage, he would insist that his prospective bride submit to a sanity hearing.

John Griffin had driven to Hattiesburg to be with East during the divorce trial. It had been several years since Griffin had stayed with his old friend in Hattiesburg, so he was unprepared for the hostility that local citizens expressed towards East. Several restaurants refused to serve the two friends and on the streets they received nothing but icy stares from passers-by. Griffin had never felt such hatred in all of his life.[136] Griffin was convinced that East, in the wake of the divorce and in the face of such public contempt, needed to get away from Mississippi for a while. He persuaded him to return to Texas for a short vacation.

While East visited the Griffins, another racist atrocity occurred, this time in Alabama. The federal courts had ordered Alabama schools to desegregate. Governor George Wallace promised to resist such requirements. He sent state troopers and eventually the National Guard to block the entrance of blacks. Local authorities resented Wallace's intrusion into a situation which they believed they could handle. Some even demanded that he desist. With tensions rising, President Kennedy federalized the Alabama guard and stopped Wallace's obstructionist efforts. The calm lasted only a few days. On Sunday, 15 September 1963, a bomb exploded in a black church in Birmingham, killing four young girls and injuring fourteen. Outraged blacks rioted throughout the next day. Just as East had blamed Wallace for the violence in the spring, Kennedy held the governor responsible for this latest incident. Kennedy declared bitterly, "It is regrettable that public disparagement of law and order has encouraged violence which has fallen on the innocent."[137]

When East and Griffin heard of the bombing, Griffin said that it was no longer a question of whether East wanted to remain outside Mississippi for a few weeks. The only question now was where he wanted to move. Racist-inspired violence had become commonplace in the South, and East's friends believed that he was a marked man in Mississippi. He already had a price on his head and, in this atmosphere, someone might be tempted to collect. A number of friends offered their homes to him either on a permanent basis or until he could find a suitable location of his own.[138]

East returned to Hattiesburg to begin the process of looking for a new home. He decided he needed to remain in the Deep South. "All human beings, I think, need roots, this being some measure of identification, of self and of surroundings. If I have roots, God help me, they're here."[139] The southern countryside, cities, and people were familiar to him, and he could not leave. The trauma of forced relocation would double if he left his native area. This need to remain in the Deep South caused him to reject Texas as a possibility. He ruled out Atlanta because of its large population. After much thought, he believed he had finally found the perfect location: Hammond, Louisiana. Hammond recommended itself to East for several reasons. With Southeast Louisiana State University located there, it might provide a good, liberal atmosphere. Also, he had several friends on the faculty, in particular, Lou Ballard. She had written numerous book reviews for the *Petal Paper* and had helped him prepare several grant proposals. East liked her very much and at one point in 1965 asked her to marry him, but she turned him down.[140] Just as he began to make plans for the move, he changed his mind. The Citizens' Council came to life in the community, and he said he did not want to trade one unbearable place for another. Depressed with this turn of events, he looked elsewhere.

Returning to his maps he started the search again. As he told his readers, "Did you ever have a like experience? I mean to have to move, absolutely have to do it, and with nowhere to go, except as you may locate on a map? It's a kind of lonely feeling."[141] One evening as he tried to relax the answer came to him. In the early 1960s, when he had spoken at Spring Hill College in Mobile, Alabama, a number of people from the nearby community of Fairhope had driven over to hear his lecture. The group had impressed him. He called Father Albert Foley at Spring Hill College to get more information about the town. Father Foley informed East that Fairhope might be the ideal location for his new home. It had started as a Single-Tax colony founded by Henry George. The second and third generation that now populated the village had retained some of that early spirit. East learned from a native that the community did not contain 6,000 liberals, but that practically everyone could tolerate differences of opinion. After talking with several other people, East decided that Fairhope would be his next home.[142]

Only one obstacle blocked his move—money. He could not afford to leave, even with his life in danger. Fiscal year 1963 had been another disaster for him. He lost $5,500.[143] John Griffin on his own initiative sent out another emergency appeal for funds. He stressed the terrible dangers that East confronted in Hattiesburg. He pleaded for money not only to keep the *Petal Paper* alive, but its editor as well.[144] People like Paul Douglas, Thomas Merton, and actor Robert Ryan responded immediately and enough money arrived from other sources to allow East to leave Mississippi for the last time in December 1963.

The move provided temporary relief. He found the atmosphere in Fairhope quite amiable. People even invited him into their homes, something that had not happened in Hattiesburg for several years. His isolation had ended, but another more subtle change occurred—one that he had neither planned nor desired. With his move to Fairhope, East became less a participant in the civil rights movement and more of an observer and commentator. From this position, East continued his attack on racism, but his comments and his example seemed to lose some of their effectiveness.

East's frustration with this new status emerged during the Summer Freedom Project of 1964. The Council of Federated Organizations (COFO), consisting mainly of SNCC and CORE members, launched a campaign to teach illiterate blacks to read and write, and to help them register to vote. Hundreds of idealistic white students from northern colleges descended on the South to carry out this mission. White Mississippians saw these youths as intruders, twentieth-century carpetbaggers. They responded with a campaign of terror and violence. Freedom workers were threatened, arrested, beaten, and killed. In all, there were eighty beatings, thirty-five burned churches, thirty dynamited homes, thirty-five shootings, and more than one thousand arrests.[145] The most appalling incident involved the brutal murder of three civil rights workers in Neshoba County, Mississippi. Despite such tactics, this children's crusade made significant progress in improving the lot of poor Mississippi blacks.[146] In July, these young workers received a great boost when President Lyndon B. Johnson signed into law the Civil Rights Act of 1964. It prohibited discrimination in hotels, restaurants, places of amusement, and in hiring practices, and it barred unequal application of voter registration tests and procedures. These advances were significant, but their cost was high.

East applauded the achievements of the Freedom Summer, but decried the violent reaction of white Mississippians. Of the many people responsible for violence, he held inconsistent southern politicians as the most important. He noted that Mississippi Governor Paul Johnson had stated upon taking office, "Hate, or prejudice, or ignorance will not lead Mississippi while I sit in the governor's chair."[147] Yet, shortly after the passage of the Civil Rights Act of 1964, Johnson advised Mississippi citizens not to comply with the law until it had been tested in court. Johnson had also joked that the letters NAACP stood for "niggers, alligators, apes, coons, possums."[148] East believed that unstable racists interpreted the governor's own ambivalence on racial issues as sanction for their most despicable crimes. It was frightening to East to think that, in his estimation, fifteen murderers walked free in Mississippi ready and willing to strike again. He closed his column with the plea, "God help us."[149]

His outrage and depression increased when a grand jury in Neshoba County failed to indict those accused in the slaying of the three young civil rights workers. The grand jury had instead attacked New York City and other major northern cities for their high crime rates. East responded,

> Hells bells! What has the crime rate in New York City, Chicago, or Podunk got to do with a specific murder in Neshoba County, Mississippi? Are we less guilty because someone else is guilty? I fail to see how we are. This attitude on our part is nothing less than an illness.[150]

What bothered East the most about the violence in Mississippi was the fact that he remained in Alabama and could do nothing to help those in trouble.

> I feel guilty as all hell for not being in Mississippi last summer. Insofar as I'm capable, I stood in the shoes of every person whose home was burned, fired on, and I stood in the shoes of every person beaten, of every person to whom an injustice was done. But I sat in the safety of Fairhope and *felt*, and that's all I did—*feel*. I didn't act.[151]

He wanted to be the P. D. East of a few years before, the Tom Joad of John Steinbeck's *Grapes of Wrath*. He wanted to be in the thick of every fight for justice and equality, but that was no longer possible. During the height of the turmoil, after the FBI unearthed the bodies of Michael Schwerner, James Chaney, and Andrew Goodman, East decided to go to Mississippi to help the Freedom Summer volunteers. On the eve of his departure, an old friend from Mississippi called and told him to stay away. "For God's sake, P. D., don't go into the state. You're a marked man in Mississippi."[152] East changed his mind reluctantly, saying that he had retreated into the shell of a coward: "I continue to feel guilty, to feel the want of courage necessary to act."[153]

East's exile from Mississippi had another and even more heart-rending consequence. It weakened temporarily his ties to his daughter, Karen. Afraid to return to Mississippi, he stayed away and saw her only when she traveled to Fairhope. In January 1965, Karen wanted her father to come to her twelfth birthday party, but he dared not attend. To make up for his absence, he telephoned her, but she still felt hurt. As her maternal grandmother, Tressie Porter, wrote to East, "She misses you, I know. And while I try to do what I can, there is a place I cannot fill."[154] Karen took her father's absences as a sign that he no longer loved her. As a result, she became indifferent toward him. Worried that Karen's apathy might trouble East, Tressie wrote to him begging his indulgence:

> I've always tried to strengthen the tie between the two of you, and actually her Mother has too. We both realize the need in her life for her father. The purpose of this letter is to ask you to be patient with her, and keep loving her.[155]

His love for Karen never wavered, and when she finally asked him to visit her, the situation became almost too painful to bear. In one letter she wrote, "I guess you think I'm being unfair to keep on asking you [to come]. But I love you, Daddy, and I want to see you like crazy. Can't you come? Maybe I *am* unfair and maybe selfish too. But I want to see you, Daddy. Please come!"[156] Despite such pleas, East regarded the trip back into Mississippi as too dangerous to undertake.[157]

East's depression over his separation from Karen and his distance from the civil rights movement diminished somewhat by late 1965. On 27 December, he married for the fourth and final time. His bride, Mary Cameron (Cammie) Plummer, a native of Mobile, met him at her parents' bookstore. At the time of their marriage, Cammie attended Wellesley College on a prestigious scholarship, but she gave this up and finished her degree at the University of South Alabama. Her entrance into East's life could not have come at a better time. As he wrote to a friend, "When I was forced to leave Hattiesburg, I was at loose ends, very restless, very lonely, until Cammie married me."[158] He described her as "the most wonderful woman I've ever known."[159] She filled a tremendous void in his life and the fact that she shared her husband's passionate concern for the rights of others made the relationship even more fulfilling.

East was nearly twice as old as Cammie but the age difference meant little to either of them. He called her his child bride or moppet, and enjoyed the good-natured kidding of his friends. When Jim Silver, by this time at the University of Notre Dame, suggested that Cammie visit him and his family in Indiana, even though East could not come, East replied, "You lecherous old bastard, I'm not about to send my child bride unless I'm there and well armed."[160]

Cammie also brought stability to East's life. She helped him reestablish contacts with his children. In early 1966, Byron and his wife, Nellwynne, paid a visit to the Easts in Fairhope. The reunion was a most pleasant occasion for all. In a thank-you note, Byron and his wife told East, "Our home is open to you anytime you can 'sneak' into Hattiesburg."[161] His ties with Karen grew even stronger as well. She now spent a considerable amount of time with her father.[162] Despite his wretched financial condition, East devoted much of his meager income to Karen's happiness and well-being. In March 1966, he purchased a piano for her and a few months later helped pay for braces on her teeth.[163] Because he, Cammie, and Karen enjoyed boating, East purchased a number of power boats over the next several years. His last and most expensive boat, which was 19 feet long with a 115 horsepower engine, cost nearly $2,000 when he bought it in 1968.[164] On each of her visits, Karen insisted on water skiing almost constantly. East willingly obliged her. He and Cammie also took her on vacation with them whenever they could afford to go. The most lavish gift he presented to Karen was a Fiat sports car. In 1969, when Karen turned sixteen, Tressie Porter could not afford to buy her granddaughter a car, so East, although still in desperate straits, assumed the debt.[165] He did not try merely to buy his daughter's affection. In addition to the many gifts, he gave her advice, someone to talk with, and, most of all, his love.

East's more satisfying domestic life in no way interfered with his stand on racial injustice. He never lost interest in what went on in his native state. Events there still affected him personally. Six months after passage of the 1965 Voting Rights Act a black friend, Vernon Dahmer, began to register large numbers of blacks. As head of the NAACP chapter in Hattiesburg, Dahmer went on a local radio station to publicize his campaign. On 10 January 1966, the morning after his speech, a group of white men fire-bombed his grocery store and his living quarters in the rear. Dahmer, burned grievously, managed to stumble out the front door and fire several shotgun blasts at the racists as they fled. The black leader survived for several days before he succumbed to severe injuries. In one of his last comments, he remarked, "I've been trying to get people to register to vote. People who don't vote are deadbeats on the state. . . . What happened to us [blacks] can happen to anyone, white or black."[166]

East echoed his friend's deathbed statement:

> I regret to appear so naive, but I'm at a loss to understand why men can't see that the murder of any single person is a direct threat to their own safety and well being. Why is it so hard to understand that the death of Vernon Dahmer threatens every single one of us? Perhaps we can't identify because Mr. Dahmer was a Negro and we aren't.[167]

The federal government shared East's concern and within three months the FBI charged fourteen white men with murder and arson. Despite well-publicized and successful benefit dinners to raise money for a defense fund, the men, one by one, found themselves convicted and sent to jail. These were the first white men pronounced guilty by an all-white jury for murdering a black man in Mississippi.[168] Such judgments, East felt, held out hope for the South.

Although East continued to print stories on Mississippi, he shifted his main focus to Alabama and Governor George Wallace. The governor made an excellent target for his barbed comments. In a letter to a South Dakota reader, he included a short poem about Wallace's supporters:

> A hillbilly farmer named Hollis
> Used possums and snakes for his solace
> His children had scales
> And prehensile tails
> And voted for Governor Wallace.[169]

East's criticisms of Wallace never ended. In the fall of 1966, Wallace, hoping to avoid further school desegregation, rejected $30 million in federal aid to Alabama's educational institutions. To replace the funds, the governor pledged to use $4 million in state money. Shocked, East lamented the adverse effect this would have on the state's children. He speculated that Wallace might try to raise the $26 million difference by selling passports to Yankees visiting Alabama. With "Little George" at the helm, Alabama had taken the lead in the race to total assdom.[170]

In April 1967, East voiced further contempt for Wallace's politics. Acting through his wife Lurleen, who had been elected governor the previous year, Wallace once again refused to cooperate with a federal court order to desegregate all Alabama schools. The ex-governor declared that only federal troops could enforce the law and, in the meantime, he would hire 500 state troopers to block any government attempt to place blacks in the state's all-white schools. Echoing Andrew Jackson, Lurleen Wallace shouted to an enthusiastic state legislature, "They have made their decree, now let them enforce it!"[171] Several days later a bomb exploded at the home of one of the federal judges who issued the order. The blast injured no one. Repeating his familiar refrain, East blamed the Wallaces for the violence:

> I am amazed at the short-sightedness of those clowns in Montgomery. It is rather apparent that they see no connection between the statements of our two governors and the act of violence directed at the Johnson home. This, I fear, is another act of irresponsible leadership. I also fear it is not the last irresponsible act we shall see.[172]

Most distressing to East was Wallace's candidacy for the presidency and the sympathetic chord it seemed to strike. Using humor to show his disgust for Wallace, he published his version of a campaign song to the tune of *Row, Row, Row Your Boat:*

> Work, work, work for George
> Help him win the race
> Merrily, merrily, merrily, merrily
> He'll keep them in their place.[173]

East found no humor in Wallace's choice for a running mate, General Curtis LeMay. As he wrote to John Griffin,

> It isn't enough that wallace [*sic*] should exploit the pent-up emotions felt by so many in the country, but now we can blow up all of Asia. If the American people are so goddamn stupid and scared as to elect this combination, then they might well deserve what they are in for.[174]

After the election, he felt relieved at Wallace's defeat, but lamented the governor's large vote total and the existence of ten million registered bigots in the United States.[175] Most frightening to East was his belief that "george wallace [sic] is far from being politically dead; he'll be with us and our political system for years to come, and therein lies one of my worst fears."[176]

Despite such condemnations, East's discussion of national race issues was spotty at best. He neglected to mention the Voting Rights Act of 1965 and the Selma marches, and paid scant attention to Watts. He did take a very strong position, however, in opposition to extremists on both sides in the struggle for equality. He was prompted to speak out on this issue when black militants started to play a more prominent role in the civil rights movement. James Meredith's June 1966 march from Memphis, Tennessee, to Jackson, Mississippi, acted as a catalyst for East. Meredith had intended to walk from Memphis to Jackson to prove to Mississippi blacks that they could go to the polls safely and vote. The march had hardly begun before a white man ambushed him, leaving him badly wounded. Members of CORE and SNCC decided that they would finish the march just as they had tried to do for Bill Moore. Mississippi whites meted out abusive and brutal treatment to the group until it reached its destination. During this march Stokely Carmichael and his supporters began to speak about black power. Carmichael told his listeners that blacks would not gain full equality until they asserted themselves physically. Dr. Martin Luther King cautioned blacks to remain nonviolent, but many turned to Carmichael out of disgust over their continued mistreatment at the hands of racist whites.[177]

The words Black Power frightened East. To him they meant that blacks claimed special rights—a claim that he saw as dangerous:

> All men have equal rights, with equal justice; no man, and I mean NO man has special rights. That's one problem now, the long standing special rights of the white, with the kind of injustice that goes with these rights. It would be stupid to switch from one evil to another.[178]

East foresaw serious problems arising from the split in the black movement between the moderates and the militants.[179] In the wake of riots in Chicago and Cleveland in 1966, he continued his argument that the threat of violence, or violence itself, could do nothing but harm to the movement. Although he easily understood what drove blacks to strike out against white society, he warned against physical force: "I understand that a person when he's held down, without hope, will make every attempt to remedy the situation, however I fear [violence] has done more harm to the man without hope than good."[180] He persisted in warning blacks against destructive behavior that would lead inevitably to white backlash. For East violence was not the answer:

> I do not believe violence is the answer to anything. Agitation, demonstration, and negotiation can provide the answers, but violence and rioting cannot. And the reaction of the whites is as foolish and useless as the militancy of the Negro.[181]

East wished that blacks would not act with the same degree of stupidity as many whites. Riots during the summer of 1967 in Detroit and Newark dispelled his hopes. When he watched television scenes of these disorders, he felt sad, distressed, and physically ill.[182] Whites and blacks had both gotten out of control and had to be stopped before they destroyed the very foundations of American society.[183] Although he showed his displeasure with blacks who engaged in violence, he remained totally sympathetic to their plight. "It grieves me deeply to think that people have to take to the streets, some of them to get killed, others to get hurt, in hopes of attaining those rights that should be granted freely and without any questions."[184] East made it quite clear that he favored, as he put it, the "Golden Mean," and opposed any extreme position whether to the right or to the left.[185]

A moderate in an increasingly militant atmosphere, East sensed that he had not kept abreast of the changing times. The acceptance of leaders like Stokely Carmichael and H. Rap Brown convinced him that his ideas about fairness and equality were quite outdated. "These are times when I feel like an ultraconservative."[186] Even when his friends told him that they too felt out of place, his sense of frustration and helplessness failed to diminish. John Griffin wrote to East describing his and Sarah Patton Boyle's alienation from the movement. He added, "I told her you felt pretty much the same way and I suppose most of us do. The goddamned racists—have won— white and black—they are triumphant."[187] Another of East's old friends, Jim Silver, felt estranged too. As he put it, "Black is not beautiful, nor is white."[188]

This new development in the racial situation baffled East completely. When he first involved himself in the fight for equal rights, he believed that good and evil were defined clearly; but this no longer held true. He still wanted to help black Americans as he had in the past, but he did not know how to accomplish the task.

> I find myself extremely depressed, as well as extremely frustrated. I feel that I am not doing anything to help people who need it. Help has to be in the form of far more than words, and all in God's earth I can offer are words.[189]

East not only had to deal with his growing feeling of irrelevance, but also with his increasingly bleak financial situation. In 1964 the paper lost $5,000, in 1965, $5,500, and in 1967, nearly $8,000.[190] By late 1968, his total indebtedness exceeded $25,000.[191] What income he had came from subscriptions and gifts from friends and supporters. On occasion, the Friends of P. D. East gave assistance but not as often nor on the scale of past donations.[192] As a result, he sent out at least two appeals for funds every year. Sometimes John Griffin wrote the letter, and if he did not, two of East's newer friends, Ethel Untermeyer and Roger Cowen, accepted the responsibility. East even sent out letters under his own signature or under Griffin's, often without Griffin's knowledge.[193] No matter who sent the appeal, it brought in less money each year as people tired of giving over an extended period. In part, this reluctance for some stemmed from the fact that East was no longer on the cutting edge of change. Other leaders seemed more effective in obtaining advances for black Americans. Some people began to question East's use of his funds.[194] Griffin got a number of complaints asking if he and East had set up a racket to defraud the unsuspecting. At this point Griffin suggested that East institute a new method for obtaining the necessary resources to keep the paper going. Unable or unwilling to develop any new ideas, East continued to mail appeals.[195] In June 1970, Griffin wrote to his old friend and asked him to refrain from using his name and letter of appeal without prior approval.[196] Griffin took this unpleasant action after a postal inspector interrogated him concerning his role in a possible mail fraud case involving East's constant solicitation of funds. East complied with his friend's wishes.

A number of loyal contributors helped keep the paper and East afloat, but they could not provide him with the necessary capital to establish a solid financial foundation. Instead, he lurched from one economic crisis to the next while going deeper into debt. His poverty restricted his travel so much that he rarely saw Griffin and lost contact with the Geismars. As he noted to a friend, "It's hell to be a charity case."[197] It was a hell he endured until his death.

Despite his desperate financial condition, East had an even more serious problem to handle, poor health. Prior to his move to Alabama he had been plagued with an ulcer, extremely painful headaches, acromegaly, and recurrent bouts of depression. His physician told him that he could gain relief from most of his ailments if he would relax and not remain so tense. East was unable to take his doctor's advice. The constant threat of bankruptcy and racial unrest kept him in turmoil. He wrote,

> I think they [ulcers] would act all right if people would stop being inhumane to each other. Conscious effort, pills, and whatever else I think of, don't seem able to stop my reacting to violence, and the only way to stop awareness of it is to find a deserted Island [*sic*] somewhere.[198]

Several physicians who subscribed to the *Petal Paper* supplied East with medicine that his doctor prescribed at cost or free. Throughout much of the 1960s, Dr. Ben Munson of Rapid City, South Dakota, sent tranquilizers, sinus tablets, and ulcer medicine. Dr. Margaret Wendell of New York City and several other physicians helped supplement Dr. Munson's shipments. Even with this assistance, East's monthly medical bills by the late 1960s averaged between $150 and $200.[199]

From 1965 until his death, East's ill health interfered constantly with his work schedule. For several months every year he contributed nothing new to his paper. He relied heavily on reprints of his old columns and the work of others. In the fall of 1970, his condition grew significantly worse.[200] His ulcer caused almost constant difficulties, and liver problems added to his woes. By early 1971, East could rarely put together an issue of the *Petal Paper* by himself. Roger Cowen, a friend he met through the paper, and Cammie assumed much of the burden. In April, East told his readers that tests during a recent hospital stay revealed that he had arthritis at the base of his skull. Combined with his sinus headaches, the pain was almost unbearable.[201] Through medication and treatments, the doctors gave him some relief from the discomfort, but within a month he went back to the hospital. He had grown extremely weak and the doctors feared that his ulcer might have hemorrhaged again. Tests showed that instead of ulcer problems he had become anemic. To remedy this condition, he received several blood transfusions, vitamins, and an iron-rich diet.[202] Recovery was a slow process, so Cammie edited the paper for May and June. East resumed his work in July, once his anemia had been brought under control, but he kept his work to a minimum.

Until December 1971, his condition remained stable, but the week before Christmas he grew exceptionally weak and entered the hospital. This time the blood transfusions and medication failed to alleviate the problem. Additional tests revealed severe liver failure, and he deteriorated rapidly. The doctors told Cammie East that they could not save him. It was merely a matter of time. Even then, when conscious, East never let his humor fail him. He and John Griffin had always argued about which of them suffered the most from illness, and East now concluded that he had won the debate. Just before lapsing into his final coma, he remarked to Cammie, "Ask Griffin if he can top this."[203] Within two days, on 31 December 1971, he was dead.

Notes

1 P. D. East to John Morsell, 17 January 1960, Box 30, P. D. East Papers, Mugar Memorial Library, Boston University. Hereafter cited as East Papers.

2 Wesley Maurer to Alfred Hassler, 20 December 1960, Box 52, East Papers.

3 P. D. East to Maxwell Geismar, no date, Box 93, Maxwell Geismar Papers, Mugar Memorial Library, Boston University. Hereafter cited as Geismar Papers.

4 P. D. East to Maxwell Geismar, no date, Box 93, Geismar Papers.

5 P. D. East to Maxwell Geismar, no date, Box 93, Geismar Papers.

6 *Billie Porter East vs. P. D. East*, Chancery Court of Lamar County, Mississippi, Number 5561, 28 June 1961, 1-2, Box 29, East Papers.

7 P. D. East to Maxwell Geismar, 23 April 1961, Box 28, East Papers.

8 Ibid.

9 Ibid.

10 Ibid.

11 Ibid.

12 Sarah Patton Boyle to P. D. East, 21 May 1961, Box 1, East Papers.

13 Ibid.

14 P. D. East to Maxwell Geismar, no date, Box 93, Geismar Papers.

[15] P. D. East to Maxwell Geismar, no date, Box 93, Geismar Papers.

[16] *Billie Porter East vs. P. D. East*, 2.

[17] P. D. East to Mr. and Mrs. Foster Hunt, 16 May 1961, Box 29, East Papers.

[18] P. D. East, "Statement of Plans for Trilby Cheek," Box 4, East Papers; P. D. East, *A Cock for Asclepius*, unpublished rough draft, Box 12, East Papers.

[19] P. D. East to Harry Golden, 29 June 1961, Box 2, East Papers. He might have added that his marital problems had complicated matters tremendously, since the letter was dated one day after his divorce.

[20] Harry Golden to P. D. East, 30 June 1961, Box 2, East Papers.

[21] P. D. East to Harry Golden, 1 July 1961, Box 2, East Papers.

[22] Harry Golden, "The P. D. East Fund," 24 August 1961, Box 2, East Papers.

[23] P. D. East, "Our Heart Weeps Over—a Misguided Mississippian," *Petal* (Miss.) *Paper*, 6 April 1961, 1.

[24] This discussion was taken primarily from Carl M. Brauer, *John F. Kennedy and the Second Reconstruction* (New York: Columbia University Press, 1977), 98–112; August Meier and Elliot Rudwick, *CORE: A Study in the Civil Rights Movement, 1942-1968* (New York: Oxford University Press, 1973), 135–210; Howard Zinn, *SNCC: The New Abolitionists* (Boston: Beacon Press, 1964), 40–61; Arthur M. Schlesinger, Jr., *Robert Kennedy and His Times* (Boston: Houghton Mifflin Company, 1978), 294–300.

[25] Walter Lord, *The Past That Would Not Die* (New York: Harper and Row, 1965), 84–85.

[26] P. D. East, *Petal* (Miss.) *Paper*, 13 July 1961, 1.

[27] P. D. East, *Petal* (Miss.) *Paper*, 24 August 1961, 1.

[28] P. D. East to third wife, 3 September 1961, Box 3, East Papers. The fictitious name Elizabeth will be used for East's third wife throughout the text. References to her in the notes will be to the "third wife."

[29] P. D. East to Maxwell Geismar, 1 October 1961, Box 30, Geismar Papers.

[30] Ibid.

[31] Third wife to P. D. East, 28 September 1961, Box 3, East Papers.

[32] Third wife to P. D. East, 30 September 1961, Box 3, East Papers.

[33] P. D. East to third wife, 8 September 1961, Box 3, East Papers.

[34] Billie Porter East to third wife, 22 October 1961, Box 3, East Papers; P. D. East to Billie Porter East, 27 November 1961, Box 29, East Papers.

[35] Billie Porter East to third wife, 22 October 1961, Box 3, East Papers.

[36] Billie Porter East to P. D. East, no date, Box 29, East Papers.

[37] P. D. East to Billie Porter East, 12 September 1961, Box 29, East Papers.

[38] P. D. East to Mary Heathcote, 31 October 1961, Box 42, East Papers.

[39] P. D. East to Irving J. Fain, 28 November 1961, Box 45, East Papers.

[40] Irving J. Fain to P. D. East, 7 December 1961, Box 45, East Papers.

[41] W. R. Innis to P. D. East, 20 December 1961, Box 45, East Papers.

[42] George E. Rundquist to P. D. East, 19 December 1961, Box 10, East Papers.

[43] New York Civil Liberties Union, "Press Release," 19 January 1962, Box 10, East Papers.

[44] P. D. East to Irving .J. Fain, 28 July 1962, Box 42, East Papers.

[45] John Howard Griffin to P. D. East, 7 February 1962, Box 2, East Papers; John Howard Griffin to P. D. East, 23 March 1962, Box 2, East Papers; P. D. East to Maxwell Geismar, 28 July 1962, Box 30, East Papers.

[46] Maxwell Geismar, to the author, 1 July 1977.

[47] P. D. East to Irving J. Fain, 28 July 1962, Box 42, East Papers.

[48] P. D. East to Ethel Clyde, 20 July 1962, Box 30, East Papers.

[49] P. D. East to Harry Golden, 19 February 1962, Box 2, East Papers.

[50] P. D. East to Steve Allen, 5 May 1962, Box 1, East Papers.

[51] P. D. East to Harry Golden, 19 February 1962, Box 2, East Papers.

[52] P. D. East to Steve Allen, 5 May 1962, Box 1, East Papers.

[53] Steve Allen to P. D. East, 8 May 1962, Box 1, East Papers.

[54] P. D. East to Irving J. Fain, 28 July 1962, Box 42, East Papers.

[55] P. D. East to Ben Munson, M.D., no date, Box 18, East Papers.

[56] P. D. East to Irving J. Fain, 28 July 1962, Box 42, East Papers.

[57] Norman Kaplan, M.D., to P. D. East, 12 July 1962, Box 27, East Papers.

[58] P. D. East to Maxwell Geismar, 28 July 1962, Box 21, East Papers; P. D. East to John Howard Griffin, 26 July 1962, Box 2, East Papers; P. D. East to Ethel Clyde, 20 July 1962, Box 30, East Papers; P. D. East to Irving J. Fain, 28 July 1962, Box 42, East Papers.

[59] John Howard Griffin to Maxwell Geismar, 10 August 1962, Geismar Papers.

[60] P. D. East to Ethel Clyde, 30 June 1962, Box 30, East Papers.

[61] Ethel Clyde to P. D. East, 2 July 1962, Box 30, East Papers.

[62] P. D. East to Mary Klopfer, 27 July 1962, Box 27, East Papers.

[63] P. D. East to Harry Golden, 28 July 1962, Box 2, East Papers.

[64] P. D. East to Irving J. Fain, 28 July 1962, Box 42, East Papers.

[65] P. D. East to John Howard Griffin, 18 August 1962, Box 2, East Papers.

[66] P. D. East, *Petal* (Miss.) *Paper*, 19 April 1962, 1.

[67] Brauer, *Second Reconstruction*, 181.

[68] Lord, *The Past*, 140.

[69] Ibid., 139.

[70] Richard Sherrill, *Gothic Politics in the Deep South: Stars of the New Confederacy* (New York: Ballantine Books, 1968), 200.

[71] Brauer, *Second Reconstruction*, 185.

[72] James Meredith, *Three Years in Mississippi* (Bloomington: Indiana University Press, 1966), 226.

[73] P. D. East, *Petal* (Miss.) *Paper*, 3 May 1962, 1.

[74] P. D. East to Arthur Schlesinger, Jr., 1 October 1962, Box 27, East Papers. He wrote practically the same letter to Senator Paul Douglas. P. D. East to Senator Paul Douglas, 1 October 1962, Box 27, East Papers.

[75] Arthur Schlesinger, Jr., to P. D. East, no date, Box 27, East Papers.

[76] P. D. East, *Petal* (Miss.) *Paper*, May 1964, 2.

[77] P. D. East to Friends, 21 October 1962, Box 30, East Papers.

[78] P. D. East, *Petal* (Miss.) *Paper*, May 1964, 2.

[79] P. D. East, "Letter from a Southern Editor," *The Independent*, April 1964, 5.

[80] P. D. East to Theron Lynd, 26 November 1962, Box 27, East Papers.

[81] P. D. East to Richard McLemore, 22 November 1963, Box 42, East Papers.

[82] Ibid.

[83] P. D. East to Maxwell Geismar, no date, Box 30, Geismar Papers.

[84] P. D. East to Friends, 21 October 1962, Box 30, Geismar Papers.

[85] Ibid.

[86] Ibid.

[87] P. D. East, *Petal* (Miss.) *Paper*, May 1962, 2.

[88] P. D. East to John Howard Griffin, 27 October 1962, Box 2, East Papers.

[89] P. D. East to Friends, 21 October 1962, Box 30, East Papers.

[90] Ibid.

[91] Maxwell Geismar to P. D. East, 21 October 1962, Box 21, East Papers.

[92] P. D. East to Maxwell Geismar, no date, Box 30, East Papers.

[93] Ibid.

[94] Harold Cubley to P. D. East, 5 December 1961, Box 30, East Papers.

[95] P. D. East to Friends, 12 November 1962, Box 30, East Papers. Katherine told her former husband the truth and the court supported her statement.

[96] Ibid.

[97] Ibid.

[98] John Howard Griffin to the author, 2 February 1976.

[99] P. D. East to Risk Detective Agency, 30 November 1962, Box 27, East Papers.

[100] Edwin Riley to P. D. East, 14 November 1962, Box 30, East Papers.

[101] P. D. East to John Howard Griffin, 27 October 1962, Box 30, East Papers.

[102] P. D. East to Richard McLemore, 22 November 1963, Box 42, East Papers.

[103] Aubrey Williams to Myron P. Berman, 3 January 1963, Box 6, East Papers.

104 P. D. East to Dear Friend, December 1962, Box 6, East Papers.

105 P. D. East to third wife, 3 January 1963, Box 3, East Papers.

106 P. D. East to Maxwell Geismar, 20 February 1963, Box 168, Geismar Papers.

107 P. D. East to third wife, 2 February 1963, Box 3, East Papers; P. D. East to third wife, 18 February 1963, Box 3, East Papers; Telegram from P. D. East to third wife, 24 June 1963, Box 3, East Papers.

108 Roger Miller, "Without Max," *Petal-Harvey Dispatch,* 3 January 1963, 1.

109 Roger Miller, "Without Max," *Petal-Harvey Dispatch,* 10 January 1963, 1.

110 Arthur Schlesinger, Jr., to P. D. East, 25 January 1963, Box 10, East Papers.

111 P. D. East to Maxwell Geismar, 26 February 1963, Box 168, Geismar Papers. As a lawyer, Higgs had been involved in the case to admit James Meredith to the University of Mississippi. The Jackson Police Department framed him on a charge of taking sexual liberties with a minor boy. The youth later admitted that the police had urged him to make the accusations. After Higgs left Mississippi to go to New York City to accept the Lasker Civil Rights Award in February 1963, he failed to return because of fear for his life. The state then found him guilty in absentia and later disbarred him from further law practice. James W. Silver, *Mississippi: The Closed Society* (New York: Harcourt, Brace and World, 1966), 96–98.

112 P. D. East to Maxwell Geismar, 20 March 1963, Box 168, Geismar Papers.

113 P. D. East to Milton Fine, 16 March 1963, Box 42, East Papers.

114 John Howard Griffin to P. D. East, 20 November 1962, Box 2, East Papers.

115 Milton Fine to P. D. East, 25 March 1963, Box 6, East Papers.

116 P. D. East to Ethel Clyde, 28 March 1963, Box 6, East Papers; P. D. East to John Howard Griffin, 20 April 1963, Box 27, East Papers.

117 P. D. East, *Petal* (Miss.) *Paper,* March 1963, 1.

118 P. D. East to John Howard Griffin, 20 April 1963, Box 27, East Papers.

119 John Howard Griffin, "Letter of Appeal," April 1963, Box 10, East Papers.

120 P. D. East to Harry Golden, 11 May 1963, Box 2, East Papers.

121 Brauer, *Second Reconstruction,* 230–39; Arthur I. Waskow, *From Race Riot to Sit-In, 1919 to the 1960s: A Study in the Connection Between Conflict and Violence* (Garden City, New York: Doubleday and Company, 1966), 233–36; Charles P. Roland, *The Improbable Era: The South Since World War II* (Lexington: University of Kentucky Press, 1975), 48–49; David J. Garrow,

Protest at Selma: Martin Luther King, Jr. and the Voting Rights Act of 1965 (New Haven: Yale University Press, 1978).

[122] P. D. East, *Petal* (Miss.) *Paper*, May 1963, 1.

[123] Zinn, *New Abolitionists*, 174–75.

[124] P. D. East, *Petal* (Miss.) *Paper*, May 1963, 1.

[125] Ibid.

[126] P. D. East, *Petal* (Miss.) *Paper*, June 1963, 1–2.

[127] Ibid.

[128] Ibid.

[129] P. D. East, "Look Back in Pain," undated text of speech given by East, 16, Box 54, East Papers; John Howard Griffin to William Boyers, 19 June 1963, Box 42, East Papers.

[130] Thomas Merton to P. D. East, 23 July 1963, Box 3, East Papers.

[131] John Howard Griffin to the author, 2 February 1976.

[132] The Reverend Paul Young to P. D. East, 7 September 1963, Box 3, East Papers.

[133] John Howard Griffin to P. D. East, 4 October 1963, Box 42, East Papers.

[134] Third wife to P. D. East, 21 November 1966, Box 22, East Papers.

[135] P. D. East to Maxwell Geismar, no date, Box 30, Geismar Papers.

[136] P. D. East to Richard McLemore, 22 November 1963, Box 42, East Papers; P. D. East, *Petal* (Miss.) *Paper*, May 1964, 2.

[137] Brauer, *Second Reconstruction*, 295.

[138] P. D. East, *Petal* (Miss.) *Paper*, May 1964, 2.

[139] P. D. East, *Petal* (Miss.) *Paper*, February 1965, 1.

[140] John Howard Griffin to P. D. East, 22 June 1965, Box 42, East Papers; Lou Ballard to P. D. East, 6 January 1965, Box 1, East Papers.

[141] P. D. East, *Petal* (Miss.) *Paper*, February 1965, 1.

[142] Ibid.

[143] East Publications Operating Statement Year 1963, Box 45, East Papers.

[144] John Howard Griffin to Friends, Fall 1969, Box 2, East Papers.

[145] Neal Peirce, *The Deep South States of America: People, Politics, and Power in the Seven Deep South States* (New York: W. W. Norton and Company, 1974), 182.

[146] Roland, *Improbable Era*, 50–51; Pat Watters and Reese Cleghorn, *Climbing Jacob's Ladder: The Arrival of Negroes in Southern Politics* (New York: Harcourt, Brace and World, 1967), 67–68; Steven F. Lawson, *Black Ballots: Voting Rights in the South, 1944–1969* (New York: Columbia University Press, 1976), 300–306.

[147] P. D. East, *Petal* (Miss.) *Paper*, November 1964, 1.

[148] Peirce, *Deep South States*, 183.

[149] P. D. East, *Petal* (Miss.) *Paper*, November 1964, 2.

[150] P. D. East, *Petal* (Miss.) *Paper*, January 1965, 1.

[151] Ibid., 2.

[152] Ibid.

153 Ibid.

154 Tressie Porter to P. D. East, 31 January 1965, Box 2, East Papers.

155 Tressie Porter to P. D. East, 11 September 1965, Box 34, East Papers.

156 Karen East to P. D. East, 21 November 1965, Box 34, East Papers.

157 P. D. East to Lewis Gott, 18 August 1964, Box 8, East Papers; P. D. East to Mr. Street, 23 March 1965, Box 48, East Papers; P. D. East to Lewis Gott, 16 August 1965, Box 28, East Papers; P. D. East to David, 20 January 1967, Box 21, East Papers. In a letter written to her father, Karen asked him to bring her back to Mississippi after her visit with him in Fairhope. She felt all the danger had passed. "My, gosh, I hate to hurt your pride, but I don't think anyone'd remember you." He still refused. Karen East to P. D. East, 17 December 1968, Box 35, East Papers.

158 P. D. East to Ben Munson, M.D., 3 September 1966, Box 25, East Papers.

159 P. D. East to Ann and Orrin Alfred, 30 September 1967, Box 24, East Papers.

160 P. D. East to James W. Silver, 10 January 1967, Box 21, East Papers.

161 Byron and Nellwynne East to P. D. East, no date, Box 17, East Papers.

162 By late 1965 and early 1966, although documentation is scarce, it seemed that Tressie Porter had assumed much of the responsibility for Karen's care. Tressie Porter to P. D. East, 8 July 1970, Box 51, East Papers.

163 Tressie Porter to P. D. East, no date, Box 21, East Papers.

164 P. D. East to Edward Warley, 9 April 1968, Box 35, East Papers. In late 1967, East tried to join the Fairhope Yacht Club but was turned down when several members objected to his membership. They charged him with being a Communist and feared he might try to integrate the club. East believed these few men were not representative of the community. P. D. East to Ben Munson, M.D., 26 February 1968, Box 23, East Papers. In a humorous vein, he sent a fake telegram to Aleksei Kosygin stating, "Infiltrated Pentagon and Cape Kennedy as instructed. Failed at Fairhope Yacht Club. Internal security too much for an expert." Telegram from P. D. East to Aleksei Kosygin, no date, Box 24, East Papers.

165 Karen East to P. D. East, 17 July 1969, Box 39, East Papers.

166 Quoted in Peirce, *Deep South States*, 184.

167 P. D. East, *Petal* (Miss.) *Paper*, June 1966, 1–2.

168 P. D. East, *Petal* (Miss.) *Paper*, April 1966, 1–2; P. D. East, *Petal* (Miss.) *Paper*, March 1968, 1.

169 P. D. East to Ben Munson, M.D., 20 September 1966, Box 23, East Papers.

170 P. D. East, *Petal* (Miss.) *Paper*, October 1966, 1–2.

[171] Sherrill, *Gothic Politics,* 347.

[172] P. D. East, *Petal* (Miss.) *Paper,* April 1967, 1.

[173] P. D. East, *Petal* (Miss.) *Paper,* January 1968, 2.

[174] P. D. East to John Howard Griffin, 3 October 1968, Box 23, East Papers.

[175] P. D. East to Al Woodbury, 11 December 1968, Box 35, East Papers.

[176] P. D. East, *Petal* (Miss.) *Paper,* November 1968, 1.

[177] Pat Watters, *Down to Now: Reflections on the Southern Civil Rights Movement* (New York: Pantheon Books, 1971), 340–55; Meier and Rudwick, *CORE: A Study,* 374–404; Stokely Carmichael and Charles V. Hamilton, *Black Power: The Politics of Liberation in America* (New York: Random House, 1967).

[178] P. D. East, *Petal* (Miss.) *Paper,* July 1965, 2.

[179] Ibid., 1.

[180] P. D. East, *Petal* (Miss.) *Paper,* July 1967, 1.

[181] P. D. East, *Petal* (Miss.) *Paper,* August 1966, 1.

[182] P. D. East, *Petal* (Miss.) *Paper,* July 1967, 1.

[183] Ibid.

[184] P. D. East to Helen Chase, 26 April 1968, Box 23, East Papers.

[185] P. D. East to James W. Silver, 4 April 1966, Box 48, East Papers.

[186] P. D. East to Sandy, 12 June 1968, Box 23, East Papers.

[187] John Howard Griffin to P. D. East, 15 January 1968, Box 24, East Papers.

[188] James W. Silver to the author, 29 June 1977.

[189] P. D. East to Gretchen Rudnick, 28 July 1967, Box 42, East Papers.

[190] East Publications Operating Statements Years 1964, 1965, 1967, Box 45, East Papers.

[191] P. D. East to James B. Ames, 21 December 1968, Box 45, East Papers.

[192] Alfred Hassler to P. D. East, 26 June 1970, Box 52, East Papers.

[193] John Howard Griffin to P. D. East, 1 June 1970, Box 48, East Papers.

[194] Maxwell Geismar to the author, 1 July 1977; John Howard Griffin to P. D. East, 10 July 1967, Box 28, East Papers.

[195] East had given up on using his novel as an additional source of income after numerous publishers turned it down. He also tried to sell his library but this failed to provide any revenue.

[196] John Howard Griffin to P. D. East, 1 June 1970, Box 48, East Papers.

[197] P. D. East to Maxwell Geismar, no date, Box 22, East Papers.

[198] P. D. East to Carol Brown, 26 April 1968, Box 23, East Papers.

[199] P. D. East and John Howard Griffin, appeal for funds, 1966, Box 45, East Papers.

[200] P. D. East, *Petal* (Miss.) *Paper,* January 1971, 1.

[201] P. D. East, *Petal* (Miss.) *Paper,* April 1971, 1.

202 Cammie East, *Petal* (Miss.) *Paper,* May 1971, 1.
203 John Howard Griffin to the author, 2 February 1976.

7

Epilogue

The problems P. D. East faced as a result of his support of
civil rights were no different than those experienced by other
southern liberals. During Senate hearings, Senator James O.
Eastland branded Aubrey Williams and Virginia Durr Communists. Both survived the accusations, but their lives became
more difficult as increased social isolation and economic pressure were brought to bear. Lillian Smith, though economically
secure, found herself isolated as a result of her criticism of
southern race relations. Professor James W. Silver of the University of Mississippi harbored a persistent fear that he would
lose his job because of his liberal stance on racial matters. East's
good friends Easton King and John Howard Griffin were
frequently targets of KKK, CCA, or police harassment. Academicians, religious leaders, journalists—anyone who dared oppose
the South's prevailing attitudes on race—could not escape the
wrath of their bigoted neighbors. They all paid a price for their
convictions.

Of all these people, East was one of those least capable of
fighting and surviving racist onslaughts. His economic and
social status were partially responsible. He never gained any
measure of financial security. The *Petal Paper* failed to make
much money even before he spoke out on behalf of civil rights,
but with no other source of income, he was totally dependent
on the paper's meager profits. This made him especially vulnerable to the CCA's economic boycotts. One other factor contributed to his financial woes. East had an extremely poor education, and he did little to improve himself. For example, he had
a remarkable sense of humor. Maxwell Geismar compared him

favorably to Mark Twain, but East failed to develop this natural gift. As a result, his writing was never as polished as that of most liberal southern journalists and therefore never as marketable.[1] Small weekly newspapers are at best an economic gamble, and East lost. His humble background proved a further handicap as it placed him outside the socially prominent class. It made his struggle for success and acceptance extremely difficult, if not impossible. By contrast, journalists such as Mark Ethridge and Ralph McGill had the wealth and prestige of large newspapers to support them. Jonathan Daniels, Hodding Carter, and Lillian Smith enjoyed comfortable incomes and privileged social status which insulated them in part from the worst excesses of their racist opponents. East clearly labored under distinctly different conditions than practically all other southern liberals.

As such, East was a unique figure because he did not fit the socioeconomic and educational mold of the typical southern liberal. Most of these people had something or someone to rely upon for support—money, social status, organizational affiliation, or family. P. D. had none of these. His few friends lived a considerable distance from him, and this made for a very lonely existence. In fact, one of his best friends, Maxwell Geismar, called him the loner of the civil rights movement.[2] When the economic pressure was applied and social ostracism came, he had to deal with much of this on his own, and he lived at best on the brink of economic and psychological disaster.[3]

Despite these hardships, some liberals, particularly those in the North, lamented that East had not been more directly involved in the civil rights movement.[4] There was some truth to these charges as East's role centered mainly on editing and publishing his newspaper. He never participated in any march, demonstration, or sit-in, and he failed to become a political party activist pressuring politicians to support legislation to end racial injustice. Even East, in one of his last editorials, voiced concern that he had not brought about more far-reaching and permanent changes in his eighteen-year fight for justice and equality. Mississippi still elected James O. Eastland to the Senate and Alabama continued to put George Wallace in the governor's chair. He recognized that although the lot of black Americans had improved, it fell far short of full social and legal justice. There was still much to do.

East might have done more, especially in the late 1960s, but given his background, his unrelenting personal problems, and the climate of fear and violence that prevailed in the South, his slowly-developing stance in favor of racial equality was extraordinary. It took great courage for him just to speak out. In doing so, he showed southern blacks that not all whites were their enemies[5] and gave courage to other white liberals. His friends in both groups emphasized that the mere presence of his liberal paper in the Deep South gave hope to those in despair. In November 1962, when East reduced the frequency of the paper to a monthly, Sarah Patton Boyle wrote him,

> What I'm trying to say is that the *Petal Paper* has given hue, life, and meaning to a struggle which without it would have been a very grim and desolate affair. Your personality and the sheet which reflects it has made a contribution to us all which is very tangible and immense. I think it is not really the frequency of the publication, but *the fact that it exists* which matters most.[6]

Virginia Durr added her support,

> I think just you being here is the important thing. The fight of the Negroes is our fight too, but so few whites tell them so. It doesn't make any difference how you say it, or whether you are good or bad or funny or not funny ... just the fact you made a decision and have stuck to it is the main thing people want to hear and to hear it gives them hope.[7]

Even after he moved from Mississippi people still had words of praise for East, although not as frequently as before. One reader remarked, "... it is not too far-fetched, for a Christian, to believe that a lot of the 'doors that have opened' in the South in recent years have opened *because of you*, even if they're not the doors of Petal or Fairhope or of the people you know."[8]

It is difficult to say what caused East to speak out. For many southern liberals there were identifiable rationales for their actions—religious beliefs, a strong sense of justice, a deep sense of compassion, to name but a few. For East the motivating forces were not so clear. His friends spoke frequently of his courage, his dedication to justice, his strong moral conscience, and his devotion to fairness.[9] All were certainly evident, but he was too complex an individual to be categorized so easily. There was also a consistent pattern of rebellion in East that held him in its grip for most of his life. He rebelled against his mother's religious and racial beliefs, Jesse Wild's dishonesty, school authorities, the army, and the racial attitudes of the South. He did not like to be told how to behave or think, whether by his mother or the CCA.

Alongside this rebellious streak ran a need to be accepted by others. Such tendencies need not be contradictory, but in East they were. At times they created extreme psychological pain for him. He wanted acceptance but on his terms. Given the racial situation in the South and East's commitment to fairness for all, such a desire was impossible. His rebellious nature was too strong to overcome. When he had to choose between being accepted or following his conscience, his beliefs held him captive. He could not do otherwise. East did not rebel just for the sake of being difficult. It went much deeper than that. He was a rebel with a cause—social justice.

In working toward that end he made a significant contribution as both a symbol and a participant. He acted in the tradition of a dedicated reformer and racial liberal, whether he consciously recognized the fact or not. People such as East cared for their ideals so much that they accepted ridicule, persecution, and physical danger. As one political commentator remarked, the civil rights acts of the 1960s were possible because countless people made personal sacrifices and even gave their lives. Only the blood and sweat of martyrs forced the politicians to act.[10]

Notes

[1] Maxwell Geismar to the author, 1 July 1977.
[2] Ibid.
[3] John Howard Griffin to P. D. East, 12 April 1960, Box 2, P. D. East Papers, Mugar Memorial Library, Boston University. Hereafter cited as East Papers.
[4] Maxwell Geismar to the author, 1 July 1977.
[5] His numerous speaking engagements at Dillard University, an all-black school, and the financial support provided by Roy Wilkins and the NAACP, demonstrated that blacks respected and appreciated his efforts on behalf of civil rights.
[6] Sarah Patton Boyle to P. D. East, 26 August 1962, Box 1, East Papers.
[7] Virginia Durr to P. D. East, no date, Box 1, East Papers.
[8] Joan Waitkevicz to P. D. East, 10 August 1967, Box 28, East Papers.
[9] Maxwell Geismar to the author, 1 July 1977; James W. Silver to the author, 29 June 1977; John Howard Griffin to the author, 2 February 1976.
[10] Garry Wills, "Feminists and Other Useful Fanatics," *Harper's*, June 1976, 35–42.

Selected Bibliography

Primary Sources

Boston, Mass. Boston University. Maxwell Geismar Papers.

Boston, Mass. Boston University. P. D. East Papers.

East, P. D. *Editorial Reprints from the Petal Paper and Personal Comments.* Pascagoula, Mississippi: By the Author, 1957.

_____. "How to be a Man of Distinction." *Harper's,* January 1959, 12–18.

_____. "Letter from a Southern Editor." *The Independent,* April 1964, 5, 8.

_____. *The Magnolia Jungle: The Life, Times and Education of a Southern Editor.* New York: Simon and Schuster, 1960.

_____. "The South, Collectively, Is a Patient Most Ill." *Vital Speeches,* 15 May 1957, 476–79.

Fischer, John to author. 29 June 1977.

Geismar, Maxwell to author. 1 July 1977.

Griffin, John Howard to author. 2 February 1976.

Griffin, John Howard. Taped response to questions submitted by the author. Fort Worth, Texas. 6 December 1976.

McMillen, Neil R. to author. 5 August 1977.

Petal (Miss.) *Paper,* 19 November 1953–January 1972.

Silver, James W. to author. 29 June 1977.

Wynes, Charles E., ed. *Forgotten Voices: Dissenting Southerners in an Age of Conformity.* Baton Rouge: Louisiana State University Press, 1967.

Secondary Sources

Abrams, Richard. "Woodrow Wilson and the Southern Congressmen, 1913–1916." *Journal of Southern History* 22 (November 1956): 417–37.

Ayers, H. Brandt, and Naylor, Thomas H., eds. *You Can't Eat Magnolias.* New York: McGraw-Hill Book Company, 1972.

Bailey, Hugh C. *Liberalism in the New South: Southern Social Reformers and the Progressive Movement.* Coral Gables, Florida: University of Miami Press, 1969.

Bailey, Kenneth K. *Southern White Protestantism in the Twentieth Century.* New York: Harper and Row, 1964.

Bartley, Numan V. *The Rise of Massive Resistance: Race and Politics in the South During the 1950's.* Baton Rouge: Louisiana State University Press, 1969.

Bartley, Numan V., and Graham, Hugh D. *Southern Politics and the Second Reconstruction.* Baltimore: Johns Hopkins Press, 1975.

Bates, Daisy. *The Long Shadow of Little Rock: A Memoir.* New York: McKay, 1962.

Berglund, Abraham, Starnes, George T., and Uyuer, Frank T. de. *Labor in the Industrial South: A Survey of Wages and Living Conditions in Three Major Industries of the New South.* Charlottesville: University of Virginia Press, 1930.

Berkman, Dave. "East of the South." *The Realist,* December 1961, 20–22.

Billington, Monroe Lee. *The Political South in the Twentieth Century.* New York: Charles Scribner's Sons, 1975.

Blumer, Herbert. "The Future of the Color Line." In *The South in Continuity and Change,* 322–36. Edited by John C. McKinney and Edgar T. Thompson. Durham, North Carolina: Duke University Press, 1965.

Brandfon, Robert L., ed. *The American South in the Twentieth Century.* New York: Thomas Y. Crowell, 1967.

Brauer, Carl M. *John F. Kennedy and the Second Reconstruction.* New York: Columbia University Press, 1977.

Campbell, Will D. *Brother to a Dragonfly.* New York: Seabury Press, 1977.

Capeci, Dominic J., Jr. "From Harlem to Montgomery: The Bus Boycotts and the Leadership of Adam Clayton Powell, Jr., and Martin Luther King, Jr." *Historian* 41 (August 1979): 721–37.

Carmichael, Stokely, and Hamilton, Charles V. *Black Power: The Politics of Liberation in America.* New York: Random House, 1967.

Carter, Hodding, III. *The South Strikes Back.* Garden City, New York: Doubleday and Company, 1959.

Cash, W. J. *The Mind of the South.* New York: Alfred A Knopf, 1941.

Chafe, William H. *Civilities and Civil Rights: Greensboro, North Carolina, and the Black Struggle for Freedom.* New York: Oxford University Press, 1980.

————. "The Negro and Populism: A Kansas Case Study." *Journal of Southern History* 34 (August 1968): 400–416.

Clark, Norman H. *Deliver Us from Evil: An Interpretation of American Prohibition.* New York: W. W. Norton and Company, 1976.

Clark, Thomas D. *The Emerging South.* New York: Oxford University Press, 1968.

Clark, Thomas D., and Kirwan, Albert D. *The South Since Appomattox: A Century of Regional Change.* New York: Oxford University Press, 1967.

Cole, Wayne S. "America First and the South, 1940–1941." *Journal of Southern History* 22 (February 1956): 36–47.

Dabbs, James McBride. *Who Speaks for the South?* New York: Funk and Wagnalls Company, 1964.

Daniel, Pete. *The Shadow of Slavery: Peonage in the South, 1901–1969.* Urbana: University of Illinois Press, 1972.

Degler, Carl. "The Peculiar Dissent of the Nineteenth-Century South." In *Dissent: Explorations in the History of American Radicalism,* 109–35. Edited by Alfred F. Young. DeKalb: Northern Illinois University Press, 1968.

_____. *The Other South: Southern Dissenters in the Nineteenth Century.* New York: Harper and Row, 1974.

Doherty, Herbert J., Jr. "Voices of Protest from the New South, 1875–1910." *Mississippi Valley Historical Review* 42 (June 1955): 45–66.

Dollard, John. *Caste and Class in a Southern Town.* New York: Doubleday and Company, 1939.

Dykeman, Wilma, and Stokely, James. *Neither Black Nor White.* New York: Rinehart and Company, 1957.

_____. *Seeds of Southern Change: The Life of Will Alexander.* Chicago: University of Chicago Press, 1962.

Eagles, Charles W. *Jonathan Daniels and Race Relations: The Evolution of a Southern Liberal.* Knoxville: University of Tennessee Press, 1982.

Egerton, John. *A Mind to Stay Here: Profiles from the South.* New York: Macmillan Company, 1970.

Ekirch, Arthur A. *The Civilian and the Military.* Colorado Springs: Ralph Myles Publishers, 1972.

Ellerbrake, Richard. "Prophet in a Magnolia Jungle." *Youth,* 14 February 1960, 12–17.

Faulkner, William. *Light in August.* New York: Random House, Vintage Books, 1972.

Fichter, Joseph H., and Maddox, George L. "Religion in the South, Old and New." In *The South in Continuity and Change,* 359–83. Edited by John C. McKinney and Edgar T. Thompson. Durham, North Carolina: Duke University Press, 1965.

Filler, Louis. *A Dictionary of American Social Reform.* New York: Philosophical Library, 1963.

Fortenberry, Charles, and Abney, F. Glenn. "Mississippi: Unreconstructed and Unredeemed." In *The Changing Politics of the South,* 472–524. Edited by William C. Havard. Baton Rouge: Louisiana State University Press, 1972.

Franklin, John Hope. *The Militant South, 1800–1861.* Cambridge: Harvard University Press, 1956.

Frederickson, George M. *The Black Image in the White Mind: The Debate on Afro-American Character and Destiny, 1817–1914.* New York: Harper and Row, 1971.

Freidel, Frank. "The Conservative South." In *The South and the Sectional Image: The Sectional Theme Since Reconstruction,* 98–116. Edited by Dewey W. Grantham. New York: Harper and Row, 1967.

Gaston, Paul M. *The New South Creed: A Study in Southern Myth-making.* New York: Alfred A. Knopf, 1970.

Gerster, Patrick, and Cords, Nicholas, eds. *Myth and Southern History.* Chicago: Rand McNally College Publishing Company, 1974.

Goodwyn, Lawrence. *Democratic Promise: The Populist Moment in America.* New York: Oxford University Press, 1976.

Grantham, Dewey W. *The Democratic South.* Athens: University of Georgia Press, 1963.

————. "The Progressive Movement and the Negro." *South Atlantic Quarterly* 54 (October 1955): 461–77.

Griffin, Clyde S. *The Ferment of Reform, 1830–1860.* New York: Thomas Y. Crowell, 1967.

Griffin, John Howard. *Black Like Me.* New York: New American Library, 1960.

Hackney, Sheldon, ed. *Populism: The Critical Issues.* Boston: Little, Brown and Company, 1971.

Hall, Jacquelyn Dowd. *Revolt Against Chivalry: Jessie Daniel Ames and the Women's Campaign Against Lynching.* New York: Columbia University Press, 1979.

Hassler, Alfred. "South by East." *Fellowship,* November 1956, 14–15.

Hemphill, Paul. *The Good Old Boys.* New York: Simon and Schuster, 1974.

Higham, John. *Strangers in the Land: Patterns of American Nativism, 1860–1925.* New York: Atheneum, 1963.

Hill, Samuel S., Jr. *Southern Churches in Crisis.* New York: Holt, Rinehart and Winston, 1966.

————. "The South's Two Cultures." In *Religion and the Solid South,* 24–56. Edited by Samuel S. Hill, Jr. New York: Abingdon Press, 1972.

Hofstadter, Richard. *The Age of Reform: From Bryan to F.D.R.* New York: Random House, Vintage Books, 1955.

Huckaby, Elizabeth. *Crisis at Central High: Little Rock, 1957–1959.* Baton Rouge: Louisiana State University Press, 1980.

Johnson, Guion Griffis. "The Ideology of White Supremacy." In *The South and the Sectional Image: The Sectional Theme Since Reconstruction,* 56–78. Edited by Dewey W. Grantham. New York: Harper and Row, 1967.

Jordon, Winthrop D. *White Over Black: American Attitudes Towards the Negro, 1550-1812.* Chapel Hill: University of North Carolina Press, 1968.

Kellogg, Charles Flint. *NAACP: A History of the National Association for the Advancement of Colored People, 1909-1916.* Baltimore: Johns Hopkins Press, 1967.

Key, V. O., Jr. *Southern Politics in State and Nation.* New York: Random House, 1949.

Killian, Lewis M. *White Southerners.* New York: Random House, 1970.

King, Martin Luther, Jr. *Stride Toward Freedom: The Montgomery Story.* New York: Harper and Row, 1958.

Kirby, Jack Temple. *Darkness at the Dawning.* New York: J. B. Lippincott Company, 1972.

Kluger, Richard. *Simple Justice: The History of Brown v. Board of Education and Black America's Struggle for Equality.* New York: Alfred A. Knopf, 1976.

Krueger, Thomas. *And Promises to Keep: The Southern Conference for Human Welfare.* Nashville: Vanderbilt University Press, 1967.

Kusmer, Kenneth. "The Functions of Organized Charity in the Progressive Era." *Journal of American History* 60 (December 1973): 657-78.

Lasch, Christopher. *The New Radicalism in America, 1889-1963: The Intellectual as a Social Type.* New York: Random House, Vintage Books, 1965.

Lash, Joseph P. *Eleanor and Franklin.* New York: W. W. Norton and Company, 1971.

Lawson, Steven F. *Black Ballots: Voting Rights in the South, 1944-1969.* New York: Columbia University Press, 1976.

Levy, Leonard W. *Jefferson and Civil Liberties: The Darker Side.* Cambridge: Harvard University Press, 1963.

Link, Arthur S. "The South and the New Freedom." *The American Scholar* 20 (Summer 1951): 314-24.

Link, Arthur S., and Patrick, Rembert W., eds. *Writing Southern History: Essays in Historiography in Honor of Fletcher M. Green.* Baton Rouge: Louisiana State University Press, 1965.

Lomax, Almena. "Some of the Differences Between Being White and Being Colored, Boy!" *Los Angeles Tribune,* 12 January 1957, 12.

Lomax, Louis E. *The Negro Revolt.* New York: New American Library, 1962.

Lord, Walter. *The Past That Would Not Die.* New York: Harper and Row, 1965.

McGill, Ralph. *The South and the Southerner.* Boston: Little, Brown and Company, 1959.

McMillen, Neil R. *The Citizens' Council: Organized Resistance to the*

Second Reconstruction, 1954-1964. Urbana: University of Illinois Press, 1971.

McPherson, James. *The Abolitionist Legacy: From Reconstruction to the NAACP.* Princeton: Princeton University Press, 1975.

————. *The Struggle for Equality: Abolitionists and the Negro in the Civil War and Reconstruction.* Princeton: Princeton University Press, 1964.

Mangum, Charles S., Jr. *The Legal Status of the Negro.* Chapel Hill: University of North Carolina Press, 1940.

Marshall, Ray. *Labor in the South.* Cambridge: Harvard University Press, 1967.

Mason, Philip. *Race Relations.* New York: Oxford University Press, 1970.

May, Robert E. "Dixie's Martial Image: A Continuing Historiographical Enigma." *Historian* 40 (February 1978): 213-34.

Meier, August, and Rudwick, Elliot. *CORE: A Study in the Civil Rights Movement, 1942-1968.* New York: Oxford University Press, 1973.

Meredith, James. *Three Years in Mississippi.* Bloomington: Indiana University Press, 1966.

Moody, Anne. *Coming of Age in Mississippi.* New York: Dell Publishing Company, 1968.

Morgan, Edmund S. *American Slavery American Freedom: The Ordeal of Colonial Virginia.* New York: W. W. Norton and Company, 1975.

Morris, Willie. *Good Old Boy: A Delta Boyhood.* New York: Harper and Row, 1971.

————. *North Toward Home.* Boston: Houghton Mifflin Company, 1967.

Mowry, George E. *Another Look at the Twentieth-Century South.* Baton Rouge: Louisiana State University Press, 1973.

Muse, Benjamin. *The American Negro Revolution: From Nonviolence to Black Power.* New York: Citadel Press, 1960.

Newby, I. A. *The South: A History.* New York: Holt, Rinehart and Winston, 1978.

Odum, Howard W. *An American Epoch: Southern Portraiture in the National Picture.* New York: Henry Holt, 1930.

Osterweis, Rollin G. *Romanticism and Nationalism in the Old South.* New Haven: Yale University Press, 1949.

Patterson, James T. *Congressional Conservatism and the New Deal.* Lexington: University of Kentucky Press, 1967.

Peirce, Neal R. *The Deep South States of America: People, Politics, and Power in the Seven Deep South States.* New York: W. W. Norton and Company, 1974.

Perry, Lewis. *Radical Abolitionism: Anarchy and the Government of God in Antislavery Thought.* Ithaca: Cornell University Press, 1973.

Raines, Howell. *My Soul is Rested: Movement Days in the Deep South Remembered.* New York: G. P. Putnam's Sons, 1977.

Reed, John S. *The Enduring South: Subcultural Persistence in Mass Society.* Lexington, Massachusetts: D. C. Heath and Company, 1972.

Roland, Charles P. *The Improbable Era: The South Since World War II.* Lexington: University of Kentucky Press, 1975.

Roy, Donald F. "Change and Resistance to Change in the Southern Labor Movement." In *The South in Continuity and Change,* 225–47. Edited by John C. McKinney and Edgar T. Thompson. Durham, North Carolina: Duke University Press, 1965.

Salmond, John A. *A Southern Rebel: The Life and Times of Aubrey Willis Williams, 1890–1965.* Chapel Hill: University of North Carolina Press, 1983.

Saloutos, Theodore. *Farmer Movements in the South, 1865–1933.* Berkeley: University of California Press, 1960.

Saunders, Robert. "Southern Populists and the Negro, 1893–1895." *Journal of Negro History* 54 (July 1969): 240–61.

Schlesinger, Arthur M., Jr. *Robert Kennedy and His Times.* Boston: Houghton Mifflin Company, 1978.

Selwa, Robert. "Predicts Much Bloodshed in Deep South this Summer." *The Michigan Journalist,* 14 May 1964, 1, 5.

Sherrill, Richard. *Gothic Politics in the Deep South: Stars of the New Confederacy.* New York: Ballantine Books, 1968.

Silver, James W. *Mississippi: The Closed Society.* New York: Harcourt, Brace and World, 1966.

Silverman, Corrine. *The Little Rock Story.* Tuscaloosa: University of Alabama Press, 1959.

Simkins, Francis Butler. *A History of the South.* New York: Alfred A. Knopf, 1965.

————. *Pitchfork Ben Tillman: South Carolinian.* Baton Rouge: Louisiana State University Press, 1944.

Sindler, Allan P., ed. *Change in the Contemporary South.* Durham, North Carolina: Duke University Press, 1963.

Skates, John Ray. *Mississippi: A Bicentennial History.* New York: W. W. Norton and Company, 1979.

Slotkin, Richard. *Regeneration Through Violence: The Mythology of the American Frontier, 1600–1860.* Middletown, Connecticut: Wesleyan University Press, 1973.

Smith, Frank E. *Congressman from Mississippi.* New York: Capricorn Books, 1964.

Smith, Lillian. *Killers of the Dream.* Garden City, New York: Doubleday and Company, 1963.

"Somber Satirist: Mississippi's East." *The Texas Observer,* 7 September 1962, 1, 6.

Sosna, Morton. *In Search of the Silent South: Southern Liberals and the Race Issue.* New York: Columbia University Press, 1977.

Spengler, Joseph J. "Demographic and Economic Change in the South, 1940–1960." In *Change in the Contemporary South*, 126–42. Edited by Allan P. Sindler. Durham, North Carolina: Duke University Press, 1963.

Spiller, Robert E., and Ferguson, Alfred R., eds. *The Collected Works of Ralph Waldo Emerson*. Cambridge: Harvard University Press, 1971.

Tindall, George Brown. *The Disruption of the Solid South*. Athens: University of Georgia Press, 1972.

————. *The Emergence of the New South, 1913–1945*. Baton Rouge: Louisiana State University Press, 1967.

————. *The Persistent Tradition in New South Politics*. Baton Rouge: Louisiana State University Press, 1975.

————. "Southern Mythology." In *The South and the Sectional Image: The Sectional Theme Since Reconstruction*, 8–21. Edited by Dewey W. Grantham. New York: Harper and Row, 1967.

Twelve Southerners. *I'll Take My Stand*. New York: Harper and Row, 1930.

Valien, Preston. "The Montgomery Bus Protest as a Social Movement." In *Race Relations: Problems and Theory*, 112–27. Edited by Preston Valien and Jitsuich Masuoka. Chapel Hill: University of North Carolina Press, 1961.

Vorspan, Albert. "The Iconoclast of Petal, Mississippi." *The Reporter*, 21 March 1957, 33–35.

————. "The South, Segregation, and the Jew." *Jewish Frontier*, November 1956, 15–19.

Walker, Robert, ed. *The Reform Spirit in America: A Documentation of the Pattern of Reform in the American Republic*. New York: G. P. Putnam's Sons, 1976.

Waskow, Arthur I. *From Race Riot to Sit-In, 1919 to the 1960s: A Study in the Connection Between Conflict and Violence*. Garden City, New York: Doubleday and Company, 1966.

Watters, Pat. *Down to Now: Reflections on the Southern Civil Rights Movement*. New York: Pantheon Books, 1971.

————. *The South and the Nation*. New York: Pantheon Books, 1969.

Watters, Pat, and Cleghorn, Reese. *Climbing Jacob's Ladder: The Arrival of Negroes in Southern Politics*. New York: Harcourt, Brace and World, 1967.

Weinstein, Allen, and Gatell, Frank Otto. *The Segregation Era, 1863–1954*. New York: Oxford University Press, 1970.

"White Mississippi Editor Pokes Fun at Jim Crow." *Jet*, 14 March 1957, 12–15.

Wilhoit, Francis M. *The Politics of Massive Resistance*. New York: George Braziller, 1973.

Williams, T. Harry. "Huey, Lyndon, and Southern Radicalism." *Journal of American History* 60 (September 1973): 268–93.

_____. *Romance and Realism in Southern Politics.* Athens: University of Georgia Press, 1961.

Williamson, Joel. *After Slavery: The Negro in South Carolina During Reconstruction.* Chapel Hill: University of North Carolina Press, 1965.

Wills, Garry. "Feminists and Other Useful Fanatics." *Harper's*, June 1976, 35–42.

_____. *Inventing America: Jefferson's Declaration of Independence.* Garden City, New York: Doubleday and Company, 1978.

Woodward, C. Vann. *American Counterpoint: Slavery and Racism in the North-South Dialogue.* Boston: Little, Brown and Company, 1964.

_____. *The Burden of Southern History.* New York: Random House, 1960.

_____. *Origins of the New South, 1877–1913.* Baton Rouge: Louisiana State University Press, 1951.

_____. *The Strange Career of Jim Crow.* 2d ed. New York: Oxford University Press, 1966.

_____. *Tom Watson: Agrarian Rebel.* New York: Oxford University Press, 1938.

Zinn, Howard. *SNCC: The New Abolitionists.* Boston: Beacon Press, 1964.

Index